001357583

HDQ

Jackson County Library Services
Medford, OR 97501

D0604195

DATE DUE			7/01
AUG 25 01			
4/15			
GAYLORD			PRINTED IN U.S.A.

A FIELD GUIDE TO

CONTEMPORARY AMERICAN ARCHITECTURE

Also by Carole Rifkind

Mansions, Mills, and Main Streets
Main Street: The Face of Urban America
A Field Guide to American Architecture

A FIELD GUIDE TO

CONTEMPORARY AMERICAN ARCHITECTURE

CAROLE RIFKIND

A DUTTON BOOK

JACKSON COUNTY LIBRARY SERVICES
MEDFORD OREGON 97501

DUTTON
Published by the Penguin Group
Penguin Putnam Inc., 375 Hudson Street,
New York, New York 10014, U.S.A.
Penguin Books Ltd, 27 Wrights Lane,
London W8 5TZ, England
Penguin Books Australia Ltd, Ringwood,
Victoria, Australia
Penguin Books Canada Ltd, 10 Alcorn Avenue,
Toronto, Ontario, Canada M4V 3B2
Penguin Books (N.Z.) Ltd, 182–190 Wairau Road,
Auckland 10, New Zealand

Penguin Books Ltd, Registered Offices:
Harmondsworth, Middlesex, England

First published by Dutton, an imprint of Dutton NAL,
a member of Penguin Putnam Inc.

First Printing, October, 1998
10   9   8   7   6   5   4   3   2   1

Copyright © Carole Rifkind, 1998
All rights reserved

 REGISTERED TRADEMARK—MARCA REGISTRADA

LIBRARY OF CONGRESS CATALOGING-IN-PUBLICATION DATA:

Rifkind, Carole.
    A field guide to contemporary American architecture / Carole
Rifkind.
       p.   cm.
    Includes bibliographical references and index.
    ISBN 0-525-94008-1
    1. Architecture, Modern—20th century—United States.
  2. Architecture—United States. I. Rifkind, Carole. II. Title.
NA712.R54   1998
720'.973'0904—dc21   98-2716
                                                      CIP

Printed in the United States of America
Set in Bitstream Carmina
Designed by Stanley S. Drate/Folio Graphics Co. Inc.

Without limiting the rights under copyright reserved above, no part of this
publication may be reproduced, stored in or introduced into a retrieval system,
or transmitted, in any form, or by any means (electronic, mechanical,
photocopying, recording, or otherwise), without the prior written permission
of both the copyright owner and the above publisher of this book.

This book is printed on acid-free paper. ∞

CONTENTS

v

3
PUBLIC BUILDINGS
101

4
ART MUSEUMS
149

5
RELIGIOUS BUILDINGS
187

ACKNOWLEDGMENTS

Many people have given generous gifts of time, effort, and expertise to the intricate and laborious process of researching, writing, and producing this book, and I am grateful to all of them.

There's no way that I can adequately express my deep appreciation to dear friends and colleagues who have critiqued, criticized, and cheered me on as this book slowly evolved: Marisa Bartolucci, Colin Cathcart, Richard Dattner, Andrew Dolkart, Bella Harris, Neil Harris, Isabelle Hyman, Mary Alice Molloy, James Stewart Polshek, Richard Rabinowitz, Mildred Schmertz, Robert Silman, Marcia Tucker, Carol Willis, and Peter Wolf.

At Dutton Books, I am extremely grateful to Hugh Rawson for his extraordinary skill and kindness. As always, my husband, Richard Rifkind, stands behind everything I do, with unflagging faith, unstinting help, and infinite patience.

I appreciatively acknowledge the many people who so willingly answered repeated requests for information, drawings, and photographs. Photography credits are given in the captions, except in certain cases where images were supplied by others and the photographers are not known, for which lapse I extend my apologies.

The matter of giving full credit to all those who built the buildings that I describe in this book is more complicated. Architecture requires extensive participation and close teamwork among individuals with many different skills and talents. The design team is likely to include a principal of the firm who may or may not also be the principal designer, project architects who translate the design intentions into detailed construction documents; structural, mechanical, and electrical engineering consultants; interior architects; landscape architects; a collaborating firm with particular expertise in local construction practices; the general contractor and many subcontractors under his or her supervision who must transform the marks of the designers into physical form. However, because the inclusion of all those would create burdensome detail, I have generally credited only the name of the principal architectural firm, not specific designers or project teams within the office, nor cooperating architects, engineers, or contractors. But this is by no means meant to diminish their roles. The making of architecture is a highly collaborative art.

INTRODUCTION

This book is written for everyone who cares enough about architecture to want to think about it, and for anyone who has never thought much about architecture who may be ready to start seeing it.

In the United States, many more buildings have been constructed in the last fifty years than in all our prior history. We find architecture fascinating, we make architects heroes, and we feature buildings in newspaper headlines and museum exhibits. Yet our downtowns are filled with ugliness, our neighborhoods dull, our countrysides ravaged. Do we lack confidence that architecture really counts?

This book presents a framework that helps the reader look at contemporary architecture with the categories helping to organize what is seen and the examples serving as surrogates for related buildings. My reason for writing this book is to help people care—to be better able to enjoy, understand, and critique architecture. The last fifty years, occupying what one historian has called "the limbo of the all-too-familiar and the not-quite-historical," requires greater awareness, closer observation, and more searching evaluation. I've tried to be evenhanded and dispassionate in my selection and discussion of buildings, hoping to free the observer to form independent opinions—but I have put my own Top Ten in the Postscript.

Buildings tell who we are—they reflect social and societal ideals, law, technology, economics, and practical necessity as well as aesthetic tastes. As Louis Sullivan wrote in *Kindergarten Chats*: "If for the word 'style' we substitute the word 'civilization,' we make at once a pronounced stride in advance toward an intelligent understanding of the 'values' of the historical monuments of architecture."

It's been estimated that our increasingly complex society requires some 270 distinct types of buildings, including such intriguing examples as the airport terminal, public garage, convention center, fast-food stand, and sports stadium. I've covered only the main building types, taking a slice from each to build the story of American architecture in the second half of the twentieth century. For dwelling places—whether single-family or multi-family—I've focused on the not always identical goals of architect and client. For government buildings, on the expression of power and tradition. For art museums and religious buildings, I've highlighted the connection between the space the architect designs and the experience the visitor enjoys. I've viewed schools and campuses as reflections of the rapid changes that have swept over our society in the past half-century. I've found tall office buildings to be revealing testimony to construction technology. The rapid changes overtaking suburbia have made it too inchoate to encompass, although I've discovered shopping centers to be eloquent about real estate speculation and consumerism as powerful forces that shape our landscape. The reader, no doubt, will want to put this picture together, personally, over time.

Our times have produced some outstanding architecture, although we may have seen more quantity than quality, greater novelty than excellence. But this is not a book about great architecture; it is about broad trends. Ultimately, it is about ourselves and what we value. I hope the book will help to deepen the observer's understanding, and thus, to raise expectations that architecture shall embody the very highest values of our society.

1

HOUSES

HOUSES

"There was something electric in the air, a particular sort of excitement that comes from the sound of hammers and saws after they have been silent too long," chronicled Esther McCoy, an astute observer of the postwar architectural scene. Indeed, architecture did seem to be headed on a new course. The Depression and war years had accumulated an enormous pent-up need for housing. Exciting possibilities arose for applying wartime improvements in production methods, plastics, steel, resins, and processed wood products. Many were stirred by the Modernist visions of Bauhaus leaders who had settled in America at the beginning of the war: "Together let us conceive and create the new building of the future . . ." declared their founding manifesto, imagining a unity of all the arts "which will rise one day towards heaven from the hands of a million workers like the crystal symbol of a new faith." Many viewed the private house as a laboratory for innovative design, expecting that solutions for the design problems of the individual house would have positive repercussions for the well-being of society at large. "A brand new set of answers were ready for the question that architecture asks of every age," McCoy reported.

Mass home ownership, a dream fulfilled in postwar America, was encouraged by federal tax incentives and affordable land along an expanding highway system. To a significant extent it was due to the housing developer, whose expertise in cost control, construction efficiencies, finance, and marketing could satisfy the family in a hurry, the would-be homeowner who needs a big mortgage, and the one who defers to the taste of the Joneses.

But it is the architect who can respond with originality to the particular and the individual—a special site, an intimate relationship with the out-of-doors, functional living, flexibility, freshness. Though there may be relatively few clients for an architect's services, they are usually sufficiently well educated, self-confident, and individualistic to believe that "architecture" is more than mere "building." And these clients have fueled the furnace of architectural thinking through the convulsive changes and rapidly shifting values of the past half-century.

ARCHITECT AND CLIENT

Both client and architect play for high stakes in the design of a house. The effort requires an intense collaboration between two parties whose differing ambitions and anticipations may pull them in opposite directions. The homeowner seeks affordability, comfort, convenience, as well as intangible qualities that respond to spiritual needs even as they signal the family's status. The architect must also make a living, gain recognition, get future work, and pursue new ideas no matter where they may lead. Bearing down on the innumerable problems, constraints, and opportunities of the project, architect and client wrestle with fundamental issues relating to possibility and practi-

3

cality, innovation and satisfaction, ego and habitation.

In the battle between "Traditional" and "Modern" that raged during the forties and fifties, the architect stood as a heroic, if sometimes intransigent figure—the noble protagonist of Ayn Rand's popular novel *The Fountainhead*, the face on the cover of *Time* or *Life*, a big draw to museums. The architect was the bold conceptualizer who imagined family life in the new technological age, who designed dwellings that bore no resemblance to any built before. Land and building costs were relatively modest postwar for ten or fifteen years, leaving the architect plenty of scope to experiment with "starter" houses as small as two thousand square feet or less. A high proportion of architect-designed houses were built in California, where a young, new population enjoyed freedom from tradition, a soft climate, casual attitudes, and the freedom of the road.

At times innovation led client and architect into troubled waters. The venturesome Dr. Edith Farnsworth was so angered by Ludwig Mies van der Rohe's behavior, so discomforted by the lack of privacy and heat control in her all-glass house and annoyed by cost overruns from the architect's insistence on expensive detailing and exquisite finishes, that she sued him. Notwithstanding the client's dissatisfaction, the house became an icon of modernism and an inspiration for generations to come.

Charismatic as he was, Frank Lloyd Wright also insisted on having his way, although he was more adept at making clients feel good about it. Writing in his book *The Natural House* (1954), he allowed that the architect had to accede to the client's needs only insofar as they "manifest intelligence instead of mere personal idiosyncrasy." Wright's implacable commitment to a hexagonal module, which he viewed as a possible prototype for industrialized housing, caused great distress to the Hanna family,

who protested the "procrustean" dimensions of rooms and hallways in their Wright-designed house. In the end, the clients forgave the architect for intransigence, added costs, and troublesome delays, praising the "subtle but true relations of form and purpose, of site and dwelling," and for the revelation "that beauty is a way of living rather than 'pictures to hang upon a wall.' "

Modern architecture's increasing diversity in the sixties paralleled that of the visual arts, which were then breaking out into Pop, Op, Minimal, Process, Earth, and Conceptual. Leadership in architectural education shifted from Cambridge, Massachusetts, and Chicago, heavily influenced by the Bauhaus, to the more permissive atmospheres of Princeton, Philadelphia, and New Haven, and beyond, to Texas, the Midwest, and the West Coast. Rising educational levels, working wives, and widening cracks in family structure shaped new visions of the family home, and rising costs put the architect-designed house out of reach of all but the truly affluent.

The high-flying sixties sagged back to earth in the seventies, when the celebration of the nation's Bicentennial was dimmed by economic instability and diminishing expectations. "Confidence in traditional values and institutions went into the trash compactor," chronicled *The Economist*, describing the worry, introspection, and conservatism that marked the "Me Decade."

A freer exchange of ideas and a more liberal give-and-take characterized the architect-client relationship in these years. Less authoritative, more collaborative, the architect led the client to imagine larger, more spirited, and definitely more eccentric houses. "The clients I get along with best, feel the happiest about, are the ones who have very much their own sense of what they want, and maintain their own veto power, and tell me no when they don't like something or want something different," explained

Charles W. Moore. "He wasn't afraid to let me design my own house," boasted one strong-willed home owner. "He gave me infinite options—'if you do this, this will happen'—and allowed me to erase whatever I wanted." Of course, there is also the loyal patronage of family and friends, which has always given the architect unusual freedom to pursue unexplored territory.

In the eighties and nineties, people worried about broadening divisions in American society and declining personal and political morality. The architect struggled with designs for affordable housing, achieving closer harmony with the environment, and nontraditional family life. Most collaborations revolved around limits and restraints, such as those described in Tracy Kidder's *House* (1985), which chronicles the practical concerns of an earnest young professional couple and the modest ambitions of architect William Rawn in creating a house that reflects sensitivity to the environment, the changing role of women, and the obligations of family, profession, and community. It bestows the understanding that good design is uplifting.

Some architects achieved celebrity status as servants to clients whose ambitions for trophy architecture added entirely new perspectives to architect-client collaboration. "The aesthetic shape that the house took was almost entirely in his hands," said client Suzanne Frank of architect Peter Eisenman's design for her country home. His was an insistently antifunctional venture into architectural theory that deferred to the client's expectations of practicality only to the extent that they didn't interfere with the "abstract principles that he cherished." Charles Gwathmey expected his clients to consider themselves fortunate to be "part of the process of making the history of architecture." Eric Owen Moss's aggressive designs were intended to challenge the clients, to confront them with issues that drove them from complacency.

Of course, the ambitious, deep-pocketed client has always expected the architect to gratify his or her ego. "I wanted to build a space where a man and woman could live together in a perfect arrangement, a place you could have grand parties, an indoor pool and the greatest bathroom in the world," one client told Frank Gehry, giving the architect unlimited freedom. "I've paid Frank whatever he's billed and told him to push the envelope." From the plain to the pretentious, the house mirrors client, architect, and culture. To contemplate such houses—better yet, to see and experience them—engages one in the making of architecture itself.

In the sense of belonging to the second half of the twentieth century, all dwellings are alike in being modern. But the term "modern" is imprecise, ambiguous, and highly charged with polemic. It does little to explain how they are different. In fact, one can follow three roads to modernity, overlapping in the work of some architects, far apart in others. The tendency to abstraction is motivated by the desire to find rational, simple, and universal solutions. Another approach, that taken by the expressionist, is highly personal, emphasizing sensation and mood. A third route, the traditional, may bear features of either or both, and something from history as well.

ABSTRACT

TECHNOLOGICAL

"The problem of the house is a problem of the epoch," wrote Le Corbusier, a profoundly influential Franco-Swiss Modernist who championed abstraction in painting, sculpture, and architecture. Aiming for a total break with the past, Modernists vowed to strip architecture of every obsolete vestige of "style," totally reinventing and rationalizing it in terms of function. "When a thing responds to need, it is beautiful," Le Corbusier insisted.

The machine-age aesthetic was seeded in America in the early thirties by a Museum of Modern Art exhibit and book, *The International Style* (1932), by Henry-Russell Hitchcock and Philip Johnson. The polemic provided instant fame for buildings produced under the influence of the Bauhaus, a visionary, multidisciplinary school that had pioneered modern design in Germany and elsewhere in Europe. In houses by an architect such as Richard Neutra, America saw demonstrations of this new architecture, no longer characterized by *mass*, weight bearing down on the earth, but, rather, by the *volume of space*, enclosed by smooth planes, sitting lightly on the ground. The new mode searched for radical innovation, ideal form, technically perfect industrialized materials, a refined system of proportion, and elimination of ornament as such.

But a broad commitment to the Modernist aesthetic flourished in America only after the Nazis closed the Bauhaus and certain of its key figures took up teaching and practice here—Mies van der Rohe, for one. Head of the Illinois Institute of Technology in Chicago, Mies argued that modern technology, as both shaper and symbol of our epoch, established a historical movement in its own right, such as Classic or Gothic architecture were in historic times. "Technology is far more than a method," Mies instructed a graduating class in 1950. "It is a world in itself . . . whenever technology reaches its real fulfillment, it transcends into architecture." The mastery of technology, Mies held, leads the architect into "the highest sphere of spiritual existence, into the realm of pure art."

Planned as early as 1946 but completed only in 1950, the Farnsworth house (figures 1, 2), on the outskirts of Chicago, exalts leanness, high finish, precise detail and proportion, and tight control of every design aspect. Rising from a podium on only four pairs of spare steel columns, the house's form is strictly derived from structure and is an insistent polemic on Mies's ambition to create "maximum effect with minimum means." Aloof from the natural site—*on* rather than *of* the landscape—it consists of a single glass-enclosed space around a central service core containing bath, kitchen, and storage. The "free plan" was intended to permit different spatial arrangements by reconfiguring movable furniture or dividers.

Influenced by Mies, Philip Johnson's own bachelor home (1949) in New Canaan, Connecticut, is also a glass-enclosed rectangular volume, but it sits squarely on the ground and has operable sash windows. This closeness to nature as well as the nod to practicality made the dwelling a useful point of departure for architects in America. (Now owned by the National Trust for Historic Preservation, the house is open to the public.) Variations on the Miesian theme could be seen in many homes designed by architects for themselves: George Matsumoto's 1954 home in Raleigh, North Carolina, had glass window walls alternating with planar wood sheathing to increase the flexibility and privacy of interior spaces; Charles M. Goodman's 1955 home in Alexandria, Virginia, was raised in height for greater presence and better natural lighting.

California was home to a number of prototype steel-and-glass dwellings, mainly under the sponsorship of the journal *Art and Architecture.* One highly attention-getting, if not widely copied, demonstration of steel framing was Charles Eames's for his own home in Los Angeles in 1949. Eames selected off-the-shelf industrial parts, such as steel bar joists and sash windows, from a hardware catalog but, having changed his mind about the orientation of the dwelling, was able to improvise a new configuration with almost exactly the same parts. Raphael Soriano's commitment to the steel-and-glass pavilion form was based on the importance of modular planning in producing cost savings, "particularly important in steel," he explained, "where logic and economy are usually identical." Soriano added vivacity to the industrial vocabulary by painting columns in primary colors and using tinted corrugated plastic sunscreens. Pierre Koenig experimented with steel beams, joints, sections, and decking. The simplicity and purity of "skin-and-bones" construction became its own aesthetic reward in the designs of Craig Ellwood, an engineer who tried to popularize steel framing and industrial components as a new American domestic vernacular. "The spirit of architecture is truthfulness to itself, the clarity and logic with respect to its materials and structure," he declared.

In the later fifties the demands of active family life and progressively higher standards of living led to a softening of Miesian austerity. One variation on the rectangular pavilion paradigm is a courtyard scheme that created separate zones for private time and family life. The 1956–57 Eliot Noyes house (figures 3, 4, 5) in New Canaan, Connecticut, which the architect designed for his own family, was formed of two parallel wings enclosing a landscaped court. End walls of rustic local fieldstone were joined by steel-framed glass walls with sliding glass doors that open the interior to the court in good weather. The stone provides a sense of shelter, ties the house to its setting, and evokes traditional connotations of "home." A two-story plan created a living zone beneath a sleeping zone at the Graf house (1956) in Dallas, Texas, designed by Edward Durrell Stone. A cast-concrete grille set in front of the facade fulfills needs for ventilation and privacy, while it also advertises the growing interest in decorative qualities. The split-level plan of the 1959 dwelling designed by Charles Colbert for his own family in Metairie, Louisiana, provides intimacy in the one-story kitchen-children's wing and spatial drama in the double-height entertainment-adult wing.

In the sixties houses grew larger in scale, more dynamic in shape, and increasingly dramatic in their encounter with the site. The Payne residence (1961) in Pleasant Valley, Pennsylvania, by Keck & Keck, is a dramatic arc form whose curving facade takes advantage of expansive country views. Besides local stone and slate, the construction exploits a modern welded steel frame and modular building panels. The Beadle house (1964) by Alfred N. Beadle, Dailey Associates in Phoenix, Arizona, is contained within a wide-bay modular steel frame, rising on steel stilts over the rough terrain of a natural river "wash" that serves as a rock garden in dry seasons. The Maher house (1965) in Houston, Texas, by Barnstone & Aubry, appears as a low rectangular form on the front elevation, but breaks free at the rear in a bold cross-axial thrust that cantilevers the steel-framed living room over the family's parking lot below.

Hopes that the use of steel would bring a high order of design to popularly priced dwellings were frustrated by high cost of plant investment and the resistance of the construction industry. Advances in wood construction, in contrast, entered into the American vernacular. Insisting that architects must "learn how to compose beautiful buildings" from industrialized parts, Walter Gropius influenced an entire generation from his position as head of Harvard's Graduate School of Design, where the émigré founder of the Bauhaus had been installed just before the war. The collaboration of Gropius and Konrad Wachsmann in Massachusetts provided a model for factory-built wooden houses. Wachsmann later pioneered a method of using smaller interchangeable units, rather than complete wall sections, to give industrially produced houses greater than usual variety and flexibility. In California, Richard Neutra experimented with the use of a prefabricated utility core and standardized wooden door and window units. In the Pacific Northwest, John Yeon's modular plywood panel system exploited a recently invented waterproof glue.

The cost economy of a standard rectangular module typically determined a simple pavilion form. In the Midwest, Keck & Keck developed a model prefabricated house composed of easily assembled and disassembled insulated eight-foot wall panels with fixed and movable glazing on the south face to optimize solar heat. The staggered plan of the firm's Kunstadter house of 1951 in Highland Park, Illinois, is a sophisticated variation that emphasizes the separation of different living zones.

Respecting the gentle, humane abstraction of northern European Modernism, Carl Koch experimented with wood in the Acorn house (figures 6, 7) of 1959. Located in a Boston suburb, the dwelling is faced in smooth vertical wood siding, using standard sliding-sash windows rather than entire glass window walls to improve economy, privacy, and light control. In another of *Art and Architecture*'s case studies, the La Jolla, California, Triad (figures 8, 9) of 1961 by Killingsworth, Stricker, Lindgren, Wilson & Associates, wood is employed with the thin, taut precision of steel, with only an occasional steel column to provide seismic stability. Taking advantage of a sloping site, the three houses are configured to gain maximum privacy for each. In an A-frame house, such as the McDonald house (figures 10, 11) of 1961 in Elyria, Ohio, designed by John Terrence Kelly, wood is used with great economy and structural efficiency. The use of triangular trusses permits the elimination of side walls and reasonably easy do-it-yourself construction.

Expressing a new forcefulness that developed within the minimalist aesthetic, Marcel Breuer's Starkey house (figures 12, 13) of 1955 in Duluth, Minnesota, was a structural tour de force. Supported on massive laminated wooden beams, its two wings seem to float high above ground level. Exuberant "roof" architecture in the fifties was not only a demonstration of new materials and advanced technology, but a bravura alternative to the much-criticized flat roof. The roof of a 1955 dwelling by Ulrich Franzen in Rye, New York, is based on the design of an airplane wing. Another of the same year, built for his family by Edward Catalano (figures 14, 15) in Raleigh, North Carolina, is a doubly warped hyperbolic parabola in form. In various dwellings of the fifties, Paul Rudolph designed the roof as a steel catenary arch, a plywood vault, and a concrete umbrella. "Each material has its own potential and we seek the most eloquent expression of it," said Rudolph.

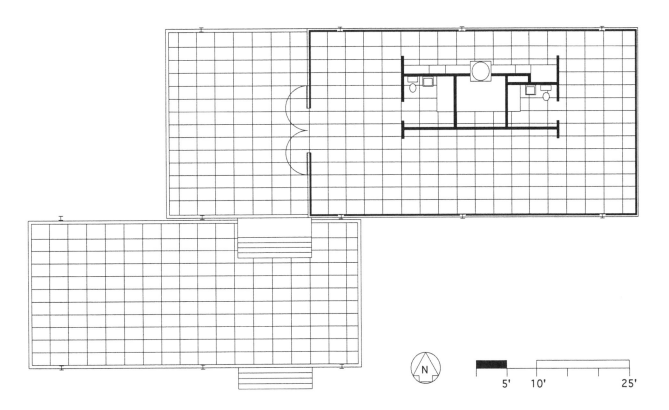

1, 2 Farnsworth house; Plano, Illinois. Ludwig Mies van der Rohe, 1946–50. *Photo: © Scott Francis/Esto.*

[PLAN] The staggered relationship of house and terrace builds formality without symmetry.

[EXTERIOR] A precise rectangular volume, the house clearly expresses steel skeleton construction. The highly finished materials propagandize industrial technology, although their fabrication actually required considerable hand craftsmanship. The architect's design control extended even to the drapery.

3, 4, 5 Noyes house; New Canaan, Connecticut. Eliot Noyes, 1956–57. *Photos: Ezra Stoller, © Esto.*

[EXTERIOR] The extension of the roof over the glass walls moderates sunlight while it also enhances the sense of shelter.

[INTERIOR COURT] Looking through the interior court toward the front entry, one sees the living-dining-study wing at the left. Bedrooms occupy a parallel glass wing at the right.

[BEDROOM] Lack of clutter and precise placement of furniture are minimalist requirements.

6, **7** Acorn house; Concord, Massachusetts. Carl Koch, 1956–59. *Photos: Ezra Stoller, © Esto.*

[EXTERIOR] A frank demonstration of low-cost factory production, the dwelling comprises two back-to-back modules. The dwelling's Modernist aesthetic is expressed in the "picture window," slatted sun screen, and crisply drawn line of the eaves.

[INTERIOR] The kitchen-dining pass-through provides convenience while it visually expands the tight space of the dining area.

8, **9**   Case Study Triad, House C; La Jolla, California. Killingsworth, Stricker, Lindgren, Wilson & Associates, 1961. *Photos: Julius Shulman.*

[EXTERIOR] The dwelling is composed of a checkerboard of interior, court, and garden spaces, all keyed to modular construction. Such a configuration makes the house adaptable to different topographies, maintaining privacy between neighboring units in a multiunit development.

[INTERIOR] The aesthetics of the design are based on transparency, reflectivity, light, and lightness.

10, 11 McDonald house; Elyria, Ohio. John Terrence Kelly, 1961. *Photos: Ed Nano.*

[EXTERIOR] Resting on eight points anchored in concrete piers, the dwelling is constructed of intersecting wood A-frames, the pointed gables entirely filled with glass.

[INTERIOR] The A-frame provides economical two-story space.

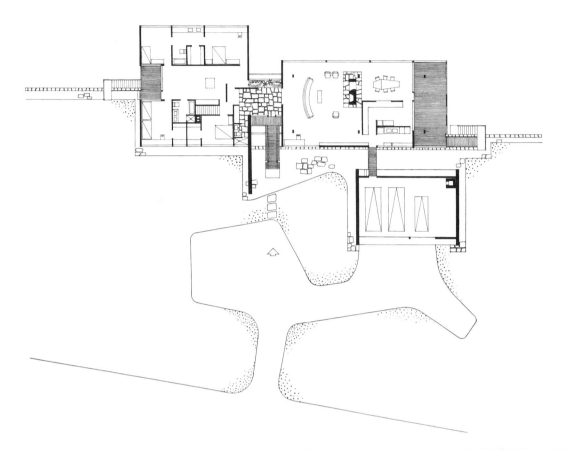

12, 13 Starkey house; Duluth, Minnesota. Marcel Breuer & Associates, 1954–55. *Photo: Warren Reynolds/Infinity, Inc.*

[PLAN] There is one wing for living and dining, another for sleeping and privacy—a so-called bi-nuclear plan. To provide free interior space, the roof is hung from two wooden beams.

[EXTERIOR] The dwelling perches on eight laminated wood posts that stand on steel pins that reach down to bedrock. The columnless area beneath the living-dining room, whose floor framing is supported by laminated wood girders, provides a sheltered space for play.

14, 15 Catalano house; Raleigh, North Carolina. Edward Catalano, 1955. *Photos: Ezra Stoller, © Esto.*

[EXTERIOR] From two concrete supports anchored in the ground, the dwelling soars upward as the double-warped plane of a laminated-wood hyperbolic-parabola roof. In this mode of construction, the skin of the structure effectively forms its own support.

[INTERIOR] The house is virtually without walls, with sliding glass doors that make a minimal division between inside and outside.

REGIONAL

Envisioning an ideal, universal building type, the Modernist was no less intrigued by the striking differences in climate, topography, and state of mind that characterize the different regions of America.

"It was a way of life and the house a frame for such a life," said William W. Wurster of living in the San Francisco Bay Area, a locale whose striking views, gentle climate, relaxed lifestyle, and pragmatic building traditions attracted adventurous clients and eager-to-please architects. Prolific and highly influential, Wurster held that it was "absolutely necessary to search for spiritual roots in the place itself and in the local way of life." The many houses produced by the firm of Wurster, Bernardi & Emmons, using plain materials and pragmatic variations in plan, proved that Bay Area architecture is "not necessarily modern with a capital M." Like Wurster, architects Gardner Dailey, Clarence Mayhew, and John Dinwiddie also respected California climate, casual living, and practical ways of building. For them, both Bauhaus innovations and Japanese wood-frame traditions were constant sources of inspirations.

In a Pacific Northwest genre very close to that of the Bay Area, Pietro Belluschi's oeuvre reflected the "mood of the countryside, the color of the soil, the shape of the trees and the textures of the grasses." Belluschi delighted in the use of a variety of natural woods and informal plans and silhouettes. Although he also designed with the Modernist's flat roof, Belluschi used pitched rooflines with particular effect, as in an Oregon ranch house (figures 16, 17, 18) of 1948, designed to be strong on its own terms while remaining a gentle presence in the surrounding countryside. Dwellings by other Pacific Northwest architects, such as Paul Thiry and John Yeon, evoked the memorable silhouette and heavy timber framing of local barns and sheds.

The climate and lush vegetation of southern California married the house to the landscape in a very particular way in the work of Gregory Ain, Harwell Harris, Jones & Emmonds, J. R. Davidson, and others. Richard Neutra's 1952 Moore house (figure 19) in Ojai, California, employs interior plantings, reflecting pools, night-time lighting, and freestanding screen walls to create pleasantly ambiguous indoor-outdoor spaces. All of these tendencies came together in the fifties and sixties in the development of a generalized California "Contemporary" style. Typically, it has a low profile, unpainted wood framing and sheathing, a gently pitched roof, large expanses of glass, and intimacy with a landscaped setting. One such is the 1960 Hunt house (figures 20, 21) in Oakland, California, by Hunt & Company, built into a hilly site to keep a low profile. Exposed redwood posts and roof rafters carry a roof that overhangs outdoor decks to create a gentle transition between interior and exterior. The increasing refinement of the Bay Area tradition can be understood in the 1963 Pence house (figure 22) in Mill Valley, California. Designed by Marquis & Stoller, the dwelling is composed of four pavilions, lightly crowned by parasol-like roofs, and casually arranged around a common deck.

East Coast Modernists could look to the example of the spare, flat-roofed house with metal sash windows and vertical wood siding that Walter Gropius built for his family in Lincoln, Massachusetts, in 1937. (The house is now owned by the National Trust for Historic Preservation and is open to the public.) Respectful of the historic character of the locale, Gropius felt that even the most tradition-bound neighbor couldn't fail to see that "the moving spirit behind it was facing the problem in much the same way in which the early builders of the region had faced it, when, with the best technical means at their disposal, they built unostentatious, clearly defined buildings that were able to withstand the rigors of the climate and that expressed the social attitude of their inhabitants."

Dedicated to machine production, the collaboration of Marcel Breuer and Walter Gropius in New England also took advantage of native stone, traditional clapboard, and familiar wood-framing techniques, producing houses that update vernacular building traditions and fit in with the landscape comfortably. "There are many possibilities in architecture provided it is not straitjacketed into narrow rules," said Breuer. "There are also many needs that our glass wall does not fulfill." Another innovator in industrial production, Carl Koch, was also interested in regional form. One result is the 1953 Gordon house (figure 23), one of a group of five wooden houses occupying a hilly site in Belmont, Massachusetts, that seem both timeless and contemporary.

In San Antonio, Texas, O'Neil Ford's "common sense architecture" found the local vernacular masonry house a model well adapted to the area's prevalent heat, bright sun, and sudden torrential rains. Ford's houses tend to be simple, boxlike forms with a thin, extended plan that captures through breezes and an overhanging roof that offers protection from rain. In response to the temperature extremes of the Midwest, architect George Keck adapted Miesian form to the requirements of solar heat-

ing. The semitropical conditions of Florida inspired Paul Rudolph to investigate new materials, such as glass louvers and watertight plastics, but mainly form itself. He found precedents in the southern raised cottage that escapes dampness; grilles and trellises that filter light and welcome cooling breezes; and screens that protect against insects. "Regionalism is one way towards that richness in architecture which other movements have enjoyed and which is so lacking today," he wrote in 1957.

Architects of the sixties reaffirmed abstraction, while they also insisted on highly personal interpretations of regional tradition. Second homes, in particular, which proliferated in those years, seemed to encourage carefree independence. A minimalist's concept of an old-fashioned farm village is apparent in the complex of buildings that make up the 1962 Cowles house (figure 24). Located in Wayzata, Minnesota, the dwelling was designed by Edward Larrabee Barnes. "A house should never melt completely into the landscape," said Barnes. "It should retain its own identity as a habitat and have its own crisp organic form." Hugh Newell Jacobsen shows irreverence as well as respect in his approach to local tradition. The architect's radical 1970 revision of a traditional pitched-roof, stone-wall Maryland house reiterates the original form to create a complex containing no less than eleven pavilions. "I endeavor to design buildings that express a sense of belonging," said the architect.

The seventies produced multiple readings of tradition and uninhibited rejoinders to the past. There was a search for symbolism, an exploding interest in architectural and landscape history, and a growing concern for historic preservation and ecology. Possibly reflecting all of these, but with sure Modernist command, the Gaffney house (figures 25, 26) in Romansville, Pennsylvania, is a 1976–80 design by Bohlin Powell Larkin Cywinski. The Nilsson house (figures 27, 28) in Los Angeles, California, seems to embody some ideal vernacular form belonging to no particular place, but to a playful realm commanded by the architect and the client. It was designed by Eugene Kupper and completed in 1979. A dwelling (figures 29, 30) by Steven Holl seems to be a metaphor of its Martha's Vineyard, Massachusetts, island location. "I was trying to get back to the spirit of New England," said the architect. The wood-framed dwelling sits on a hilltop like a beached whale, its skeletonlike exterior armature producing a visual richness that contrasts strongly with the dwelling's insistent simplicity.

By the eighties and nineties, Modernist tradition was itself valued as a part of the American heritage, even as it continued to grow and evolve. Paying homage to Mies's presence in the Midwest, the 1980 Fultz house (figures 31, 32, 33) in Porter County, Indiana, was designed by Hammond, Beeby & Babka. The lightweight, easily assembled steel truss construction system of Caryl's house (figures 34, 35) of 1995 in Point Richmond, California, by Holabird & Root, evokes Charles Eames's experiments with on-site installation of steel components. Strict minimalism governs the 1990 Croffead house (figures 36, 37) outside of Charleston, South Carolina, by Clark & Menefee. The simple cubic volume of poured concrete and concrete block, fronted by a glass-block loggia, generates an intense sense of locale. "Who can really hope to understand an entire region?" asked the architects. "We're more interested in the tangible characteristics of the *local* site: the views, the quality of sunlight, the color of the lichen on the trees. . . ."

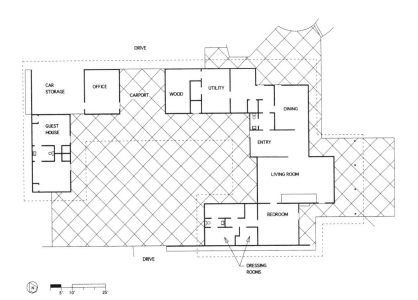

16, 17, 18 Menesee house; Yankill, Oregon. Pietro Belluschi, 1948. *Photos: Ezra Stoller, © Esto.*

[PLAN] Appearing to be an ad hoc ranch house, the complex is actually a highly functional arrangement of dwelling, guesthouse, garage, and office.

[EXTERIOR] The influence of Japanese wood framing is seen in the bold overhang of the low-pitched roof, while a commitment to modern indoor-outdoor living is represented by the expansive glass window wall that links living room and terrace.

[INTERIOR] The flush fireplace wall and the china cabinet dividing living and dining spaces reveal the Modernist aesthetic.

19 Moore house; Ojai, California. Richard Neutra, 1952. *Photo: Julius Shulman.* A response to the seductive West Coast climate and casual way of life, the staggered plan and glass walls bring a minimal dwelling into an intimate relationship with the out-of-doors.

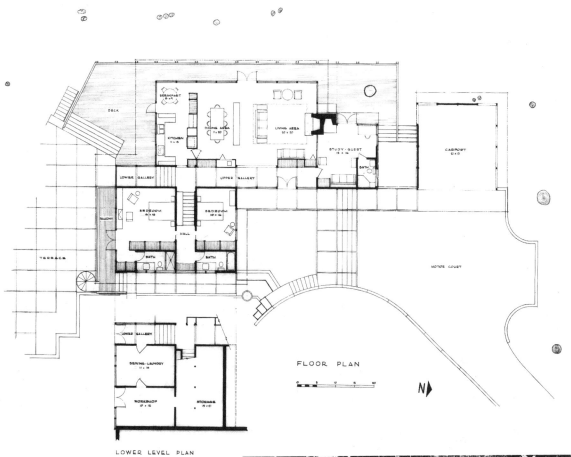

FLOOR PLAN

N▶

LOWER LEVEL PLAN

20, 21 Hunt house; Oakland, California.
Hunt & Company, 1960. *Photo: George Knight.*

[PLAN] The separate spaces are linked to each
other and the out-of-doors by a continuous
outdoor gallery.

[EXTERIOR] Redwood posts, carrying glass right
up to the eaves, are distinctive of the
"California Contemporary" genre. Kitchen,
dining, and living areas, divided only by
freestanding casework, are conceived as a
single space.

22   Pence house; Mill Valley, California. Marquis &
Stoller, 1963. *Photo: Karl H. Riek.* An ample deck
unites four separate wings. True to Bay Area tradition,
the house exploits the site for maximum views.

23   Gordon house; Belmont, Massachusetts. Carl
Koch, 1953. *Photo: Ezra Stoller, © Esto.* The living-
dining wing and open sunporch off the second-story
bedrooms display the add-on quality typical of the
New England vernacular.

24 Cowles house; Wayzata, Minnesota. Edward Larrabee Barnes, 1962. *Photo: Ezra Stoller, © Esto.* The composition encompasses separate sleeping, living, and service areas in bold abstract forms that evoke an old farm courtyard. The powerful diagonals of the rooflines hark back to an agricultural vernacular, while flat-roofed segments are insistently contemporary.

25, 26 Gaffney house; Romansville, Pennsylvania. Bohlin Powell Larkin Cywinski, 1976–80. *Photos: Sandy Taylor [exterior]; Joseph Molitor [interior].*

[EXTERIOR] Placed within the stone foundation of a burned barn, the spare forms of the dwelling seem to be an abstraction of the history of the site. Sliding-sash windows, pitched roof, wood siding, and stone wall construction all reflect local farmhouse tradition.

[LIVING ROOM] The living room is a glass-walled space, diagonally configured to create surprising views and spatial experiences.

27, 28   Nilsson house; Los Angeles, California. Eugene Kupper,
1979. *Photo: Tim Street-Porter.*

[PLAN] A highly unconventional plan arranged along one long,
formal axis.

[EXTERIOR] Making reference to some imagined vernacular, the design
employs pitched-roof shapes, a heavy chimney, an imposing front
door, and thick walls.

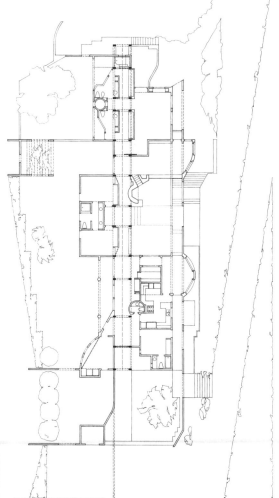

29, 30   House; Martha's Vineyard, Massachusetts. Steven Holl Architects, 1989. *Photos: © Paul Warchol Photography [exterior]; © Steven Holl Architects [interior].*

[EXTERIOR] The wood-framed dwelling sits on a hilltop like a beached whale, its skeleton producing a visual richness that contrasts strongly with the dwelling's insistent simplicity.

[INTERIOR] Like the prow of a boat, the triangular dining area seems to be floating toward the sea. "The site of a building is more than a mere ingredient in its conception," said Holl. "It is its physical and metaphysical foundation."

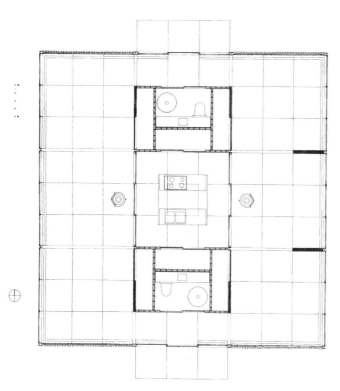

31, 32, 33 Fultz house; Porter County, Indiana. Hammond, Beeby & Babka, 1980. *Photos: Harold N. Kaplan, © HNK Architectural Photography.*

[PLAN] The square plan is based on a strict four-foot grid, with a central utility core containing an open kitchen flanked by two bathrooms.

[INTERIOR] The exposed ceiling decking and stove heater add an improvised quality to the Miesian paradigm.

[EXTERIOR] The design is a showcase for industrialized building components such as sliding garage doors, steel wall panels, and metal joists.

34, 35 Caryl's house; Point Richmond, California. Holabird & Root, 1955. *Photos: Gerald Horn.*

[EXTERIOR] Built over a boat slip in San Francisco Bay, the steel-framed cubic dwelling has wood sun screens and siding.

[INTERIOR] The diagonal alignment of the stair and the double height of some rooms create a variety of interior spaces.

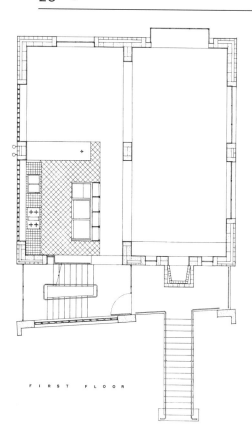

F I R S T   F L O O R

36, 37 Croffead house; Charleston, South Carolina. Clark & Menefee, 1990. *Photo: © Timothy Hursley.*

[PLAN] On three levels to take up the minimum of ground space, the house conforms to the building line of the suburban block while it optimizes river views. The strict geometry of the volume is broken only by the slanted front wall that aligns the dwelling to the mature trees that front the site. This first-floor plan contains the living areas and kitchen.

[EXTERIOR] Frontality, formality, and river orientation are in the tradition of the Carolina low-country villa.

EXPRESSIONIST

ORGANIC

While abstraction reflected a search for the universal, rational, and ideal, modernism also wanted to express the unique, intuitive, and romantic. As different as they are from each other, the architects who worked in an expressionist mode shared a common interest in creating an emotional response: exaggerating light, space, and mass; enjoying the contrast of boldly articulated geometric forms; and exploiting the sensual quality of materials, especially those close to nature.

Frank Lloyd Wright's Organic architecture conceived the house as growing from the ground like a living plant. The "new sense of building on American soil," he wrote in *The Natural House* (1954), would "*grow* building forms not only true to function but expressive far beyond mere function in the realm of human spirit."

The Wrightian house is sensitive to climate, orientation, and site conditions. Seemingly anchored by a massive chimney, it is low to the ground, seeking the protection of a hillside or berm. Wright's principles of Organic architecture dictated that elevation and ornament evolve from the geometry of the floor plan. Rectangular, hexagonal, or triangular plans, for example, generated corresponding treatments of window openings, framing patterns, built-in furniture, and lighting.

"Architecture must learn to see brick as brick, learn to see steel as steel, see glass as glass," declared Wright, who determined each dwelling's mass, proportions, and detailing in relation to the properties of the principal building materials. Wright's walls are not like sides of a box, but, rather, piers or partial screens that permit space to flow freely. "Light is the beautifier of architecture," said Wright, who used daylight to make small spaces seem more spacious.

Wright produced dozens of "Usonian"—that is, United States-ian—dwellings in many parts of the country in the forties and early fifties. Small and relatively inexpensive, their more or less standardized building features and consistent modules made them adaptable to diverse clients, sites, and building codes. A modest example is the L-shaped Pope-Leighey house (figures 38, 39, 40) of 1939–41 in Mount Vernon, Virginia. (Owned by the National Trust for Historic Preservation, the house is open to the public.)

Based on circular plans, several larger houses by Wright dramatically exploit the roughness, solidity, and weight-bearing qualities of unfinished fieldstone. The Friedman house (figures 41, 42), completed in 1949 in Pleasantville, New York, is developed from two intersecting circles, with massive, randomly set sloping fieldstone walls that add emotional warmth to hard stone. The David Wright house of 1950 in Phoenix, Arizona, is a powerful sculptural form, generated by ramps that spiral up from the desert floor. Circular patterns add decorative qualities to concrete block piers and mahogany boarding.

Wright felt sure that Organic principles permitted each architect to find his own way, accurately predicting that the tradition would produce "as many different kinds of houses as there are people." The Organic tradition has continued to evolve, after Wright's death in 1959, through the closing years of the century.

Certainly, there have been cross-influences between the Organic tradition and the Modernist mode. An encounter that produced a distinct hybrid is seen in the 1955 Duff house (figures 43, 44, 45) in Wayzata, Minnesota, by Close Architects. The hexagonal module and hovering roof are close to Wright, while the glass walls and smooth surfaces remind one of Mies. The 1986 House-in-the-Woods (figures 46, 47) in Sheboygan, Wisconsin, by Weese Langley Weese continues the Organic tradition while simultaneously reflecting both the passage through modernism and a renewed interest in local history. The heightened emotional impact of hearth and roof—symbols of warmth and shelter—is a constant feature in the work of those who practice in the Organic tradition. In Houston, Frederick MacKie and Karl Kamrath designed a number of hearth-centered dwellings of overwhelming horizontality. In Elm Grove, Wisconsin, William Wenzler and Associates' theatrically roofed 1965–67 Gerlach house (figures 48, 49, 50) is wrapped in curved glacial stone walls that culminate in the interior in a massive chimney.

The Organic tradition has permitted certain free spirits to exercise individuality to the point of eccentricity. Exploiting profoundly expressive shapes and bold silhouettes, Wright's son, Lloyd Wright, designed the Bowler house (1963) in Palos Verdes, California, with steeply pitched gable ends and a tall anchoring chimney that have all the dynamism of an alighting bird. Bruce Goff pushed the boundaries of building with nonconventional materials such as egg cartons, waste glass, cork, dime-store ashtrays, and fishing net. He preferred free, nonmodular plans, such as that of the 1966 Jacquart house in Sublette, Kansas, which centers around the heavy stone forms of a cavelike atrium. "There is never just one solution," said Goff, placing intuition ahead of logic. "The creative artist works intuitively and instinctively with the one he feels best with."

The Organic tradition also exploits the emotional properties of structure, John Lautner's work being outstanding in this respect. Lautner's Elrod house (1968) in Palm Springs, California, is a curvaceous extravaganza roofed by a self-supporting dome that permits vast glass window walls. The Organic tradition's romance of nature establishes "a reference and radiance for living, a unique, yet universal experience" in the work of Fay Jones, whose Eden Island, Arkansas, residence of 1964 is a tall, erect form with taut wood framing that seems to intensify the drama of an extraordinary grotto setting.

Increasingly sophisticated and self-confident clients have stretched the Organic tradition in various directions. James Howard Fox's (1987) Jackson house (figure 51) in Cashiers, North Carolina, was designed for a wheelchair-bound client who held strong convictions about privacy and views. Bart Prince was asked to design a "sculptural biography" of the inhabitants of the 1984–88 Price house (figures 52, 53) in Orange County, California. Besides communal family spaces, the plan allots eccentric, indeterminate, and highly individualistic spaces for individual family members.

Concerns for saving fuel, reducing pollution, "natural" ways of building, and hand craftsmanship have been adding new dimensions to Organic architecture since the sixties. "We are trying to find our way back into the earth family . . . to unite the inner and the outer man," declared Berkeley professor Sim Van Der Ryn, one of those who brought the architectural counterculture onto the main stage. It's essential "that we look upon the world, listen and learn," wrote Ian McHarg, a landscape designer and pioneering environmentalist, in the immensely influential book *Design with Nature* (1969).

Energy conservation measures such as earth berming, thickened walls, rationalized ventilation, and south-facing glass windows are now commonplace. The Green Mountains, Vermont, Crowell house (figure 54) by Moore Grover Harper sits deep in an earth berm on its north side, while it opens a glazed face to the south. Completed in 1975 on a compact plan, the dwelling has an eighteen-inch-thick sod roof that helps to minimize its intrusion on the open landscape. Built with a similar toolbox in Sharon, Connecticut, Alfredo DeVido's 1986 Moore house (figures 55, 56, 57) is banked into retaining walls that suggest natural stone strata, enhancing the intimacy of the house in its setting.

The Southwest, especially southern California and New Mexico, can probably claim the most sophisticated energy-conservative designs. In the Sandia Mountains outside of Taos, Edward Mazria's Stockbrand house of 1980 (figures 58, 59, 60) achieves almost complete energy self-sufficiency by means of berming, a heat-collecting swimming pool, rooftop photovoltaic cells, sawtooth-shaped clerestory windows, and reflecting surfaces. In putting it all together, he explained that "the architecture in this building does most of the work." A Sandia Mountains, New Mexico, dwelling of 1977 by Antoine Predock makes a strong design statement with the steeply sloping solar-heat-collecting roof. A sheltered roof garden and overhung windows advertise the need for protection from the sun. A Santa Cruz Mountains, California, dwelling of 1979 is an ecologically sensitive house that almost disappears into its scenic mountain setting. Designed by Jersey Devil (Steve Badanes and Jim Adamson), the house is carved directly into the hillside site and is covered by a grass-covered roof following its contours.

Unconventional do-it-yourself craftsmen-builders have flourished in second-home or warm-climate sites, sometimes commanding considerable wit and ingenuity. William Bruder, for one, masterminded several such projects in Arizona. The owner's hands-on renovation (1981–88) of the Rotharmel house in Glendale followed Bruder's seven-year master plan that eventually turned the ordinary tract house into a sculptured circular concrete fantasy intricately configured with the setting. In the privately planned community of Star, New Mexico, Michael Reynolds used rammed earth, old tires, and beer cans to create handmade dwellings that are practically energy self-sufficient, with additional environmentally sensitive features such as a catchwater roof and recycled-waste-water systems. The architect's goal: "To evolve humanity into an earthen harmony."

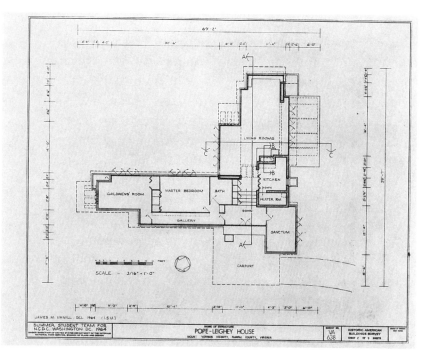

SCALE — 3/16" = 1'-0"

JAMES M. HAMILL · DEL 1964 · (L.S.U.)

SUMMER STUDENT TEAM FOR
N.C.D.C. WASHINGTON D.C. 1964
UNDER DIRECTION OF UNITED STATES DEPARTMENT OF THE INTERIOR
NATIONAL PARK SERVICE, BRANCH OF PLANS AND DESIGN

NAME OF STRUCTURE
POPE-LEIGHEY HOUSE
MOUNT VERNON VICINITY, FAIRFAX COUNTY, VIRGINIA

SURVEY NO.
VA
638

HISTORIC AMERICAN
BUILDINGS SURVEY
SHEET 2 OF 9 SHEETS

38, 39, 40 Pope-Leighey house; Mt. Vernon, Virginia. Frank Lloyd Wright, 1939–41; relocated and rebuilt, 1964. *Photos: Jack Boucher, Historic American Buildings Survey, Library of Congress.*

[PLAN] In this L-shaped plan, the service core, incorporating kitchen, bath, heater room, and fireplace, serves as a pivot between family gathering spaces and individual bedrooms.

[EXTERIOR] "I like the sense of shelter in the look of a dwelling," said Wright. The dwelling's ground-hugging quality is emphasized by horizontally grooved cypress boarding, seemingly continuous from interior to exterior. A powerful visual element, the roof is raised higher over the living-dining area than over the kitchen and bedrooms.

[INTERIOR] Note the changing ceiling height, which lends intimacy to the dining area and spaciousness to the living area. The patterned grilles in the clerestory windows demonstrate Wright's conception of integral ornament, "as natural to architecture as plumage to a bird."

41, 42 Friedman house; Pleasantville, New York. Frank Lloyd Wright, 1949. *Photos: Ezra Stoller, © Esto.*

[EXTERIOR] The two-story dwelling rises on two intersecting circles, with the main living area at a lower level, bedrooms above. The stone wall creates continuity with a circular-roofed carport at the left.

[INTERIOR] The energy of the dwelling seems to emanate from the rough-textured mass of the stone fireplace and chimney.

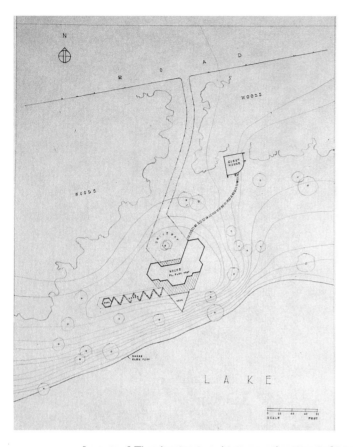

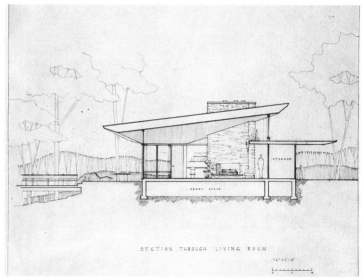

43, 44, 45 Duff house; Wayzata, Minnesota. Close Architects, 1955. *Photo: Walter Zombine.*

[PLAN] Contrary to Wright's dictum that a house should be built *around* a hill, never *on* it, the dwelling occupies a hilltop site that takes advantage of lake views.

[SECTION] The massive stone hearth creates a sheltered, cavelike ambience, while the lift of the roof and the glass window walls seem to lead out-of-doors.

[EXTERIOR] The dominating chimney and active roof stem from Wright, although the smooth, vertical sheathing is a favored minimalist motif.

46, 47 House-in-the-Woods; Sheboygan, Wisconsin. Weese Langley Weese, 1986. *Photo: Harold N. Kaplan, © HNK Architectural Photography.*

[PLAN] The entry foyer with stairway and fireplace niche holds one in the heart of the house. Lateral extensions and cross axes produce an additive character not typical of Organic design.

[EXTERIOR] The dwelling evokes the early-twentieth-century Prairie School architecture.

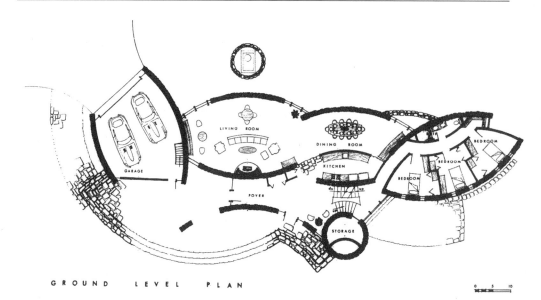

GROUND   LEVEL   PLAN

48, 49, 50   Gerlach house; Elm Grove, Wisconsin. William Wenzler and Associates, 1965–67. *Photos: Bill Engdahl/Hedrich-Blessing.*

[PLAN] The plan is an exuberant repetition of an arc-shaped module.

[ENTRANCE] Entry into the house is a dramatic experience, the front door being deeply recessed within projecting stone piers.

[INTERIOR] One encounters a protected, welcoming hearth.

51 Jackson house; Cashiers, North Carolina. James Howard Fox, 1987. *Photo: James Howard Fox.* Providing privacy on the front elevation, the tight row of small squared window openings seems to belt in the powerful mass of the sloping stone walls. The yawning circular opening at the eaves captures a view of a wildflower garden.

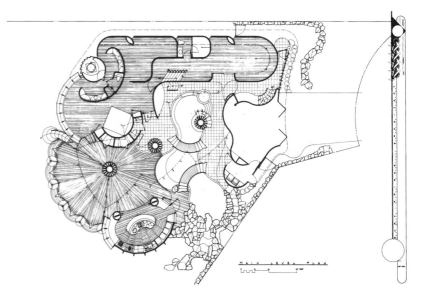

52, 53 Price house; Orange County, California. Bart Prince, 1984–88. *Photo: © Scott Frances/Esto.*

[PLAN] Spaces, not really definite rooms, radiate outward from the three circular structural supports. The plan is dynamic in three dimensions, having two curving stairways that cross over an amoeboid pool, cutouts to an upper floor, and openings onto decks and terraces. The kitchen and living-dining areas are at the left side of the plan, sleeping spaces at the top.

[EXTERIOR] The dwelling twists up and around the spiral stairways. The owner's office occupies the writhing tower at the right.

54   Crowell house; Green Mountains, Vermont. Moore Grover Harper, 1975. *Photo: Robert Perron.* The "handmade" aesthetic is strong in ecological design.

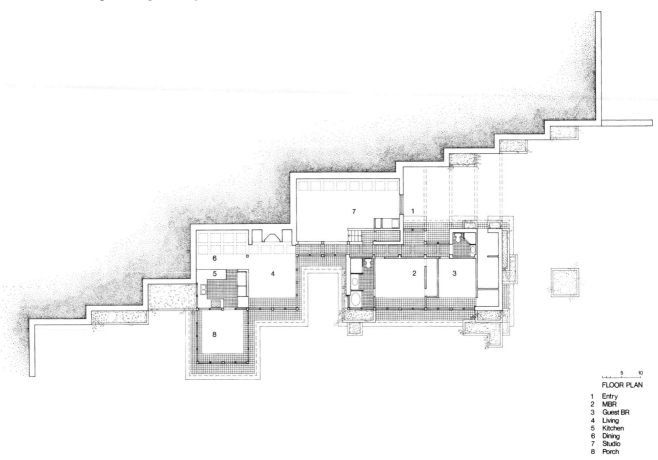

5   10
FLOOR PLAN
1   Entry
2   MBR
3   Guest BR
4   Living
5   Kitchen
6   Dining
7   Studio
8   Porch

55, 56, 57   Moore house; Sharon, Connecticut. Alfredo DeVido Associates, 1986. *Photos: © Norman McGrath.*

[PLAN] Only the bedrooms and porch have windows, other rooms being lit by skylights.

[EXTERIOR] The north side of the house is dug into the ground; the glazed porch opens to the south. Sod roofing, skylights, overhanging eaves, and south glazing optimize the mix of protection and exposure.

[INTERIOR] Though the fireplace is dug into the hillside, skylighting dramatically illuminates the hearth.

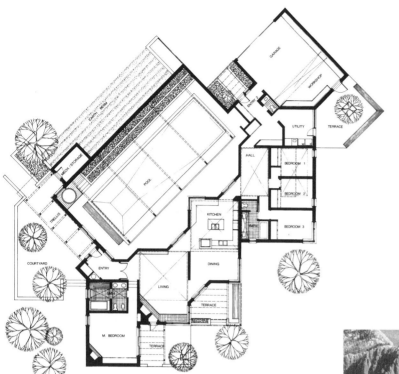

58, 59, 60 Stockbrand house; Sandia Mountains, Taos, New Mexico. Edward Mazria, 1980. *Photos: Tim Street-Porter.*

[PLAN] All rooms but the kitchen face the southern sun.

[EXTERIOR] Close to the ground, with a jagged silhouette that echoes the mountain range, the house is at one with the site.

[INTERIOR] Clerestory windows exploit solar heat.

MANIPULATED SPACE

The charismatic Louis I. Kahn, having experienced a protracted period of development that enabled him to fuse the architecture of ancient Rome and Egypt with that of the Organic tradition and the Modernists, learned to address architecture as "life emerging from the inseparable aspects of mind and heart." Aiming to uncover what the "building wants to be," Kahn exploited the drama of light and shadow and expressive shapes, always upholding the primacy of space. "In the nature of space is the spirit and the will to exist in a certain way," Kahn taught.

No follower of Kahn has had more impact on house design than Charles Moore. "You can capture space and let it go, define or explore it," Moore proclaimed. "Space is one of those things that you have more of after you have 'exploded' it, but it seems to thrive in captivity too." The 1965 Karas house (figure 61) in Monterey, California, by MLTW/Moore Turnbull, is a stunning demonstration of the drama of verticality. The house pushes space through three interpenetrating levels crossed by bridges and lofts and opened by cutaways.

Moore's interest in the excitement of space, as well as his fascination with the vernacular, was widely shared. Bold picturesque shingle forms became part of a playful American idiom, typically in second homes at seaside and rural locations. One such is the 1966 Oestreicher house (figure 62) in Sausalito, California, designed by Esherick, Homsey, Dodge & Davis with a tall, picturesque mass, steep roof pitch, angular projections, and eccentric window openings. Hardy Holzman Pfeiffer Associates' 1967 shingled Hadley house (figures 63, 64) in Martha's Vineyard, Massachusetts, is a frisky ensemble of gable ends, chimney stacks, and towers that irreverently paraphrases New England's late-nineteenth-century Shingle Style. The McCune house by Hobart Betts in rural Londonderry, Vermont, engages in a "spatial ball game . . . space going in, out, up, down, and ducking around." The genre enjoyed particular popularity in the Hamptons, the eastern Long Island playground of well-to-do New Yorkers. Norman Jaffe's 1971 Perlbinder house in Sagaponack plays with the vertical dimension in a shingled, four-story, slant-roof form.

Deepening admiration for Louis Kahn, and Paul Rudolph, joined with a fascination with Le Corbusier's work of the fifties, contributed to the popularity of heavily articulated forms that dramatized mass as well as space. Among those who worked in the idiom were Ulrich Franzen and Ralph Rapson as well as Earl R. Flansburgh, who designed the Lyman house (figures 65, 66) of 1966 in Dover, Massachusetts. It is a tense composition of thrusting, boxlike forms, held aloft from the rocky site by an emphatic concrete foundation. Gentler, and coming down to the site, Don Hisaka's 1969 design for his own house (figures 67, 68) in the Cleveland, Ohio, suburb of Shaker Heights composes four wood-sheathed, rectangular volumes to create an interior court. Designed by Levinson, Zaprauskis Associates, the 1972 Arbor house (figures 69, 70, 71) in suburban Philadelphia, Pennsylvania, is surrounded by a latticelike enclosure that envelops the cross-axial dwelling in complex indoor-outdoor relationships.

Fascinated by the properties of space, certain architects were drawn to an earlier phase of Le Corbusier's modernism—the abstract, white cubic dwellings of the twenties and thirties. "Spatial interpenetration, overlap and intersection interests us," said Charles Gwathmey, whose work explores "the nature and the whys and wherefores of space." Gwathmey Siegel & Associates' 1979 house in Cincinnati (figures 72, 73, 74) uses exquisite details and high finishes to present the walls as abstract planes. Intricately interlocked in both the vertical and horizontal dimensions, the dwelling, courtyard, outbuildings, swimming pool, and tennis court form a villagelike setting. Richard Meier & Partners' pristine, cubic dwellings, such as the Douglas house of 1973 in Harbor Springs, Maryland, are explorations of processional space, spatial hierarchy, diagonal rotation, and layered space. "Beyond theory, beyond historical reference, my meditations are on space, shape, light and how to make them," said Meier, continuing this investigation into the eighties and nineties. Other architects who took this approach include Anthony Ames, in Atlanta, Georgia, and Batter Kay Associates, in Solano Beach, California.

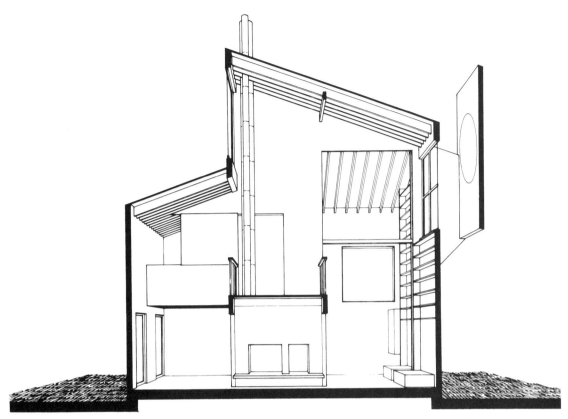

61 Karas house; Monterey, California. MLTW/Moore Turnbull, 1965. The three-story-high living room space is activated by light from a huge window at the highest point of the wall as well as by reflected light from the exterior baffle seen at the right.

62 Oestreicher house; Sausalito, California. Esherick, Homsey, Dodge & Davis, 1966. *Photo: Barbeau Engh.* Continuous shingle cladding endows the dwelling with a strong sculptural presence, made even bolder by the assertive geometry of window openings and balconies.

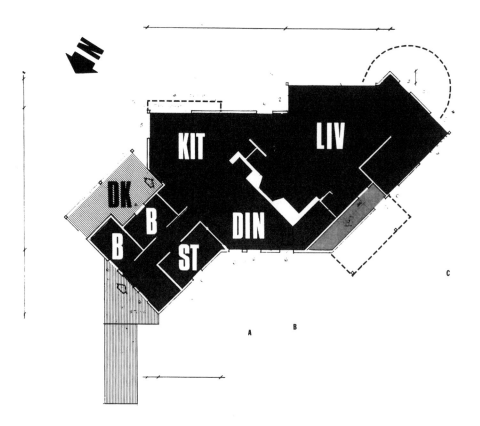

63, 64 Hadley house; Martha's Vineyard, Massachusetts. Hardy Holzman Pfeiffer Associates, 1967. *Photo:* © *Norman McGrath.*

[PLAN] Insistent diagonality energizes the interior. The bedroom wing (at the left) joins the kitchen-dining wing (in the center) at a precipitous forty-five-degree angle, while the connection to the living room (at the right) is skewed by the diagonal placement of the massive chimney stack.

[EXTERIOR] Seeming serendipity governs the shape and pitch of the roofline and the size and location of the window openings.

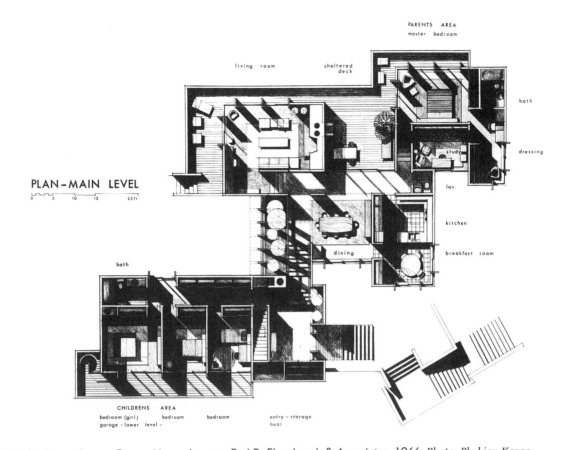

PLAN - MAIN LEVEL

PARENTS AREA
master bedroom

living room

sheltered
deck

bath

dressing

study

lav.

kitchen

dining

breakfast room

bath

CHILDRENS AREA
bedroom (girl)   bedroom   bedroom   entry - storage
garage - lower level -   heat

65, 66 Lyman house; Dover, Massachusetts. Earl R. Flansburgh & Associates, 1966. *Photo: Phokion Karas.*

[PLAN] Four separate wings are vigorously articulated into a pinwheel configuration.

[EXTERIOR] The deep window openings make the walls seem like thick masonry, although they are actually of wood.

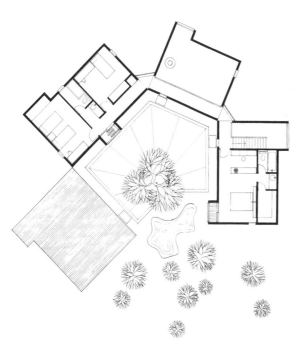

67, 68 Hisaka house; Shaker Heights, Ohio. Don Hisaka, 1969. *Photo: © Thom Abel—Abel Photographics.*

[PLAN] The dwelling is composed of children's bedrooms, the master bedroom suite, a living-dining area, and an attached garage.

[EXTERIOR] Decisively expressed on the exterior, separate stairways serve the master bedroom and children's bedroom wings.

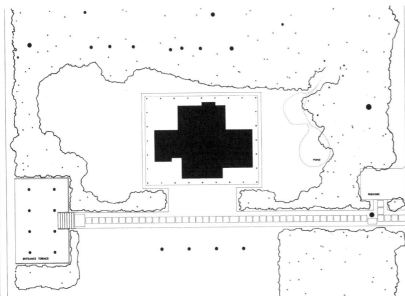

SITE PLAN

69, 70, 71 Arbor house; suburban Philadelphia, Pennsylvania. Levinson, Zaprauskis Associates, 1969–72. *Photos: © Lawrence S. Williams, Inc.*

[PLAN] The plan is a dynamic cross shape.

[INTERIOR] The two-story height of the ceiling and the indeterminacy of the wall seem to set space free.

[EXTERIOR] A lattice wall wraps the dwelling in a permeable envelope.

EAST ELEVATION

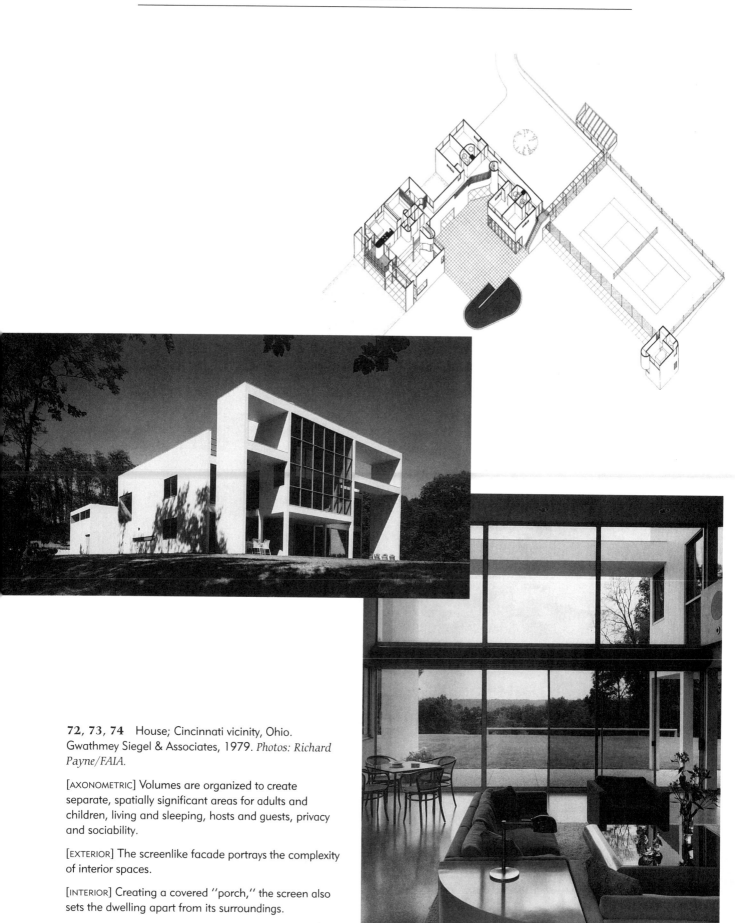

72, 73, 74 House; Cincinnati vicinity, Ohio. Gwathmey Siegel & Associates, 1979. *Photos: Richard Payne/FAIA.*

[AXONOMETRIC] Volumes are organized to create separate, spatially significant areas for adults and children, living and sleeping, hosts and guests, privacy and sociability.

[EXTERIOR] The screenlike facade portrays the complexity of interior spaces.

[INTERIOR] Creating a covered ''porch,'' the screen also sets the dwelling apart from its surroundings.

DECONSTRUCTIVIST

The eighties generated an expressionistic tendency sometimes described as Deconstructivist. In the work of diverse architects, it is an attempt to expand the boundaries of architecture, to focus on fragmentation, assemblage, ad hoc change, incoherence, and the process of building—or unbuilding.

One innovator in this vein has been Peter Eisenman, a philosopher-architect who looks beyond function and structure to explore meaning, tension, and conflict. Repudiating Euclidean geometry as inadequate to explain "the uncertainty and relativity of the modern world," Eisenman has favored skewed lines and indeterminate forms, such as the Moebius strip, which has no real inside and outside, whose forms move "simultaneously towards completion and dissolution . . . at once becoming and disappearing."

By contrast, Frank Gehry, an artist-architect, took his inspiration from other artists, but also from the streets, from a culture that's made up of running for airplanes, throwaways, fast food, and advertising. Pragmatic and irreverent, Gehry said he preferred "the sketch quality, the tentativeness, the messiness if you will, the appearance of 'in process,' rather than the presumption of total resolution and finality."

Gehry's flight into fantasy in the 1979 remodeling of his funky Santa Monica, California, bungalow (figures 75, 76) set Deconstructivism on its course. Bursting with energy, Gehry's addition wrapped a rakish timber-and-wire-mesh envelope around the original building, leaving doubts about what is just begun or already completed, solid or void, old or new. Like his heroes Frank Lloyd Wright and Bruce Goff, Gehry exploited the craft potential of materials, glorifying the ticky-tacky stuff of commonplace culture, such as corrugated metal, chain-link fencing, bright plastic, and raw plywood.

A related California design by Coy Howard is the Ashley house of 1987, in Chino, apparently sculpted to its site by varied floor levels, wall profiles, and room heights. The 1993 remodeling by Eric Owen Moss of the Lawson/Westen house (figures 77, 78, 79), a mundane ranch in West Los Angeles, California, seems to explode a new kitchen and stairway core right through the roof, challenging basic understandings of building. The Dan house in Malibu, California, of 1994–96, an investigation of discordant forms that has little interest in stable right angles, flat planes, or conventional window shapes, was designed by Frank D. Israel Design Associates. It is "a combination of an Airstream trailer and some Santa Barbara farm buildings" said the architect.

A rather more cerebral, if less exuberant, approach prevails outside of southern California. Thinking of building as the making of art, Bausman-Gill conceived the design of the Pritchett house of 1988 (figures 80, 81, 82) in Conanicut Island, Rhode Island, as an investigation into the nature of planes and the differentiation of painterly surfaces, generating individuality for each separate element. Inspiration came from a broad range of vernacular sources—"the planar relief of New England wooden churches, the exposed structural systems of the surrounding barns and the sloped roof shape of early colonial houses so symbolic of domestic form." Lee Skolnick's own 1992 house (figures 83, 84) in North Haven, New York, is an intricate configuration of idiosyncratic elements that each, in a different way, reflects on eastern Long Island vernacular tradition. His architecture is about "reconstruction," said Skolnick, who endowed different elements with different meanings.

Increasingly concerned with architectural theory, Steven Holl visualized "an architecture of strange and mysterious beginnings with the hope of original and unique meanings in each place." Holl's 1991 Stretto house in a Dallas, Texas, suburb broke out of the Modernist fold to enter fully into the realm of sensation. Holl composed the dwelling as four cubic volumes that step down a slope in tandem with four dams on the creek that flows through the site. His interest in architecture as frozen music influenced the use of curving, overlapping, and hovering rooflines.

75, 76 Frank Gehry house; Santa Monica, California. Frank O. Gehry & Associates, 1979–88. *Photos: © Grant Mudford.*

[EXTERIOR] The expansion of an existing dwelling involves the apparent collision of glass, corrugated tin, and chain-link fencing.

[INTERIOR] Preserving an exterior wall on the interior to reveal change over time, the addition opens an indeterminate wall/ceiling and window/wall.

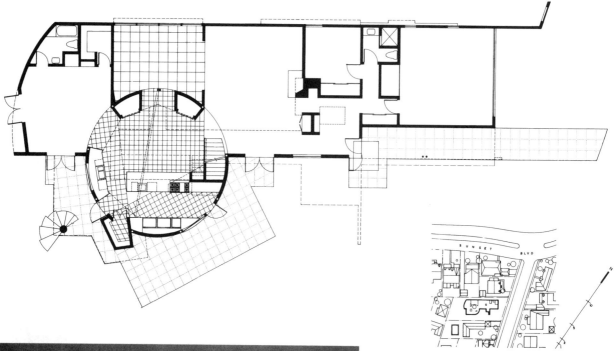

77, 78, 79 Lawson/Westen house; West Los Angeles, California. Eric Owen Moss Architects, 1993. *Photos: Tom Bonner.*

[PLAN] The kitchen-stairway core rises in elevation as a four-story, off-center cone that provides vantage points for dramatic interior vistas.

[EXTERIOR] The intervention sets windows, walls, and rooflines at rakish angles.

[INTERIOR] Seen from above, the shape of the stairway seems to set the house in motion.

80, 81, 82 Pritchett house; Conanicut Island, Rhode Island. Bausman-Gill Associates, 1988. *Photos: © Jeff Goldberg/Esto.*

[EXTERIOR] Vertical supports that project in front of the wall emphasize the individuality of each component. Skylights reveal interior roof trusses.

[PLAN] The complex is disjointed into three components: main house, pool house, and guest wing.

[INTERIOR] The entry foyer leads one past the slanting wall of the kitchen enclosure along a thrusting pathway that culminates in the hearth.

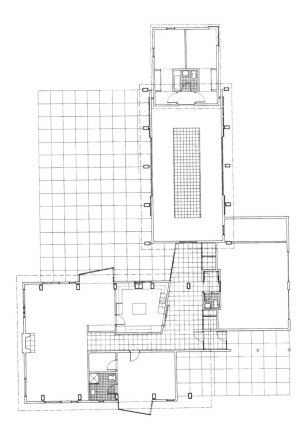

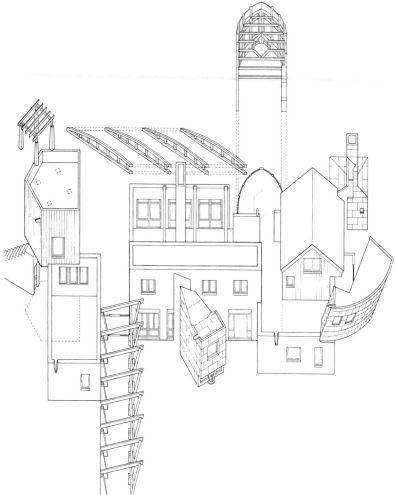

83, 84   Skolnick house; North Haven, New York. Lee H. Skolnick Architecture + Design Partnership, 1992. *Photo: © Peter Aaron/Esto.*

[EXTERIOR] The curved cantilevered form contains the master-bedroom-and-bath suite (at the right). The cube projects the stair forward of the living room in the main part of the house, where the children's bedrooms occupy the second floor. The tower contains a studio. Each segment is differentiated by the combination of materials—brick, fieldstone, vertical cedar planks, cedar clapboards, and copper.

[AXONOMETRIC] A collage of almost familiar forms that settle in to feel like the local vernacular.

TRADITIONAL

POSTMODERNIST

Americans understand the symbolism of the traditional dwelling. A pitched or overhanging roof promises shelter. A prominent front door signals welcome. A regular pattern of windows signifies an orderly family life. The use of conventional materials, whether stucco in Florida, concrete block in Texas, or shingle in New England, shows a shared sense of community. A neat, predictable appearance pays respect to neighborhood property values. In more than two hundred years of history, in all the many styles of American dwellings, from provincial Spanish Baroque to polite English Neoclassic and sophisticated Gothic Revival, style, itself, can be seen as a powerful symbol of status and success.

Resisting the advances of modernism, traditional design stubbornly survived the forties and early fifties. A taste for the familiar was shared by clients who yearned for a return to normalcy after World War II, architects with big reputations to maintain, and tract-house developers who knew what would sell. Only in the sixties had the modern house become sufficiently familiar to have developed a widely understood symbolism of its own. But by then, the seeds of reaction had already been sown.

"Architects can no longer afford to be intimidated by the puritanically moral language of orthodox Modern architecture," wrote Robert Venturi in *Complexity and Contradiction in Architecture* (1966). In compelling theoretical explorations that ventured into new territory, Venturi highlighted the decorative, symbolic, and emotional potential of architecture. With the discerning eye of a connoisseur and the quick draw of a cowboy, Venturi rescued his-

tory and idiosyncrasy from the wastebasket, snatching funky Pop Art from the Las Vegas strip, quirky Mannerist detailing from seventeenth-century Rome, and picturesque carpenter treatments from small-town America. "I am for the richness of meaning rather than clarity of meaning," Venturi declared. "A valid architecture evokes many levels of meaning and combinations of focus: its space and its focus become readable and workable in several ways at once." This new Postmodernist tendency flourished through the seventies and eighties, paralleling the interest in historic preservation and the growing nostalgia for small-town and rural living.

The strong measure of irony that pervaded the Postmodernist movement got an early start in Robert Venturi's design for his mother's house (1962–64) in Chestnut Hill, Pennsylvania. The dwelling is modest in size and materials, but of vaulting ambition, bearing conspicuous ornamental motifs that allude to Palladio and Michelangelo. The design of Venturi, Rauch & Scott Brown's 1967–68 Lieb house (figures 85, 86, 87, 88) pays homage to the very ordinariness and banality of a Long Beach Island, New Jersey, streetscape. The plain, boxlike dwelling, far from ordinary, is eloquent of Venturi's inclusivist philosophy, mocking pretentions to "class" while it mocks the exclusiveness of modernism itself. "It stands up to, rather than ignores, the environment of utility poles," the architects asserted.

The Postmodernist mindset demonstrated humor, irreverence, even satire, in ever more diverse responses both to the local setting and the idiosyncrasies of the client. Ueland & Junker's Heckscher house (figure 89) in the posh Chestnut Hill suburb of Philadelphia of 1974–75 added tacky aluminum siding and rakishly angled doors and windows to an otherwise staid configuration. In Washington, Connecticut, Robert A. M. Stern and John S. Hagmann tacked enigmatic moldings on the 1974 Lang house, a dwelling whose quirky floor plan, unsettling approach, and twisted axes assert the freedom to fantasize. Hugh Newell Jacobsen's 1977 duplicate addition to a staid Victorian house in Chevy Chase, Maryland, seems to mock the seriousness of the original.

Moore Ruble Yudell's Rodes house (figures 90, 91) of 1979–80 in Los Angeles played with the illusion that the quite modest house is really the grand climax of a formal processional entry. The fan-shaped plan creates a stagelike setting, and there are make-believe remains of a grand Baroque stair from which to watch the drama. A saucy free-spirited response to tacky surroundings is Tigerman McCurry's 1992 Artist's Studio and Residence (figures 92, 93, 94) in La Conchita, California. Intended to show how "disgruntled" the architects were with traditional architecture, the complex imposes itself on its surroundings in the guise of a pink stucco "basilica" flanked by two miniature look-alikes that serve as garage and carport.

In a more restrained and sober mood, the Postmodernists also revisited indigenous building forms. Southern respect for tradition, together with a solid respect for the vicissitudes of the climate, distinguish the Tampa, Florida, Logan house of 1980, designed by Rowe Holmes Associates. The house is based on the historic dog-trot form, with an open breezeway in the center to maximize air circulation. A 1981 dwelling in Door County, Wisconsin, was designed by Nagle, Hartray & Associates to recall the region's distinctive lighthouses.

But "style" was most seductive to the Postmodernists. "To build within a tradition is to tip one's hat to the community—and to honor its evolution over time," explained Robert A. M. Stern, one of those who revived the late-nineteenth-century Shingle Style on Long Island, New York. Stern's 1980 Bozzi house (figures 95, 96) packs what would have been a romantic assembly of oddly shaped rooms into a neat contemporary configuration. Forms that evoke the past—turret, tall chimney, eyebrow dormers, and oculus windows—"suggest that some things, like the pleasures of a month in the country, have never really changed," said Stern. Paul Segal, Eugene Futterman, and Francis Fleetwood are others who have reined in Modernist sensibilities while developing new versions of the Shingle Style on Long Island and in other vacation communities.

In countless landmark districts across the country, requirements for public oversight have engaged local officials and concerned citizens in the design process. In Nantucket, Massachusetts, for example, Bissell & Wells's Flintoft house (figure 97) of 1978 was required to keep in line with the historic district commission's line on scale, massing, materials, and details.

Postmodernist adaptations and renovations of the late-nineteenth-century Victorian Stick Style have generated never-seen-before dwellings that seem, nevertheless, to be genuinely historic. In the Seaside, Florida, resort community planned by Andres Duany and Elizabeth Plater-Zyberk elaborate design controls encourage a fine-textured, high-density setting. The 1985 Rosewalk Cottages (figures 98, 99), by Robert Orr & Melanie Taylor, include three different interpretations of historic small town carpenter style. Exploiting such twentieth-century innovations as open plans and loft balconies, the designs use woodwork and garden treatment to add fun and fantasy. The picturesque qualities of open woodwork also characterize Kiss + Cathcart's 1993–94 additions to an original Stick Style house (figures 100, 101) in Hastings-on-Hudson, New York. The spirited articulation of stick framing goes along with a pragmatic approach that attempts to resolve "piecemeal problems in piecemeal ways," said Cathcart.

Inevitably, Postmodernists have been drawn to classicism—although with widely diverging intentions and very different results. Certain architects have created opportunistic encounters between classicism and local vernacular. "The tradition of Classic meeting Farm that seems to run in a direct line from Vicenza to Virginia" was not ignored in the 1983 Mere house (figures 102, 103, 104) in Flint Hill, Virginia, maintained its architects, Ben Benedict and Carlo Pucci (Bumpzoid). Rising on a steep hill from a lakeside site, the house is a spare rectangular form, its lake facade embellished by a columned pediment that evokes the dignity of an ancient temple. A similar tongue-in-cheekiness inspired the 1990 Hanley/McGuire house in Head of Westport, Massachusetts, by Perry Dean Rogers & Partners, who designed a tiny shingled cottage with a majestically raised entry level.

Serious scholarship has put the renewal of classicism in contemporary America on firmer ground. Thomas Gordon Smith made a close study of classicism to rediscover its forgotten sensuality. The evocative colors and intriguing detailing of Smith's 1980 Tuscan house in Livermore, California, for example, seem to express a Californian attitude toward the good life. Smith's own house (figures 105, 106, 107) in South Bend, Indiana, of 1989–91, an eloquent, highly personal dialogue between past and present, is based on a rigorous study of ancient Roman precepts and their changing interpretations over time. Adhering closely to canonic proportions and details, Allan Greenberg sought to create "something new and immediate" in the Classic tradition by the use of modern planning and building techniques. Staying close to a historic Virginia prototype for a Georgian-style house of the early nineties in Connecticut, Greenberg exploited the thickness of the walls to hide ducts and conduits, altered the usual room configuration to create an extra-large kitchen and master bedroom, and added a dormered skylight on an upper floor.

Classicism is a sometime thing in the conception of Robert A. M. Stern's "Dream house," a prototype house commissioned by *Life* magazine in 1994. With crowd-pleasing innovations in room configurations, the dwelling's envelope is impressive in its Classic details. But, true to nineteenth-century eclectic tradition, the house appears equally well dressed in Tudor, Craftsman, Dutch Colonial, or Spanish Colonial garb.

Other architects are joining in this dating game, but it's too early to know if the courtship of classicism will culminate in a wedding—or drift on in an aimless affair.

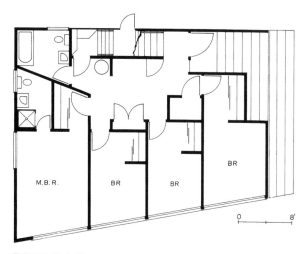

FIRST FLOOR

SECOND FLOOR

85, 86, 87, 88 Lieb house; Long Beach Island, New Jersey. Venturi, Rauch, 1967–78. *Photos: Stephen Hill.*

[PLAN—FIRST FLOOR] Intentionally unceremonious, the entry foyer is an awkward space, cut up by doorways and a washing machine nook.

[PLAN—SECOND FLOOR] The notched plan separates kitchen and living room while zoning the uses of the outdoor deck.

[EXTERIOR—REAR AND SIDE] The dwelling is sheathed in the commonplace two-tone asbestos shingle typical of the 1940s builders' houses around town. There's a cheeky intention in the apparently ad hoc fenestration, including a circular window that alludes to a 1930s radio loudspeaker.

[ENTRANCE] An overscaled numeral and a stair that narrows from grand to intimate are among the "big" statements that distinguish the dwelling as "serious" architecture.

89 Heckscher house; Chestnut Hill, Philadelphia, Pennsylvania. Ueland & Junker, 1974–75. *Photo: Mark Ueland.*

[EXTERIOR] Picturesque massing and native fieldstone relate the dwelling to the locality.

90, 91 Rodes house; Los Angeles, California. Moore Ruble Yudell, 1979–80. *Photo: © Timothy Hursley.*

[PLAN] In a novel plan that responds to the owner's interest in the theater, the living room opens to an oval, stagelike patio.

[EXTERIOR] Although the double rank of windows suggests otherwise, the curved living room is actually a dramatic, two-story space, the formal entry to the house.

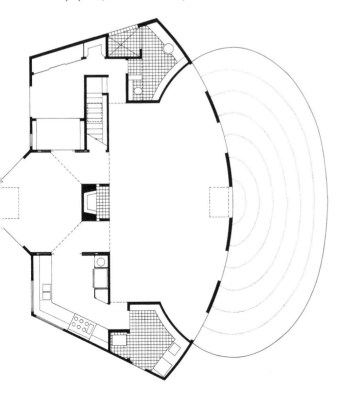

92, 93, 94   Artist's studio and residence; La Conchita, California. Tigerman McCurry Architects, 1988–92.
Photos: © Tigerman McCurry Architects.

[EXTERIOR] The architects echo a nearby Mission church, adding palm trees to add a humorous touch.

[INTERIOR] The south wall is a "view altar," where a cruciform painting by the artist-owner hangs over doors and windows that command sweeping ocean views.

[PLAN] In another show of levity, the cross-arm plan evokes that of a church. The living room-studio occupies the nave; kitchen and bathroom fill the crossing; two bedrooms are located in the apse area; the side "chapels" are given over to a garage and a carport.

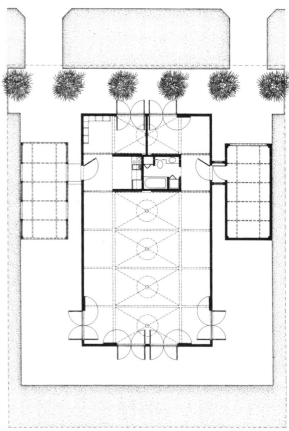

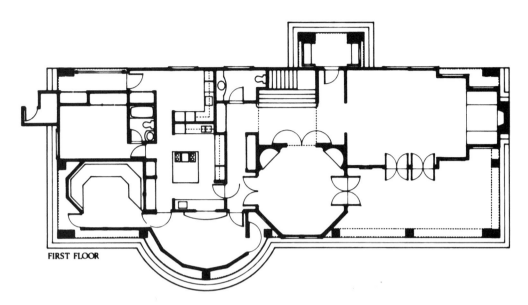

FIRST FLOOR

95, 96 Bozzi house; East Hampton, New York. Robert A. M. Stern Architects, 1980. *Photo: Roberto Schezen.*

[PLAN—FIRST FLOOR] With the exception of the rounded turret, rooms of diverse shape and size are encompassed within a neat rectangular plan.

[EXTERIOR] Picturesque detail embellish the simple volume.

97 Flintoft house; Nantucket, Massachusetts. Bissell & Wells, 1978. *Photo: © David Franzen/Esto.* Although the shingles and saltbox shape belong to Shingle Style vocabulary, the dwelling's expansive scale, large outdoor deck, and rakish widow's walk testify to its late twentieth-century date.

98, 99 Rosewalk Cottages; Seaside, Florida. Robert Orr & Melanie Taylor, 1985. *Photos: © Mick Hales.*

[EXTERIOR] The dwellings have turrets and widow's walks that not only contribute to the picturesque quality, but also bring light into the interiors.

[INTERIOR] Broad porches and flowing interior spaces are up-to-date interpretations of Victorian space.

100, 101 Impert-Germaine house; Hastings-on-Hudson, New York. Kiss + Cathcart Architects, 1993–94. *Photo: © Norman McGrath.*

[PLAN] An updated plan reorganized a rear entry, added a music room that buffers the house from a too-close neighbor, widened the living room into the central stair hall, and joined the kitchen to casual living areas.

[EXTERIOR] Boldly highlighted by exposed Stick Style framing, the expanded, triple-gable porch reorients the main entrance toward a new terraced lawn.

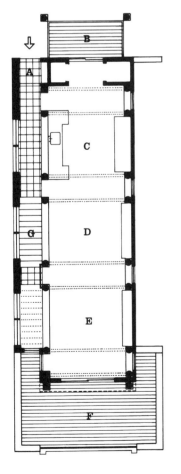

102, 103, 104 Mere house; Flint Hill, Virginia. Bumpzoid, 1983. *Photos: © Langdon Clay.*

[EXTERIOR] The glazed gable and solar wall are frank expressions of modernity.

[PLAN] The entry in the short end of the rectangular plan (indicated by the arrow) takes the visitor down a side hall that opens, successively, to the kitchen (C), dining room (D), living room (E), and rear deck (F)—a procession at once dignified and convenient.

[INTERIOR] The expression of the dwelling's hybrid nature continues in the juxtaposition of columns and exposed framing.

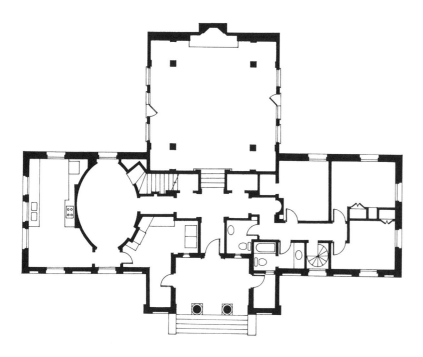

105, 106, 107 Smith house; South Bend, Indiana. Thomas Gordon Smith, 1989–91. *Photos: Langdon Clay.*

[PLAN] Entering the house, one traverses a cruciform foyer and another set of steps to reach a square living space that the architect associates with an ancient multipurpose Greek room. The left side of the plan contains an oval dining room and a kitchen, while the right side has bedrooms and bathrooms.

[INTERIOR] Portraits of architects on the living room's vaulted ceilings, from ancient Greece to twentieth-century America, continue the dialogue between past and present.

[EXTERIOR] In the spirit of the American mid-nineteenth-century Greek Revival, the facade is enriched by inventive ornamental motifs. The use of brick is an allusion to the dwelling's dual midwestern and classical heritage, while pigmented concrete block on the side wings is a modern alternative to ashlar stone.

NEW VERNACULAR

From the eighties on, as already noted, regional Modernists, Postmodernists, and certain of the Deconstructivists grew increasingly interested in the investigation of the qualities of particular places. The tendency is most vivid in work that may be described as New Vernacular, which is sensitive to the sensual properties of the setting (sight, smell, sound), to natural history (seasons, climate, topography, vegetation), and to human history (local tradition and lore). Deferential to the act of living as well as to the art of building, such architecture also engages memory, anticipation, and the sense of time.

"An old split rail fence . . . the owner's favorite destination on her walks as a young girl among these hills . . . is now the symbolic heart of the house," explained Jefferson Riley of Centerbrook Architects, regarding the evolution of the 1982–83 Elliott house (figures 108, 109, 110) in western Pennsylvania. Well versed in the attributes of vernacular architecture, Riley took his inspiration from local manors, stables, hunting lodges, and family farms.

On a sandy dune of Fire Island, New York, it's not history but the happy spirit of summertime that pervades the 1981–82 Peitsky beach house (figure 111), designed by Peter Wilson. The formally landscaped garden at the center is a stage set for lighthearted recreation, while the house itself becomes the actor on stage, appearing to the passerby in four totally different guises on different sides of the house—a saltbox, an Italian villa, a formal garden, and a continuing construction site.

On a river bluff above Wimberley, Texas, Lawrence Speck's 1985 Tapp-McGrath house (figures 112, 113) is an aggregation of individual elements, in the tradition of central Texas. Life as lived in that locale is most vividly materialized in the kitchen, the tallest and broadest room in this house, because that's where frequent and abundant meals are required. Responsive to climate in its siting, the ranch also respects local custom in its use of materials—stone, exposed wood structural struts, and metal roof. Plaster walls are painted rose to respond to changing light conditions, and trim is painted green to mirror local vegetation.

Exploration of its Catskill Mountain setting—to learn where a stream softens the breeze and how pine trees scent the woods—was essential to James Cutler's design of the Wright house (figures 114, 115) in Lew Beach, New York. Built in 1991, and designed to look as if it were "almost there forever," the pavilion resembles some north-country lodge, with wood and stone elements that evoke the passage of time. "One senses time by decay," said the architect. Surely no setting could be more different than the semisuburban Houston, Texas, neighborhood of the Saito house. Nevertheless, the 1992–93 remodeling of that plain postwar house by Carlos Jimenez/Architecture was similarly based on respectful "listening" to the mood and character of the place. The renovation let the house's profile remain as it was, but employed new fenestration to reflect the reconfiguration of the interior.

Reverence for the history and traditions of the site blends with a cheeky determination to express one's own individuality in the work of Brooks & Carey. In Monkton, Vermont, the 1989–90 Dennison-Peek house (figures 116,

67

117, 118, 119)—familiar in profile, built of commonly available materials, and economically constructed—appears at first glance to be another old-time farmhouse. The illusion is quickly shattered when one notes the quirky way in which the house seems to perch in the landscape and how it bulges outward on the south facade to catch a view of the lake. In Westby, Wisconsin, Brooks & Carey's Lombard/Miller house of 1994 echoes its board-and-batten farmhouse neighbors, but it is painted yellow as a tongue-in-cheek allusion to the area's butter production.

A profound sense of the Illinois prairie landscape—and also the architect's sense of play—breathes life into Booth/Hansen's 1990 "Chicken Coop" house (figures 120, 121, 122, 123) in Lake Bluff, Illinois. A small, neat rectangular form with low-pitched roof, the exterior portrays the dwelling as a simple farm building—a possibility denied by the sophisticated vaulted interior. "Vernacular construction around the world connects people to their landscapes in diverse, yet profound relationships," asserted Larry Booth. "This is the true, common, democratic architecture."

"We improvised idiosyncratically on the chaotic urban context," said Richard Fernau of Fernau & Hartman, designers of the 1995 Steven Tipping Building (figures 124, 125, 126). Visually framing a gateway to downtown Berkeley, California, the building combines "living over the store" with retail and office use, adding liveliness to the already mixed-bag neighborhood. Responding in the vernacular manner to the client's demand "for a building that was me," as well as to strict regulatory controls, tight financing, and the opinions of neighborhood residents, the building gives an honest description of "how construction works in the 1990s," he said.

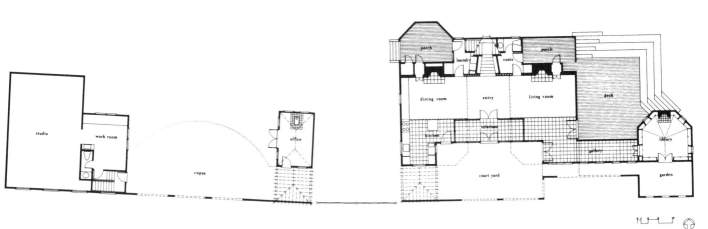

FIRST FLOOR

108, 109, 110   Elliott house; Ligonier, Pennsylvania. Centerbrook Architects, 1982–83. *Photos: © Norman McGrath.*

[PLAN] Semiscreened from the south, the extended plan creates diverse indoor-outdoor places: a hexagonal library with its own garden; the living room, dining room, and kitchen off an outdoor deck and solarium; two separate offices surrounding a wooded area.

[EXTERIOR] The dwelling is configured like a village main street, facing south along an east-west axis. In the center, linking living and work spaces, an old split-rail fence.

[LIBRARY] The sensory richness of the room relates to its idiosyncratic shape, florid scroll ornamentation, dominating hearth, abundance of books.

111 Peitsky house; Fire Island, New York. Peter Wilson, 1981–82. *Photo: © Peter Aaron/Esto.* The real focus of the house is a garden room framed by lattice screens and trellises.

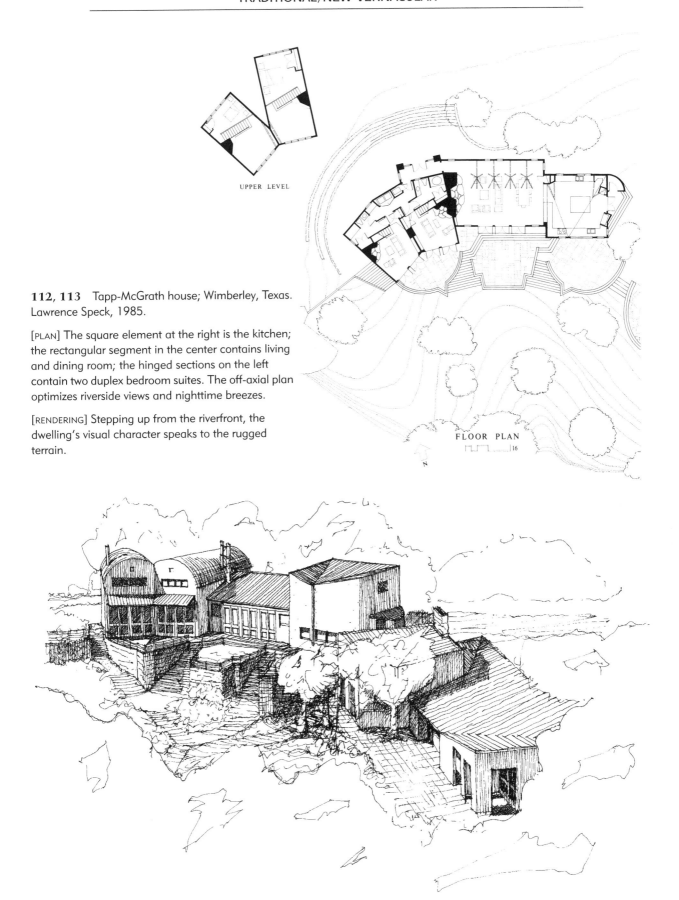

UPPER LEVEL

112, 113 Tapp-McGrath house; Wimberley, Texas. Lawrence Speck, 1985.

[PLAN] The square element at the right is the kitchen; the rectangular segment in the center contains living and dining room; the hinged sections on the left contain two duplex bedroom suites. The off-axial plan optimizes riverside views and nighttime breezes.

[RENDERING] Stepping up from the riverfront, the dwelling's visual character speaks to the rugged terrain.

FLOOR PLAN

N

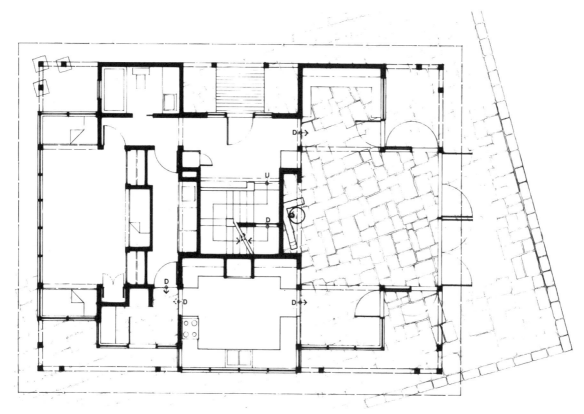

114, 115 Wright house; Lew Beach, New York. James Cutler, 1991. *Photo: © Peter Aaron/Esto.*

[PLAN] The house rests on a new foundation that incorporates a fragment of an old stone wall. Off the center hall, the living room is at the right, a bedroom at the left. The kitchen is at the center bottom of the plan, adjacent to the screened dining room and outdoor porch.

[EXTERIOR] Heavy timber piers permit the walls to open up to the out-of-doors, while the deeply overhanging eaves protect against the sun.

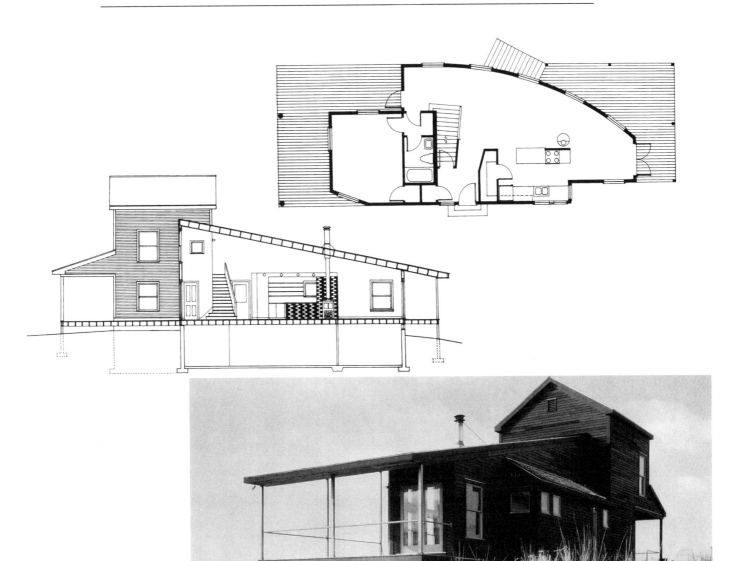

116, 117, 118, 119 Dennison-Peek house; Monkton, Vermont. Brooks & Carey, 1989–90. *Photos: © Scott Frances/Esto.*

[PLAN] A small house, containing a single space for living, dining, and cooking as well as a separate bedroom and bath on the first floor.

[SECTION] The high shed roof visually expands the tight family living space.

[EXTERIOR] Seen from the rear, the dwelling seems to hover over the landscape.

[INTERIOR] The fenestration is traditional in feeling, while it also conveys modern freshness and preference for feeling close to the out-of-doors.

120, 121, 122, 123 "Chicken Coop" house; Lake Bluff, Illinois. Booth/Hansen & Associates, 1990. *Photos: © Bruce Van Inwengen.*

[SITE PLAN] In a wooded corner of the eight-acre site, the dwelling intrudes minimally on the grassy landscape.

[PLAN] A simple, linear arrangement of space: a single living-room-dining-room-kitchen, two bedrooms, sleeping loft, and bath.

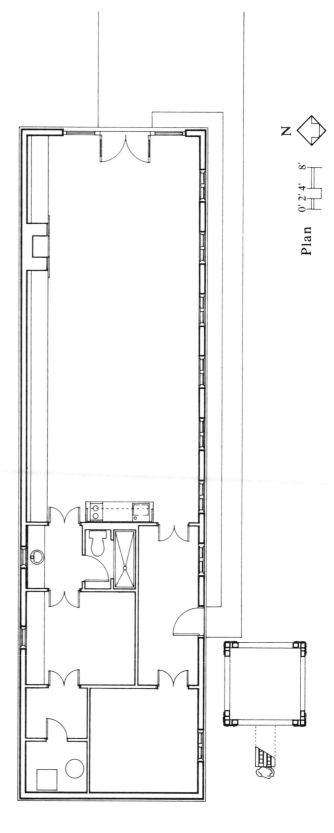

Plan

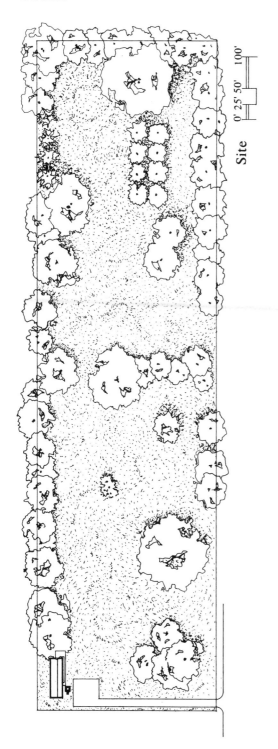

Site

[EXTERIOR] The dwelling is low to the ground, partially built on the foundations of an old farmhouse. It is painted black to recall the burning of the prairie each spring, while the viewing tower is painted yellow, to match the summer grasses.

[INTERIOR] The view toward the front door displays the closeness of house and setting.

124, 125, 126   Steven Tipping Building; Berkeley, California. Fernau & Hartman, 1995. *Photo: © Richard Barnes.*

[PLAN] In addition to the owner's apartment and garden (at the left side of the plan), the building encompasses a café, parking, and landscaped alley at street level, as well as the owner's offices at the second and mezzanine levels.

[SECTION] Domestic tranquility is provided by the apartment's side-street location and protected rear garden.

[EXTERIOR] Echoing the ragged quality of the neighborhood, the building is a seemingly ad hoc ensemble of humble materials.

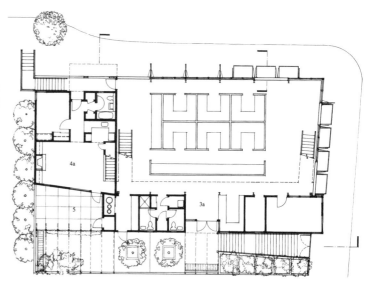

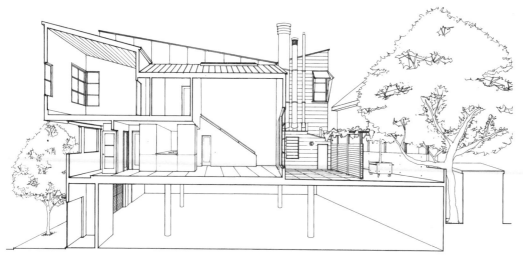

2

HOUSING

HOUSING

There is the house. And there is housing. A house is for middle-class people who have free choice. Housing is for the poor—the way people live when they have no choice. Now, as fifty years ago, a large minority of our population cannot afford to buy or rent a decent place to live. "Housing is pride and joy, status and sanctuary for some," wrote urban planner Peter Marcuse. "It is shame and fear, stigma and prison for others." Nothing can be more revealing of our society's attitudes toward race, age, gender, income, and status than what we build, or don't build, for those who need help.

Poor people have had to make do with improvised or "hand-me-down" housing for most of our history. Theirs were the musty cellars, subdivided single-family houses, jerry-built shanties crammed at the rear of building lots, and poorly lit, malventilated, and ill-serviced five- and six-story tenements. In turn-of-the-twentieth-century New York and Boston, low-income families were housed at a density hardly known at any other time or place. Living was less crowded in Philadelphia, but slum conditions were almost as bad. Racial prejudice worsened the lot of African-Americans streaming out of the rural South to Chicago and other industrialized cities, where nervous home owners sold residential property at bargain prices to real estate agents and speculators reaped windfall profits in the rapid conversion of prosperous neighborhoods into poorly maintained slum ghettos.

Meager was the number of philanthropists and reformers able to produce successful model housing projects. Miserable living conditions compelled New York and other large municipalities to pass laws against overcrowded, unhealthy, and unsafe housing, but government was slow to accept a role in generating decent housing at affordable cost. Architects also tended to withdraw from the scene, finding status, remuneration, and satisfaction in City Beautiful issues rather than in designing accommodations for the poorest third of the nation.

The social utopianism of the twenties and thirties, influenced by progressive practices in England, Holland, and Germany, finally brought government, reformers, and architects together. The federal government produced experimental housing for World War I workers. Insurance companies and others responded to tax incentives that made it more attractive to invest in large, moderate-cost housing projects. Labor unions, philanthropies, and socially conscious architects contributed support, funding, and new design ideas. Ultimately, the advent of World War II, following on the heels of the Great Depression of the 1930s, put the lid on such efforts—even as it opened an extraordinary new era in housing production.

PROJECTS

1940s–1960s

Compelling visions of morality, modernism, and capitalism were fundamental to the federal government's support of low-income housing in the Depression thirties. Shame at the miserable living conditions of poor families and desire to get the economy going spurred the New Deal administration to push housing reform, producing a variety of new prototypes, funding mechanisms, and legal tools. As a way station, not a permanent stopping place, publicly built and managed housing would, it was thought, give the worthy poor a helpful push into the American free enterprise system.

Works Progress Administration demonstration projects gave hope for humane solutions to mass housing needs. Building some thirty thousand emergency housing units for defense workers in the Second World War, the federal government awarded architects with strong social vision the opportunity to explore site planning, housing design, and construction techniques to produce a higher standard of living at lower cost. The 250-unit Aluminum City Terrace (figure 127) in New Kensington, Pennsylvania, following a flat-roofed Modernist design by Walter Gropius and Marcel Breuer, exploited an experimental prefabricated wood-panel construction system. Among other innovative architects, Eliel and Eero Saarinen explored neighborhood planning issues in a project in Center Line, Michigan; George Howe, Oscar Stonorov, and Louis I. Kahn, in a project in Middletown, Pennsylvania, suggested new possibilities for pleasant and sociable outdoor space and more efficiently used inside space. "A close study had to be made of what people want, rather than what standards allow," the architects concluded.

It didn't happen that way. Instead, the urgent need for affordable shelter and the ambitious scope of federal programs created an entirely new class of client—public functionaries, whose miserly limits on quality reduced the design of publicly assisted housing to standardized mediocrity. Future occupants would rent not own, be screened by bureaucrats, and be kept in line by rules and regulations. Housing officials thought the living habits of poor people disqualified them from expressing preferences—so they provided that social workers did it for them.

Empowered by sweeping housing, highway, and urban renewal legislation in the forties and fifties, the federal government condemned large swaths of land occupied by tired industries and the aged slum housing that was all the poor could afford. Keenly aware that such properties stood right in the path of downtown modernization, municipalities generally gave the replacement of low-income housing a lower priority than commercial redevelopment or housing for upper-income people.

If public housing was shaped by minimal standards for space and amenity—no doors on closets, for example, and only a galley kitchen—the low building height and abundant outdoor space of the 1940s projects were a distinct improvement over the dark and congested tenement blocks that they replaced. Completed in the Bronx, New York, in 1944, Clason Point Gardens (figures 128, 129) consisted of forty-six exceedingly basic, two-story garden-apartment-type buildings on a self-contained, carefully landscaped superblock site. The space of the streets closed by the project added to its generous expanse. "I have always believed that men and women were not intended to live in tall, crowded buildings and that children can best enjoy a happy and healthy childhood if, instead of being crowded into six-, eight-, and ten-story buildings, they are enabled to live amid the surroundings that you see as you look about you today," declared housing administrator Nathan Strauss at the 1942 groundbreaking. By contrast, the scale and sameness of the Ida B. Wells housing project in Chicago, developed by the Chicago Housing Authority in the same years, was oppressive. In a phalanx-like array on a huge flat site, the project encompassed more than 1,650 units of insistently plain two-story row houses and three- and four-story walk-up apartment houses. It was such tight sense of control that was to become typical of the public housing projects.

Technological advances in concrete framing and elevator design made high-rise construction the cheapest and therefore the most expedient method of building low-cost housing. The 1937–40 Queensbridge Houses (figures 130, 131, 132) in the borough of Queens, developed by the New York City Housing Authority, was composed of more than three thousand units in twenty-six virtually identical red-brick, flat-roofed, six-story apartment houses. The site plan created ample open space, but no sense of neighborhood. The configuration as end-to-end Y's represented an experiment in the efficient utilization of the elevator core, reduced corridor length, and improved ventilation and light. Investigating the same issues, other projects produced high-rise apartment houses in variations of X, H, T, and L configurations.

Hailed as the perfect congruence of modern functionalism and social vision, Le Corbusier's slab-shaped apartment house, Unité d'Habita-tion in the south of France, was highly influential in America during the fifties and sixties. One sorry descendant was the slab-shaped Harold Ickes Homes (figure 133) in Chicago, designed by Skidmore, Owings & Merrill for the Chicago Housing Authority and completed in 1955. Constructed of exposed concrete framing and floor plates, and emphatically stripped of detail, its imagery suggested the factory, not the home. Another Chicago project that exploited the slab shape—the largest housing development ever built anywhere at the time of its completion in 1962—was the plain brick Robert Taylor Homes (figure 134), designed for the Chicago Housing Authority by Shaw, Metz Associates. One segment of a continuous four-mile stretch of public housing, the project comprised twenty-eight identical sixteen-story buildings, containing more than four thousand apartments and covering only seven percent of the site. "We live stacked on top of one another with no elbow room," a resident told the *Chicago Daily News* in April 1965. "Danger is all around. There's little privacy or peace and no quiet. And the world looks on all of us as project rats, living on a reservation like untouchables."

Through the early sixties, some half-million federally supported housing units were built in some three hundred communities across the country, to ever-lower standards of pleasantness. By the end of the decade, the number had grown to more than nine hundred thousand. Proponents of public housing could point to such benefits of project living as fireproof construction, ample light, good ventilation, fully equipped kitchens, private baths, incinerated garbage, spacious outdoor settings, off-street parking, regular maintenance, and carefully chosen neighbors. And they could reject the warnings that meanness, sameness, and institutionalism were creating the slums of tomorrow.

127 Aluminum City Terrace; New Kensington, Pennsylvania. Walter Gropius and Marcel Breuer, 1943. *Photo: Gottscho–Schleisner Collection, Library of Congress.* In terrace formation on a hillside site, the project consisted of 250 strictly Modernist row houses demonstrating open interior planning and modular construction technology.

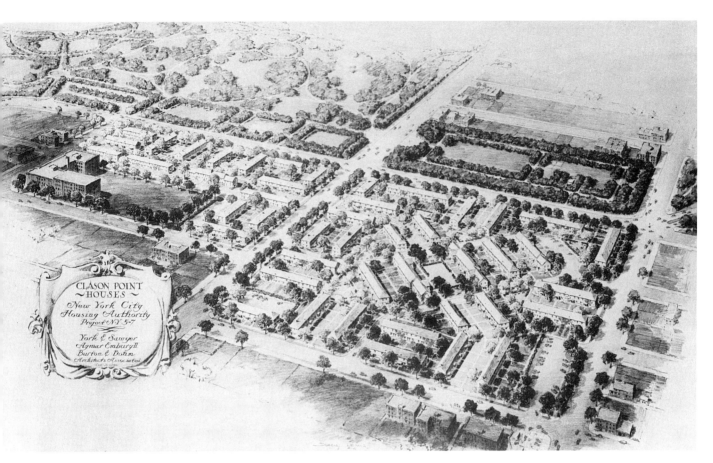

128, 129 Clason Point Gardens; Bronx, New York. New York City Housing Authority (York & Sawyer, Aymar Embury II, and Burton & Bohm), 1942–44. *Photo: New York City Housing Authority.*

[RENDERING] Groups of two-story town houses were arranged in pairs to create intimate neighborhoods.

[EXTERIOR] Barrackslike in their bareness, the buildings' small scale and traditional pitched roof do, nevertheless, suggest domestic life.

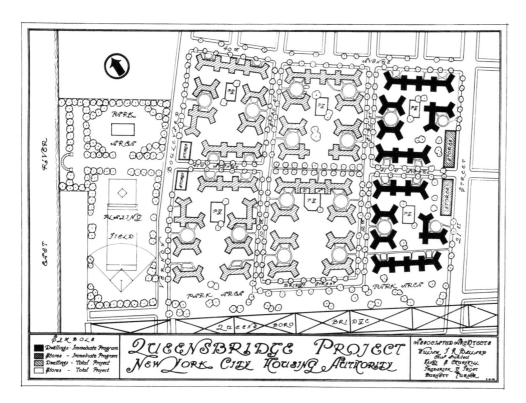

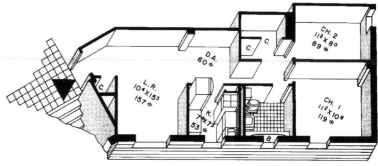

130, 131, 132 Queensbridge Houses;
Queens, New York. New York City Housing
Authority, 1937–41. *Photo and plan: New York
City Housing Authority.*

[SITE PLAN] The plan is large, generic, and
repetitive, although the riverside park and
Y-shaped housing blocks open the site to light,
air, and views.

[PLAN] The small size of rooms and corridors,
the tight eating alcove, and the lack of closet
doors and cross ventilation reflect the stinginess
of the public purse.

[EXTERIOR] The red brick buildings are
relentlessly plain.

133 Harold L. Ickes Homes; Chicago, Illinois. Skidmore, Owings & Merrill, 1955. *Photo: Murphy Photography, Inc.* The structure's imposing scale and monolithic shape diminish the appeal of its outdoor space.

134 Robert Taylor Homes; Chicago, Illinois. Chicago Housing Authority (Shaw, Metz Associates), 1960–62. *Photo: Chicago Housing Authority.* One of the largest housing projects ever built, Robert Taylor Homes consisted of twenty-eight identical sixteen-story buildings containing more than four thousand apartments. The buildings covered only seven percent of a site that stretched a quarter of a mile in width and two miles in length.

CIVICS

1960s–1970s

Aesthetics entered into the struggle to keep cities alive in the sixties. "Good urban design can be built into projects designed for any income level," declared Urban Renewal Commissioner William Slayton, who was charged with implementing the Kennedy administration's commitment to better planning and design. Retreating from the position that public housing had to be stigmatized by meanness and banality, public policy began to welcome innovation, originality—even urbanity.

But the problems of low-income families were growing more oppressive. Among other low-income people, African-Americans victimized by racial discrimination and Hispanics frustrated by cultural and language differences experienced a shrinking job market, declining civic life, burgeoning drug use, and deepening social dysfunction. Rising costs squeezed the tight operations budgets of public housing. After 1965, when the projects had to be opened to people on welfare without the screening that had previously ensured social stability, management problems grew even more severe. Residents of what was once considered one of the best-designed public housing projects in the country, the Pruitt-Igoe Houses (1955) in St. Louis, Missouri, were reported to be depressed and pessimistic, feeling that "doing ill is more natural than doing good," according to Giles Rainwater's 1967 study *Fear and the House-as-Haven in the Lower Class.* In the "long, hot summers" when poor people raged against ghetto life, planners started to think about bottom-up social welfare programs, participation of poor people in planning their own environments,

and the kinds of places where people can thrive, not just survive. Spawning the myth that design was the root cause of the projects' failure, rather than the desperate lives of the occupants, Pruitt-Igoe was leveled in 1972. It was the first of such high-rise housing projects to be demolished, but not the last.

"The luxuries of the rich are the necessities of the poor," declared Robert Marquis, of Marquis & Stoller, designer of the 1963 St. Francis Square (figures 135, 136) in San Francisco. Creating an exceptionally attractive and urbane totality, the project consisted of 299 units cooperatively owned by low-income families. Varied materials, including the clapboard sheathing so typical of San Francisco and richly textured brick and concrete paving, also helped to humanize the environment. Designed by Lawrence Halprin & Associates, the outdoor setting focused on the landscaping, decks, terraces, walks, and fences that made the project unique. (A users' study undertaken by Clare Cooper about a decade later revealed that sixty percent of the residents thought the landscaping features were more important than a larger living room or kitchen.)

Excellent site planning also helped to overcome the "project look" at the 228-unit Warren Gardens housing (figure 137) in Roxbury, Massachusetts. Designed by Hugh Stubbins & Associates, it was completed in 1969. Clusters of two- and three-story units were composed to emphasize both the individuality of the residences and the totality of a closely integrated social community. In New Haven, Connecticut, the 301-unit Church Street South housing of

1974, by Charles W. Moore, was developed around a central spine that encourages the sense of community, while it also links the project to the surrounding New Haven urban grid. Definitely domestic in scale and detail, three-story textured-concrete-block dwellings are arranged in clusters of two to eight units, each of which relates to a particular landscape feature—a plaza, grassy lawn, meadow, or park.

Reversing the tendency to value open space per se, planners began to recognize that space had to be designed to encourage positive attitudes, promote the sense of community, and stimulate "territoriality." Oscar Newman's influential book *Defensible Space* (1972) stressed the importance of surveillance, security, child supervision, street-level amenities and activities, avoiding no-man's zones, and encouraging a sense of order on the urban street. Planners discovered that with greater ground coverage, low-rise housing could achieve about the same density as conventional tower-in-the-park schemes and, with good planning, could create finer-textured, safer, and more sociable environments.

In Boston, planners moved in with the residents of old tenement houses to study the way they lived and how they liked to live. New York State undertook similar research, discovering that poor people require quality features just like well-to-do apartment dwellers: places to store bicycles and baby carriages, kitchens big enough for family time, the possibility of making changes to their apartment over time. Families wanted to live in a good neighborhood—and even in the suburbs.

Implementing some of these new understandings, the low-rise 625-unit Marcus Garvey Park Village (1973–76) in Brooklyn, New York, comprised units that faced the public street as well as ones that faced interior mews. Private gardens, balconies, and stoops where people could socialize also allowed convenient supervision of outdoor play. A New York State Urban Development Corporation demonstration project, it was planned in cooperation with the New York City–based Institute for Architecture and Urban Studies. "Feelings of dignity, self-esteem, and worth are human needs equal in value to comfort, security, and safety," said UDC architectural chief Theodore Liebman, insisting on features that comfort any dweller, regardless of income.

Approaches to mid- and high-rise housing required even more rigorous attention to density and diversity. "No good for cities or for their design, planning, economics or people can come of the emotional assumption that dense city populations are, per se, undesirable," Jane Jacobs taught in *The Death and Life of Great American Cities* (1961). "The task is to promote the city life of city people, housed, let us hope, in concentrations both dense *and* diverse enough to offer them a decent chance at developing city life."

The first New York City project to reverse the tendency to design with the lowest possible site coverage, the 625-unit Riverbend (figures 138, 139), in Manhattan, was based on a fine-textured, big-city scale. A cooperative (rather than a rental project) for people of limited means, it was completed in 1967 to the designs of Davis, Brody & Associates. Resisting standardized solutions, the design took serious account of the needs of the future occupants. "We became less interested in building landmarks and more interested in building buildings that were good for people," explained the architects. "We became less interested in breaking the urban mold and more interested in urban continuity and context; and we became less interested in innovation for its own sake and more interested in permanence and lasting values." Housing entered the realm of architecture, not just building.

To avoid the antisocial monotony of homogeneous low-income housing, new projects were opened to people of various income levels and a wider range of activities. Roosevelt Island, in New York City, was master-planned by Philip Johnson and John Burgee (1969–75) to be a mainly pedestrianized setting, with housing for different income levels, schools, retail shops, and expansive promenades and recreational areas. In Minneapolis, Minnesota, the federal government's ambitious New-Town-In-Town concept, which placed enormous confidence in total, large-scale design, was behind Cedar Square West (figure 140) by Ralph Rapson & Associates, considered a prime example of enlightened city planning. Initiated in 1971, a 3,500-resident section had been intended as only the first phase of a 25,000-resident community diversified by a good deal of commercial and institutional uses. However, the overwhelming size and insistent totality of the project stirred the ire of the community, causing protracted legal battles that eventually won less density, lower height, and greater preservation of existing neighborhood fabric.

Grassroots appreciation for serviceable old building stock and familiar neighborhoods deflected urban renewal's "start-with-a-clean-slate" mentality. Gentrification, that is, the replacement of low-income occupants by well-to-do people able to afford the rehabilitation of older houses, as well as the sweat-equity efforts of low-income families preserved many blocks of town houses and small multiple-family dwellings in places like Manhattan's Upper West Side, Brooklyn's Bedford-Stuyvesant, Boston's North End, and Baltimore's Fell's Point.

Gathering strength in the seventies, the historic preservation movement grew on the understanding that neighborhoods are complex cultural and social organisms whose stability is essential to urban viability. One project that maintained the continuity of a community was the 1970 Park Danforth (figure 141) in Portland, Maine. The new residence for eighty-five elderly occupants, to the designs of Stecker LaBau Arneill, was an addition to a rehabilitated 1810 mansion. The project also maintained a historic use, since the mansion had been a boardinghouse for the elderly since shortly after it was built.

In the seventies, changing attitudes opened neighborhoods previously denied to low-income housing projects. Completed in 1976 in a "desirable" residential zone, the thirty-four-story Elm Street Plaza in Chicago, Illinois, was designed by Ezra Gordon–Jack M. Levin & Associates for the Illinois Housing Development Authority. A mix of low- and moderate-income families could enjoy design features usually found only in luxury housing, including a swimming pool and parking garage. In Manhattan, the 1971–83 Taino Towers, designed by Silverman & Cika, consisted of four thirty-five-story towers so well built and so richly provided with high-quality features—including floor-to-ceiling windows, spacious closets, and large, centrally air-conditioned rooms—as to avoid the project stigma altogether.

In 1973, facing a conservative reaction to government social programs, runaway costs, and a sluggish economy, Washington virtually froze new low-income housing construction, insisting, despite evidence to the contrary, that subsidies of market-rate rentals would fill the need.

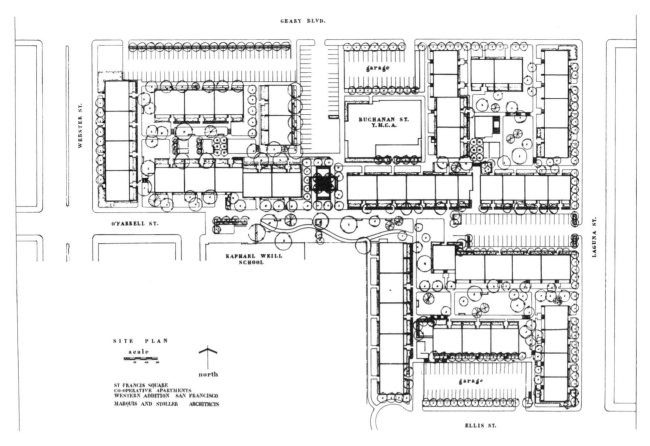

SITE PLAN
scale
20 40 50

north

ST FRANCIS SQUARE
CO-OPERATIVE APARTMENTS
WESTERN ADDITION SAN FRANCISCO
MARQUIS AND STOLLER ARCHITECTS

135, 136   St. Francis Square; San Francisco, California. Marquis & Stoller, 1963–65.

[SITE PLAN] The site design emphasizes outdoor appeal, sociability, and parental supervision. The perimeter of the superblock site is defined by terraces of three-story apartments and parking facilities; the center, by heavily landscaped common spaces. Each apartment unit has its own front and back doors, as well as a shared stair hall that encourages neighborly encounters.

[EXTERIOR] The exceptional livability of the site stems from the subtle interweaving of public, semiprivate, and private spaces.

137 Warren Gardens; Roxbury, Massachusetts. Hugh Stubbins & Associates, 1969. *Photo: © Jonathan Green.* Private yards give each dwelling an identity. Pitched rooflines, clapboarding, and closeness to the contours of the site are echoes of New England tradition.

138, 139 Riverbend; New York, New York. Davis Brody & Associates, 1967. *Photo: © Norman McGrath.*

[EXTERIOR] Oriented both to the surrounding city and the river, a U-shaped arrangement of seven buildings of various heights encloses a landscaped plaza that forms the heart of the development. Two-story private balconies face outdoor corridors that function as elevated "streets."

[SECTION] Arranged in an innovative interlocking fashion, duplex units provide a homey spaciousness.

140 Cedar Square West, Cedar Riverside New Community; Minneapolis, Minnesota. Ralph Rapson & Associates, 1971–90. Ranging in height from four to forty stories, the buildings hold 222 semi-luxury, 960 middle-income, and 117 low-income units in a design intended to create no stigma for the poor.

141 Park Danforth; Portland, Maine. Stecker LaBau Arneill, 1970. *Photo: Bill Maris.* Designed for compatibility, the modern addition echoes the historic mansion in its relationship to the street, materials, fenestration, and eaves line.

INCREMENTS

1980s–1990s

"With the demise of nearly fifty years of federal subsidy launched by the New Deal, low-cost social housing has largely been left to the same mechanisms as . . . used cars," grumbled Rutgers University urbanologist George Sternlieb about the drastic and sustained cuts in government support for housing. However, various strategic programs aimed at maximizing government's leverage, coupled with the get-up-and-go of both the not-for-profits and the profit-hungry, produced new low-income housing generally distinguished by human scale, interesting variety, and standards-defying innovation. The quantity, however, remained woefully inadequate.

Increasingly, housing design addressed occupants' needs to be emotionally invested in their dwelling place, community, and neighborhood. Architects could no longer design for the bureaucrat but for the occupant as client. And the occupants were less likely to be the generic working-class family of mother, father, and 1.8 children than the homeless, substance dependents, abused women, new immigrants, AIDS victims, and the mentally ill, who like everyone else hold high hopes for a "nice place to live."

Appreciation for the character and stability of neighborhood life deepened. Hoping to maintain some social and economic heterogeneity in the city's rapidly gentrifying historic neighborhoods, the Charleston Housing Authority, in South Carolina, assigned 113 low-income rental units to eight scattered sites. Designed by Bradfield Associates, the 1981–82 Radcliffeboro Historic District Houses (figure 142), which constitute about half the project, are modern-day evocations of the eighteenth-century Charleston "single house," having a plan and orientation that reflect local climate and tradition. In San Francisco, a project that resembles indigenous row housing, complete with flower boxes and wrought-iron railings, is the 177-unit Delancey Street project of 1991, designed by Backen, Arrigoni & Ross and built with the help of donated time and materials. The development includes a residential rehabilitation program for recovering addicts and former convicts along with a health club, swimming pool, screening room, retail space, and a restaurant to provide both work opportunities for residents and funds to keep the operation going. In San Diego, California, the 202 Island Inn (figure 143) received a different treatment on each facade. It boasts a front porch connecting the hotel lobby to a corner café that provides a meeting place for the locals. A single-room-occupancy hotel for approximately two hundred men of limited means, the 1992 project was designed by Rob Wellington Quigley to be contextual with the widely disparate character of several adjacent communities.

At the scale of the city, assertive urban design has made once anomalous land parcels into strong neighborhood settings. The fifty-unit Charlestown Navy Yard Row Houses (figures 144, 145) of 1988 were built on the site of a disused shipyard on the edge of the Boston Harbor, where William Rawn Associates drew on the tradition of waterfront industrial buildings to invent a new city landmark. It was made affordable to low-income, first-time home buyers through the joint efforts of the lenders, the city, and the not-for-profit developers. Pairs of houses are interlocked in elevation in order to provide both with private entries and outdoor spaces. The provision of kitchen-dining rooms large enough to serve as family rooms meant doing without certain other design amenities, which, it is hoped, residents will manage to devise for themselves over time. Also in Boston, the same architects' 1990 Back of the Hill Complex, consisting of 165 brick town houses, draws on established patterns of use and sociability in a site design that provides a clear definition of sidewalks as public, stoops as semipublic, and entries as private.

Lining the perimeter of an entire city block in a once burned-out section of Brooklyn, New York, the 1991 H.E.L.P. Houses (figure 146) is a 150-unit four-story complex that reasserts the traditional city grid. Designed by Cooper, Robertson, the project has a single entry in order to preserve the security of the central courtyard, where, divided into a variety of outdoor "rooms" on two levels, attractive recreational and social space encourages a sense of community for the low-income and formerly homeless families who live in the project.

The rehabilitation of aging and increasingly dysfunctional housing projects became a critically important undertaking. In Dorchester, Massachusetts, the high-rise, low-income Columbia Point Housing project was transformed by Goody, Clancy & Associates into the mixed-income Harbor Point (1988–90) through a combination of renovation and new low-rise construction that has created a mixed urban-suburban setting. In Chicago, the Chicago Housing Authority in 1991 started the redevelopment of the Robert Taylor Homes (see page 81 and figure 134) to serve a mixed-income community in the first phase of a billion-dollar plan that aims to transform the city's vast stock of public housing. Following the plans of

Johnson & Lee, certain buildings were improved by secure lobbies, better landscaping, and quality interior finishes intended to hint at "upward mobility." In 1997 the housing agency announced that seven of the high-rises would be demolished and replaced with new town houses. In the Fort Greene neighborhood of Brooklyn, New York, a derelict sixty-year-old apartment building that lends character to a zone otherwise dominated by public housing was rehabilitated in 1991. Known as Brooklyn Gardens, it focuses on a common courtyard and houses three different communities: a transitional residence for single mothers and their children, a single-room-occupancy hotel, and a residence for the mentally ill.

To help free troubled people from dependence, new projects have given importance to job training, social services, and the users' participation in decision-making. The thirty-unit Amandla Crossing (figure 147) in Edison, New Jersey, was developed by Middlesex Interfaith Partners with the Homeless in 1991 primarily as a one-year stopping place for single mothers and children, frequently the victims of abuse. Adjacent to a community college that offers the women courses and job training, the development, designed by Michael Mostoller and Fred Travisano, is composed of several buildings whose rural imagery and natural materials relate to the locale.

A complementary mix of uses addressed to strengthening the sense of community, encouraging economic independence, and enlivening sidewalk activity was developed at the 1995 Hismen Hin-Nu Terrace (figure 148), designed by Pyatok Associates for an Oakland, California, nonprofit organization representing African-, Asian-, and Latino-American constituencies. Designed with intense community participation, the project created ninety-two units for low-income families and elderly people. In a systematic approach to the problems of the poor, the project also included a market hall and side-walk spaces that encourage local people to engage in vending activity and start-up businesses. Another project by Pyatok, the 1992 James Lee Court, is a publicly subsidized housing development for twenty-six previously homeless families in a nearby Oakland neighborhood. Shaped by the preferences of future occupants, the scheme contains a mix of apartment sizes (no two apartments are alike), ample living rooms by virtue of space "borrowed" from bedrooms, and outdoor play areas modeled on New York City–style "stoops." There are no common facilities here, because homeless people "wanted nothing that resembled a shelter or transitional housing," explained the architect. "They wanted real apartments, no matter how small."

142 Radcliffeboro Historic District Houses; Charleston, South Carolina. Bradfield Associates, 1981–82. *Photo: Paul Beswick.* The relaxation of federal standards permitted the architect to produce a design that reduced the stigma of the public housing project while it preserved the character of the historic district.

143 Island Inn; San Diego, California. Rob Wellington Quigley, 1992. *Photo: © Hewitt/Garrison.* No aloof institutional presence, this housing facility contributes to the liveliness of the street.

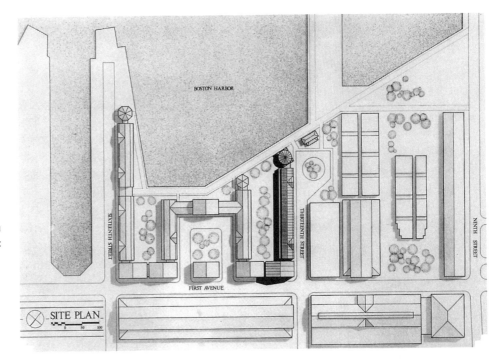

144, 145 Charlestown Navy Yard Row Houses; Boston, Massachusetts. William Rawn Associates, 1988. *Photo: © Steve Rosenthal.*

[SITE PLAN] Like a traditional finger pier in its long, narrow configuration, the project asserts a strong presence on both the public street and Boston Harbor.

[EXTERIOR] Each town house has either a small yard or a private deck at the rear. Most units enjoy a view of the harbor.

146   H.E.L.P. Houses; Brooklyn, New York. Cooper, Robertson, 1991. *Photo: © Peter Mauss/Esto.* Oriented to both the public street and an interior courtyard, the project is enriched by corner towers, pitched rooflines, gables, and diverse materials.

147 Amandla Crossing; Edison, New Jersey. Michael Mostoller and Fred Travisano, 1991. *Photo: Leigh Photographic Group.* Containing five apartments each, six pitched-roof houses radiate from an L-shaped building that houses the common lounge, social workers' offices, library, and day-care facilities.

148 Hismen Hin-Nu Terrace; Oakland, California. Pyatok Associates, 1995. *Photo: Michael Pyatok.* Strongly articulated and embellished with decorative detailing and artwork, the building asserts the occupants' individuality. Through the gateway, interior open space is divided into three courtyards that serve neighborly activities.

3

PUBLIC BUILDINGS

PUBLIC BUILDINGS

Since the beginnings of the American republic, buildings of Classic Greece and Rome have symbolized civilization's highest values—the rule of law, citizenship, patriotism, honor. Thomas Jefferson appropriated the form of a Roman temple for the Virginia State Capitol (1785–89) to bestow the legitimacy of tradition on the revolutionary young nation. Jefferson also insisted that the plan of the nation's capitol be based on "one of the models of antiquity which have had the approbation of thousands of years," considering the Classic tradition essential to an education in civic values, its authority established down through the centuries.

Classicism stands for idealism, reason, and moderation. It also represents power and authority. Classic architecture depends on the refinement and precision with which each element is developed, expressed, and subordinated to the unity of the whole. Details are of critical importance in Classic architecture, for it is the clarity of articulation and expressiveness of ornament that help the observer to relate to size, composition, proportion, and way of building. Classic tradition builds on precedent, but it also permits flexibility, encouraging fresh responses to changing time and circumstance.

The basic unit of Greek architecture is the "order," each with its own personality: the vigorous Doric, gentle Ionic, luxuriant Corinthian.

The order comprises a vertical column—consisting of base (usually), shaft, and capital—and a horizontal entablature (the elaborated beam carried by the column). Each order determines a particular scale, proportion, and ornamental system for the entire building. The Romans elaborated the wall as a formal composition based on the use of the orders. They also introduced the pier, arch, vault, and dome.

"In the whole art of building the column is the principal ornament without any doubt; it may be set in combination, to adorn a portico, wall, or other form of opening, nor is it unbecoming when standing alone. It may embellish crossroads, theaters, squares; it may support a trophy; or it may act as a monument. It has grace, and it confers dignity," declared Leon Battista Alberti, the fifteenth-century Italian Renaissance theoretician who gave new impetus to Classic tradition. "Beauty is that reasoned harmony of all the parts within a body, so that nothing may be added, taken away, or altered, but for the worse." Mannerist sensibility in the sixteenth century, Baroque in the seventeenth, Rationalist in the eighteenth, Romantic in the nineteenth—each added new possibilities to classicism, carrying it forward into the modern era and to its revival in America.

In Jacksonian America, the spare classical forms of Robert Mills's Treasury Building (Washington, D.C., 1836–42) evoked constitutionalism itself. "Let us compare our government to a plain, unadorned column, whose base is the people; the shaft the constitution; and the capital the laws," one politician declared. In the late nineteenth and early twentieth centuries, the grand civic ambitions of the so-called American Renaissance encompassed visions of a City Beautiful, with grand axial avenues, imposing classical monuments, and gracious parks and promenades.

In mid-twentieth century, the radical Modernist demanded complete freedom from the bounds of tradition, insisting that a profoundly new age be expressed by an architecture based on the rigorous analysis of function and the bold exploitation of new materials and technology. The use of clean lines, flat surfaces, and simple geometric shapes would create a style that ended all styles. If Classic architecture exploited the symbolism of ornament, Modernist architecture would convey meaning by the very lack of ornament. If Classic architecture's masonry masses asserted permanence and authority, the Modernist's steel and glass would celebrate innovation, freedom, and flexibility.

Such polemic aside, respect for the authority and monumentality of Classic tradition endured, easing its penetration into Art Deco, regional styles of the twenties, and Cubist tendencies of the thirties. A modernized classical ensemble composed with a soaring tower in place of a traditional low dome, Bertrand Goodhue's Nebraska State Capitol (1922–32) helped to establish both a new image for the public building and a new canon for the tall building.

In the course of the growth and development of cities over the second half of the twentieth century, commercial buildings appropriated the visual dominance once claimed by public buildings; in the burgeoning suburbs, the public realm remained virtually inconsequential. In public buildings everywhere, the observance of ceremony and celebration yielded to broad and complex bureaucratic functions; the representation of authority ceded to the signs and symbols of participation. Seesawing between classicism and modernism, the buildings and spaces that make up the public realm both serve and symbolize the changing goals and grasp of government.

ROOSEVELT-TRUMAN-EISENHOWER YEARS

The unprecedented growth of government during the presidency of Franklin Delano Roosevelt (1932–45) was vividly portrayed in severely abstract classical public buildings that symbolized both the authority of tradition and the promise of modernity. A grandiose project accomplished with extraordinary speed, the building of the Pentagon (1941) integrated slum clearance with massive new construction and efficient access roads—a portent of how government would transform the face of American cities in the next decades.

Shifting power from local and state offices to Washington, the New Deal moved the federal government into business regulation, social reform, agricultural subsidies, electrification, land reclamation, and massive public works projects, multiplying by many times the number of bridges, roads, waterworks, electric systems, town and city halls, post offices, schools, and courthouses. Becoming a patron of contemporary art, the federal government commissioned artworks for hundreds of public buildings nationwide. But perhaps no work of public art is more suggestive of the ambitions of the era, however, than John Russell Pope's Jefferson Memorial (1943) in Washington, D.C., commanding all the grandeur and authority of ancient Rome.

Having earned stunning victories over Fascism and Nazism, the nation cast off its traditional isolationism to become the protector of democracy around the globe, supporting the establishment of the United Nations in 1945 in the hope that reason, rather than arms, would govern future world affairs. Instead, the lower-ing of the "Iron Curtain," the advent of the Cold War, and deep-seated fears of Communism drove a sharp wedge of caution and conservatism into American attitudes. "You can tell a lot about a country by the kind of building it has," said President Harry Truman (1945–52). "I don't understand fellows like [Frank] Lloyd Wright," he admitted. "He started this whole business of chicken-coop and hen-house architecture, and I don't know why in the world he did it."

Accepting "new influence and new responsibilities," Truman sent strategic aid abroad through the Marshall Plan, which was meant to demonstrate that nations of the world could live together in peace and prosperity. But he reacted to Communist aggression by bringing America into armed conflict in Korea in 1950. Watching the profound changes taking place in American society, Truman promised a "Fair Deal" to all, including higher minimum wages, expanded civil rights, and more ambitious government-sponsored social welfare.

This era saw the beginning of determined efforts to reorganize the city for more and better government, as seen in such places as Borough Hall Civic Center, in Brooklyn; Capitol Hill, in Nashville; Independence Hall, in Philadelphia; Golden Triangle, in Pittsburgh; and civic centers in Mobile, Los Angeles, and elsewhere. A standard formula rapidly evolved: condemn slum areas, demolish old buildings, enlarge city blocks, widen streets, build underground garages, add access highways and traffic signals. Notions of a decentralized city were boosted by Frank Lloyd Wright's mile-wide Broadacre City and the futuristic plan of Brasilia, Brazil, as well as by Cold War fears of the atomic bomb. "For the first time since the Middle Ages, weapons of war are again of paramount influence in the planning and building of cities," *Architectural Record* editorialized in 1950.

Ending the Korean War shortly after he took office, President Dwight David Eisenhower (1952–60) faced fears of advancing Communism abroad and feelings that government had to step back and let ordinary citizens take control of their lives at home. "We view the nation's strength and security as a trust upon which rests the hope of free men everywhere," declared Eisenhower. Committed to a massive arms buildup, Eisenhower forged regional military alliances around the world even as he ac-commodated to "peaceful coexistence" with the Soviet Union. At home, Ike followed the path of "dynamic conservatism," confident that businessmen were the best-qualified guardians of the nation's unprecedented prosperity. Building projects characteristic of Eisenhower's administration were military bases, bomb shelters, hospitals, schools, urban renewal districts, and a vast highway construction program that used enough concrete to lay "six sidewalks to the moon," as the president later boasted.

The polite fifties saw classicism sink into disfavor because of the taint of association with strong-arm governments, while a still tentative modernism rose as a symbol of America's progressivism.

STRIPPED CLASSIC

Modern Classic, or so-called Stripped Classic because of its tendency to reduce classical forms and motifs, was the style common to many public and quasi-public buildings of the thirties and early forties. The strong effect of mass achieved a sense of monumentality, presence, and permanence, while simplified detailing satisfied the current taste for sleekness. The apogee of the style is seen in Paul Cret's 1937 Federal Reserve Building (figure 149) in Washington, D.C., a monument that impresses the viewer with the great breadth of its marble facade and formal entry. This quasi-official Classic style was emulated around the country, but it proved most enduring in Washington, D.C., where a grandiose example was produced as late as 1965, the marble-clad Rayburn House Office Building, by Harbeson, Livingston and Larson.

Stripped Classic became a city and suburban neighborhood vernacular in the frenzy of public works projects undertaken by the federal Works Progress Administration. Completed in 1940 to WPA designs, the Woodhaven Station of the United States Post Office in Queens, New York (figure 150), employs simple but up-to-date materials in a severe, balanced composition that adds dignity to the streetscape.

Since soaring height disturbs classicism's sense of repose, tall buildings designed in the Stripped Classic manner employ bold massing and heavy-seeming masonry to restore the effect of rootedness. Such devices are vivid at the seventeen-story Criminal Courts Building and City Prison (figure 151) in Manhattan, designed by Harvey Wiley Corbett and completed in 1941. Rising from a back-to-back-E plan, the smooth-limestone–sheathed building assumes an impressive dignity. A rather modest building, designed by Leslie S. Hodgson, the 1940 Weber County Court House (figure 152) in Ogden, Utah, similarly exploits symmetry, formal composition, and heavy masonry effects to achieve Classic monumentality.

149 Federal Reserve Building; Washington, D.C. Paul Cret, 1937. *Photo: Horydczak, Library of Congress.* A dignified and imposing presence close to the sidewalk, the building is symmetrically composed, with crisp spatial divisions and prominent cornice lines.

150 United States Post Office, Woodhaven Station; Queens, New York. Louis Simon, Works Progress Administration, 1940. *Photo: New York Landmarks Conservancy.* Public purpose is announced by emphatic signage and the monumental scale of window and door openings.

151 Criminal Courts Building and City Prison; New York, New York. Harvey Wiley Corbett, 1941. *Photo: Gottscho–Schleisner Collection, Library of Congress.* Strong stepped-back forms and massive entry piers add formality and symbolism.

152 Weber County Court House; Ogden, Utah. Leslie S. Hodgson, 1940. *Photo: Ellen Land-Weber, Seagram County Court House Archive, Library of Congress.* The careful balance of horizontal and vertical elements contribute to the Classic sense of composure.

MODERNIST

Exploiting Modernist design as the symbol of a new political order, the Secretariat building at the United Nations Headquarters (figure 153) in Manhattan is a bold, free-standing slab form. The design is eloquent on the modernity of glass over stone: glass provides transparency and reflectivity, rather than light and shadow; the quality of glass is apparent from its surface, rather than its mass; glass is light, not heavy; glass is industrially produced, rather than worked by hand. Built between 1947 and 1950, the complex was designed by an international committee that included Le Corbusier but which was led by the American architect Wallace K. Harrison. The simplicity of the Secretariat building announces its function as an office building. "The world hopes for a symbol of peace," said Harrison. "We have given them a workshop of peace."

Notwithstanding the stunning example of the U.N., public officials usually eyed modernism warily. Only in 1954 did the federal government seek out advanced architecture as a way of advertising America's benign progressivism in an ambitious embassy-building program. Such commissions gave new scope to those willing to move modernism in personal directions, which included such architects as Ralph Rapson, Eero Saarinen, and Edward Durrell Stone.

At home, taking up the rear guard, civil servants more concerned with efficiency and economy than aesthetics typically produced buildings that ranged from totally utilitarian to cautiously Modernist. One example of the former is the rigorously simplified St. Mary Parish Court House (figure 154) of 1950–51 in Franklin, Louisiana, by John Baker and Neild-Somdal Associates, made of plain materials and having a blunt unceremonious entrance. A demonstration of the latter is Welton Becket Associates' 1955 Police Station (figure 155) at the Los Angeles Civic Center. The International Style's entry into establishment circles, the station is light, trim, and spare, composed of neatly detailed rectilinear volumes that define minimal, landscaped plazas. Modernity made a rendezvous with monumentality at the 1960 New York City Civil Courthouse and Municipal Courts Building (figure 156), designed by William Lescaze and Matthew Del Gaudio. Here limestone sheathing alternates with glass window walls in differing ratios on each facade.

153 United Nations Headquarters; New York, New York. Wallace K. Harrison, supervising architect, 1947–50. The low silhouette of the General Assembly Building, crowned by a domelike element, sets off the insistent height and rectangularity of the tall Secretariat. Standing free in an open space, completely enclosed in tinted green glass on two long sides, the thirty-nine-story broad rectangular slab adds a bold silhouette to the skyline.

154 St. Mary Parish Court House, Franklin, Louisiana. John Baker and Neild-Somdal Associates, 1950–51. *Photo: Geoff Winningham, Seagram County Court House Archive, Library of Congress.* The functionalism of the design is apparent in the simply expressed piers and window grilles.

155 Police Station, Civic Center; Los Angeles, California. Welton Becket Associates, 1955. *Photo: Julius Shulman.* Exposed framing raises upper stories above the recessed base, an intentional contrast to the rootedness of traditional masonry.

156 Civil Courthouse and Municipal Courts Building; New York, New York. William Lescaze and Matthew Del Gaudio, 1960. *Photo: Joseph Molitor.* Windowless courtrooms hide behind limestone; offices are lighted through aluminum-framed windows. Unlike Classic ornament, the sculpture does little to impart a sense of scale to the facade.

KENNEDY-JOHNSON-
NIXON-FORD YEARS

The brief, hopeful presidency of John F. Kennedy (1961–63) envisioned a New Frontier that would "truly light up the world," an administration that would "explore the stars, conquer the deserts, eradicate disease, tap the ocean depths, and encourage arts and commerce." Amid crises overseas, the Peace Corps promised a new alternative to armed conflict. An ambitious domestic agenda focused on economic growth, full employment, federal support for the arts, broadened educational opportunity, and medical care for the aged. "The times they are a'changin'," sang Bob Dylan. "I have a dream," chanted the Reverend Martin Luther King. The *Guiding Principles for Federal Architecture* (1962) rejected any official government style in favor of "the finest contemporary American architectural thought."

As history would have it, the sweeping Great Society legislation of Lyndon B. Johnson (1963–68) exceeded that of both FDR's New Deal and JFK's New Frontier. Washington took on an increasingly active role in child care, education, aid to low-income families, medical care for the aged, racial integration, job training, urban redevelopment, mass transportation, and land conservation. Established in 1965, the National Endowment for the Arts and, in 1967, the Arts in Public Places program, created unprecedented initiatives in architecture, urban design, and public art. The Great Society is spurred by "the excitement of becoming, trying, probing, failing, resting, and trying again," declared Johnson, "but always trying and always gaining."

The activist political climate of the sixties

witnessed new commitment to civic values, higher expectations for government leadership, and a thirst for creativity and individual expression. A profusion of public buildings bore eloquent testimony to government's vastly enlarged scope and enhanced style, while angry graffiti on the walls spoke about economic inequality, social strife, and protest against America's war in Vietnam.

The protest movement embraced issues of feminism, gay rights, ethnic and racial identity, consumer protection, economic equality, historic preservation, and environmentalism during the administrations of Richard M. Nixon (1969–74) and Gerald Ford (1974–76), who attempted to tone down angry rhetoric, reduce dissension, and protect "law and order." Nixon established diplomatic relations with Communist China and achieved detente with the Soviets and arms reduction abroad. But he faced quickening inflation, runaway energy costs, economic recession, and deepening feelings of doubt and disenchantment at home. Government withdrew from many social programs, while actually expanding activity in community economic development, health care, higher education, and historic preservation. "Let each of us ask—not just what will government do for me—but what can I do for myself?" asked Nixon at his second inauguration, setting the tone for the seventies as the "Me Decade."

From Boston to San Bernardino, federal and local governments applied the vast powers of urban renewal to create a new, heroic scale for older inner-city government centers. In the burgeoning Sun Belt, campuslike civic settings helped to organize dispersed urban regions and anomalous suburban sprawl. Increasingly, design had to demonstrate that even if government was to be bigger, it could also be accessible, responsive, and inclusive. Growing sophistication can be glimpsed in the choice of such works of civic art as Pablo Picasso's metal abstraction of the artist's wife and dog at the Chicago Civic Center, Alexander Calder's colorful abstract stabile in Grand Rapids, Michigan, and Claes Oldenburg's cheeky chunk of Pop Art in Philadelphia. In architecture, we see modernism break into the "establishment" during the 1960–75 period. At first, it searches for roots in classicism. Later on, it strikes out for individuality, even eccentricity.

MODERNIST CLASSIC

A maturing modernism asserted many commonalities with classicism: a uniform construction grid, a carefully organized hierarchy, a clarity of geometric form. Searching for symbolic meaning, Modernist architecture grasped Classic precedent in the use of travertine or marble sheathing, the colonnade as a compositional device, and the elevated podium.

The inherent structural logic of the colonnade links it to both Classicist and Modernist schemes, a fact that is apparent at Edward Durrell Stone's 1963 State Legislative Building (figures 157, 158) in Raleigh, North Carolina, where highly simplified, marble-clad steel columns surround the entire perimeter. Stone's New City Hall (1967) in Paducah, Kentucky, and Kennedy Center (1971) in Washington, D.C., carry this tendency into a Baroque phase.

Not strictly speaking public, but just the same encouraged by all manner of government incentives, the cultural and performing arts centers that became so significant a part of the American public landscape in the postwar era were progeny of the marriage of classicism and modernism. Pacing this development, Lincoln Center for the Performing Arts (figure 159) in Manhattan centers around a public square of ceremonial proportions, framed by colonnades and an arcade on three sides, opening to the city on the fourth. Developed on urban-renewal land parcels, the formalistic ensemble represented New York City's bid for cultural leadership of the nation and world. Comprising three travertine-sheathed performance halls of 1962–66 that form a unified enclosure for the highly formal plaza designed by Philip Johnson

(1966), the complex explicitly recalls the formal order of Michelangelo's Piazza del Campidoglio in Rome.

By contrast, Hawaii's colonnaded State Capitol (1965–69) in Honolulu, by John Carl Warnecke & Associates, exploits both Classic scale and Modernist space in a design that eschews historic precedent. It boasts a six-story-high colonnade and glass window walls on two adjacent sides that boldly expose legislative chambers to public view. Similarly, the carefully balanced 1969 Milwaukee Center for the Performing Arts (figures 160, 161), by Harry Weese & Associates, employs a colonnade on three facades but allows boldy simplified forms to portray its essential modernity.

The organizational principles used by Classicists also proved useful to Modernists in organizing large, varied, and complex building programs. The 1963–65 Los Gatos Civic Center (figures 162, 163) in Los Gatos, California, is based on a checkerboard keyed to an elevated podium, effectively integrating a multiplicity of activities into a unified whole. Designed by Stickney & Hull, the complex is monumental even though the scale is small. The position of the council chamber beneath a raised park maximizes the use of the site. In the case of Oregon's 1964 Eugene City Hall (figure 164), the plaza sits atop a belowground parking garage. Using the Classic circle-within-a-square device, Stafford & Morrin and James Longwood designed right-angled wings and landscaped areas around a drum-shaped council chamber that serves as the central focus.

The expression of the tall building as a Classic column was a definite achievement of Modernist architecture. One distinguished example is Chicago's Civic Center (now Richard J. Daley Center), (figures 165, 166, 167), a stunning realization of a classical order in steel designed by C. F. Murphy Associates with Loebl, Schlossman & Bennett and Skidmore, Owings & Merrill (1963–66). The podium anchoring the steel columns serves as base, the repeating floors become the shaft, grilles at the upper stories act as entablature. Reflecting glass and subtly protruding mullions create a rich surface with an effect analogous to Classic ornamentation.

As the column and beam expressed the constructional realities of ancient times, the structural cage expressed those of the modern era. In Oklahoma, the 1969 Tulsa Civic Center Municipal Building (figure 168) is constructed on a sturdy, well-proportioned, and clearly stated concrete frame, which rises directly from the podium to form an open colonnade at ground level. Designed by Murray Jones Murray, it is sited in an expansive plaza, the twelve-story height helping to balance the prevailing horizontality of other buildings in the complex. The 1973 New York City Police Headquarters (figure 169), by Gruzen & Partners, is eloquent on the rationality and strength of a reinforced concrete frame. Classic principles of composition are expressed in the complex's three-part composition of base, middle, and top, its strong patterns of light and shadow, and the clarity of its cubic form.

157, 158   State Legislative Building; Raleigh, North Carolina. Edward Durrell Stone Associates, 1963. *Photos: Ezra Stoller, © Esto.*

[EXTERIOR] Making two stories appear as one, the colonnade supports overhanging eaves that serve as an abbreviated entablature. Offices are on the ground level; the council chambers above are reached by a ceremonial stair.

[INTERIOR] The skylit interior courtyard makes use of the classical circle-within-a-square composition.

159 Lincoln Center for the Performing Arts; New York, New York. Avery Fisher Hall (right), Max Abramovitz, 1962; Metropolitan Opera House (center), Wallace Harrison, 1966; New York State Theater (left), Philip Johnson, 1964. *Photo: © Katrina Thomas.* The uniform roof and entrance height, common use of travertine facing, repeating colonnade, and formal plaza dramatize classicizing ambitions.

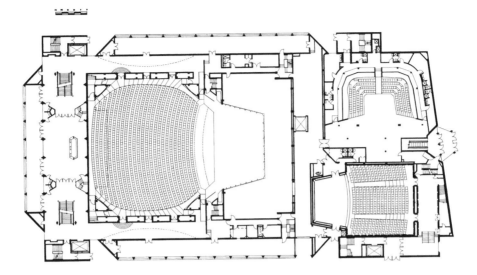

160, 161 Milwaukee Center for the Performing Arts; Milwaukee, Wisconsin. Harry Weese & Associates, 1969. *Photo: Balthazar Korab.*

[PLAN] The variety of interior spaces include three theaters and extensive support space. Note the use of the colonnade on three sides of the building.

[EXTERIOR] The staccato rhythm of the colonnade plays against smooth wall surfaces.

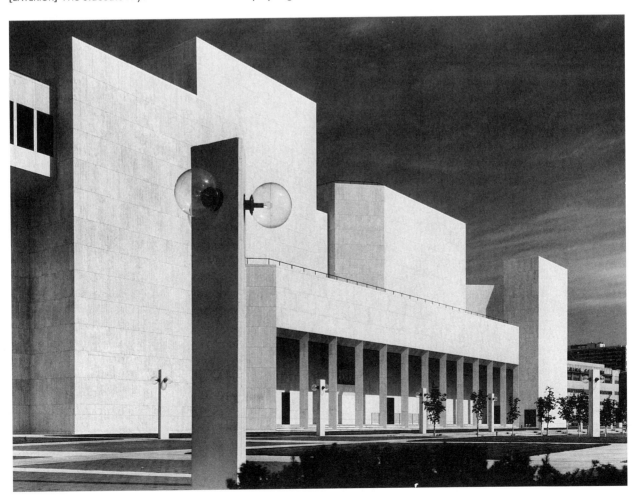

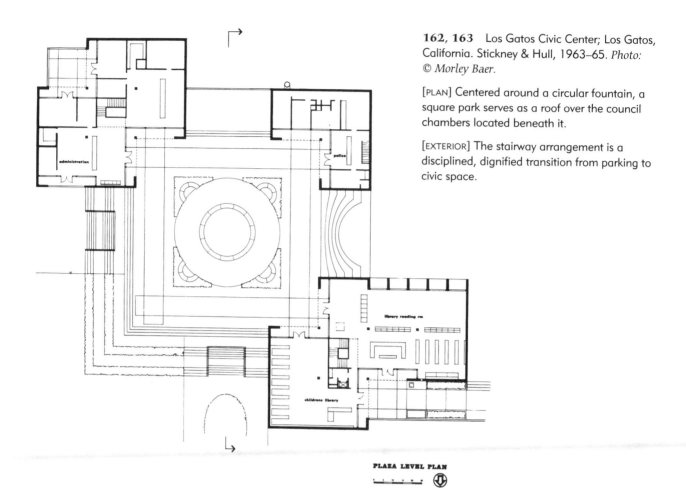

PLAZA LEVEL PLAN

162, 163   Los Gatos Civic Center; Los Gatos, California. Stickney & Hull, 1963–65. *Photo: © Morley Baer.*

[PLAN] Centered around a circular fountain, a square park serves as a roof over the council chambers located beneath it.

[EXTERIOR] The stairway arrangement is a disciplined, dignified transition from parking to civic space.

164 Eugene City Hall; Eugene, Oregon. Stafford & Morrin and James Longwood, 1964. *Photo: Hugh N. Stratford.* The extended colonnade, formal approach, and precise articulation interpret Classic methods of composition in Modernist terms.

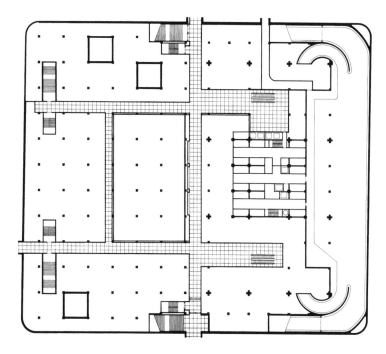

165, 166, 167 Chicago Civic Center (now Richard J. Daley Center); Chicago, Illinois. C. F. Murphy Associates; Loebl, Schlossman & Bennett; Skidmore, Owings & Merrill; 1963–66. *Photo: Hedrich-Blessing.*

[PLAN] The clearly expressed regular grid of structural columns follows classical principles of composition.

[SECTION] Preserving the desired regularity of the facade, the fenestration conceals the double-story height of courtrooms.

[EXTERIOR] Looking at the city setting, one sees the building in its open plaza as analogous to a Classic temple precinct. Studying the details, one imagines the spandrels as friezes, I beams as moldings, and the patterns of light and shade as ornament.

CONCOURSE LEVEL PLAN

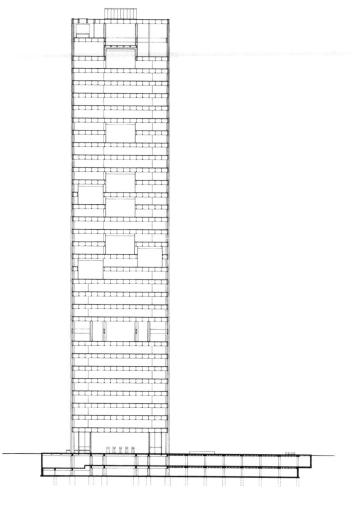

TRANSVERSE SECTION FACING EAST

168 Tulsa Civic Center Municipal Building; Tulsa, Oklahoma. Murray Jones Murray, 1969. *Photo: Bob Hawks, Inc.* A constant thirty-foot module integrates buildings and plaza.

169 New York City Police Headquarters; New York, New York. Gruzen & Partners, 1973. *Photo: David Hirsh.* Set above the busy tangle of city streets, the building is composed in a manner to suggest a base, shaft, and entablature.

ABSTRACT MONUMENTALITY

Neither lingering classicism nor limping modernism could hold a candle to the powerful imagery and expressive abstract form of such seminal edifices as Louis Kahn's Richards Medical Research Building at the University of Pennsylvania, Frank Lloyd Wright's Guggenheim Museum and Marin County Civic Center, and Le Corbusier's Government Center in Chandigarh, India. Embracing originality, change, and complexity, the architectural imagination searched for monumentality in entirely modern terms.

Two civic landmarks significant in this evolution were the 1963–69 Boston City Hall (figures 170, 171), an assertive sculptural mass, and the 1963–68 United States Department of Housing and Urban Development (figures 172, 173) in Washington, D.C., arresting in its structural energy. Designed by Kallmann, McKinnell & Knowles, the Boston City Hall is a complex configuration of interlocking concrete trusses and cross trusses that rises nine stories high. The looming mass and complexity of the building dominate the broad open space developed around it. By contrast, the HUD office building by Marcel Breuer Associates is compelling by virtue of the swaggering efficiency of the construction system. The modular cast-concrete wall units, which contain windows and utility ducts, provide a rich surface for light and shadow.

Rejecting an "enfeebling, narrow interpretation of functionalism," Paul Rudolph designed the 1968–70 Orange County Government Center (figure 174) in Goshen, New York,

so as to defy the norms and values of classicism. The eccentric assemblage of thrusting concrete forms and dynamic spatial volumes seems capricious, but it actually encourages the efficient conduct of bureaucratic and ceremonial activity. Another muscular building is John M. Johansen's Mummers Theater (1970) in Oklahoma City, which breaks out of rectangularity in an apparently random piling-up of heavy raw-concrete boxes, ducts, decking, and towers. Ulrich Franzen's Alley Theatre (1968) in Houston, Texas, sets one intersecting, curving shape against another so that no coherent sense of the unity of the whole can be obtained.

One observes that even glass can be used to convey the effect of weight rather than lightness, solidity rather than transparency. The dark glass curtain wall of San Bernardino City Hall (figure 175) in San Bernardino, California, designed by Victor Gruen Associates in 1969–72, forms a flowing skin around the six-story concrete structure. The scalelessness of the building's geometry eschews classicism to reveal the values of its own era.

Into the seventies, the search for monumentality remained entirely without reference to Classic precedents, producing ever simpler, bolder, and more memorable silhouettes. Designed by John Carl Warnecke & Associates, the 1976 Hennepin County Government Center (figures 176, 177) in Minneapolis, Minnesota, encompasses two towers, one for judicial facilities, the other for offices. The two segments confront each other across a twenty-four-story atrium space, while the broad surrounding plaza seems to create psychological as well as physical distance from an adjacent late-nineteenth-century courthouse. The eight-story Dallas City Hall (1975–78), designed by I. M. Pei & Partners, is an impressive concrete monument. Wedge shaped and cantilevered forward at a seemingly precarious angle, it projects boldly into an expansive public plaza cleared for it.

170, 171 Boston City Hall; Boston, Massachusetts. Kallmann, McKinnell & Knowles, 1963–69. *Photo: © Cervin Robinson.*

[EXTERIOR] Vigorous articulation dramatizes diverse activities within: public lobbies at the ground level; space for ceremonial, executive, and legislative uses above; offices for the bureaucracy at the top.

[SECTION] The fact of the building's nine-story height is confused by complex spatial relationships.

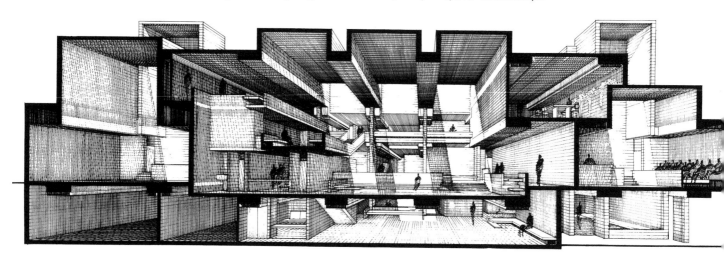

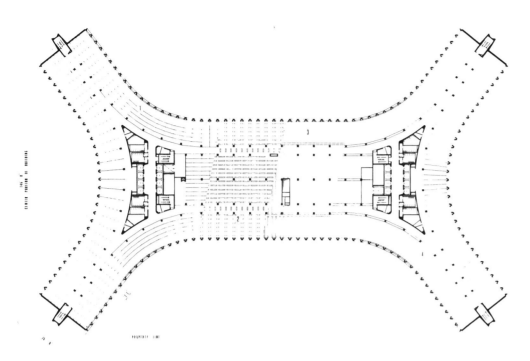

172, 173 United States Department of Housing and Urban Development; Washington, D.C. Marcel Breuer Associates, 1963–68. *Photo: Ben Schnall.*

[PLAN] The building is configured as a pair of toe-to-toe Ys, each one with a cast-concrete "tree" as the principal structural member.

[EXTERIOR] The monumentality of the effect is achieved by sheer bulk, without resorting to any hint of columnar construction.

174 Orange County Government Center; Goshen, New York. Paul Rudolph, 1968–70. *Photo: Joseph Molitor.* The complex is made to seem small in scale in deference to its suburban surroundings, while its importance is asserted by the treatment of mass, space, light, shadow, and texture.

175 San Bernardino City Hall; San Bernardino, California. Victor Gruen Associates, 1969–72. *Photo: Balthazar Korab.* Signaling civic purpose and public accessibility, the building rises up on columns to create an open plaza.

Section B

176, 177   The Hennepin County Government Center; Minneapolis, Minnesota. John Carl Warnecke & Associates, 1976. *Photo: Philip M. James.*

[SECTION] The truss-framed atrium creates a dynamic interaction between the two parts of the complex.

[EXTERIOR] The impression of strength derives from bold massing and solid end walls.

CARTER-REAGAN-BUSH-CLINTON YEARS

In these years, an uncertain electorate vacillated between Republicans promising to curtail the incursions of government and Democrats struggling to maintain the dignity of the needy. Amid growing pessimism about the future, America's standard of living declined relative to that of other advanced economies. The presidency of Jimmy Carter (1977–80) attempted to put America back on the moral high road, advocating international human rights and the resolution of the Arab-Israeli conflict. Resigned to an economy of growing constraints, Carter began his term in office telling the American people, "We have learned that 'more' is not necessarily 'better' . . . we can neither answer all questions nor solve all problems." This administration encouraged energy conservation and increased incentives for preserving revenue-producing historic buildings.

The presidencies of Ronald Reagan (1981–88) and George Bush (1989–92) attacked "tax and spend" government, emphasizing self-reliance and self-sufficiency as the stuff of the American Dream. Reagan insisted that government had "grown beyond the consent of the governed," promising to cut social programs even as he undertook a massive arms buildup. Liberal tax policies encouraged rampant development of hotels, office buildings, and shopping centers. Taking a "kinder, gentler" stance, Bush edged away from a strongly ideological position, calling for less spending on defense and more on education, rallying Americans to find the solution for homelessness, drug use, crime, and poverty in "the exercise of free will unhampered by the state," and volunteerism.

Bill Clinton's presidency, starting in 1993, wavered on the notion that he was a different kind of Democrat. Shrugging off the "liberal" label, Clinton promised that his administration would stimulate the economy while reducing the federal debt, ensure fuller medical coverage while containing runaway costs, and provide job training, educational opportunities, and environmental protection while staying out of people's lives. "Raised in unrivaled prosperity, we inherit an economy that is still the world's strongest, but is weakened by business failure, stagnant wages, increasing inequality, and deep divisions among our own people," Clinton told the nation. "To renew America we must revitalize our democracy." The need for courthouses, jails, and government office buildings spurred the biggest federal building campaign since the New Deal. Since 1994 it has followed procedures specifically intended to ensure high-quality architectural design that contributes to urban vitality and shows sensitivity to the character of local places.

There are certainly fewer parades these days. Public life is typically informal, self-initiated, and conducted in the most casual possible state of dress. Shunning monumentality, this era's public art explores the spirit of the local place, as can be seen in Robert Venturi's suggestive archeology of the Benjamin Franklin house site in Philadelphia and in Alice Aycock's investigation of the dynamics of the city at Manhattan's East River Pavilion. Beyond patriotism, public art has examined some of the most searing and complex issues of the nation's life, as in the case of Maya Lin's earth-slashing Vietnam Memorial in Washington. There is growing conviction that government must be more accountable to the citizens it serves. Some expect City Beautiful bravado, others prefer Radiant City ingenuity. Most probably accept the inevitability of only modest, incremental change, but there is no clear consensus on form or symbolism.

ANTIMONUMENTAL

The design of public buildings became increasingly responsive to expectations for cost-conscious, nonauthoritarian, sensitive, and inclusive government. For example, the representation of government as welcoming and participatory can be seen as a central theme of the Scottsdale Civic Center (1968–75) in Scottsdale, Arizona, designed by Gonzalez Associates. The result of extensive community involvement over a prolonged period, the complex is executed in a heavy-walled adobe that recalls local history. The city hall focuses on a central council chamber whose openness seems to reflect the nature of the planning process itself. Zimmer, Gunsul, Frasca Partnership's 1976 Douglas County Justice Services Building (figures 178, 179) in Roseburg, Oregon, sits modestly behind a column-fronted Greek Revival courthouse, staggered in mass and stripped to essentials so as to be distinctly more casual than the historic facility. The design and siting of Wolf Associates' 1977 Mecklenberg County Courthouse (figure 180) also enhance the perception of government as accessible. Planned as a new visual focus for the expanded Charlotte, North Carolina, civic center, the low structure, lightly poised on the ground, shows glass-faced corridors to public view. A benign role for government is suggested by the oasislike setting of the Federal Building-U.S. Courthouse in Jacksonville, Florida (figures 181, 182), whose location on a heavily trafficked city thoroughfare is softened by semitropical plants and waterworks. Completed in 1979 to the designs of William Morgan, the facility is at a nonimpos-

ing, human scale, stepping back as it rises to a four-story height around an expansive central landscaped court.

A significant crop of public buildings are intimately related to the streetscape instead of taking an aloof stance, subjecting the design to the visual and cultural features of the neighborhood. One such contextual design in Tallahassee, Florida, is Heery & Heery's 1983 City Hall (figure 183), whose evocative portico relates to a nearby monumental building, while its brick cladding and agglomerative massing sympathize with the neighboring commercial main street. The 1989 Orlando Park Village Center (figure 184), in a suburb of Chicago, was designed by Perkins & Will in a villagelike configuration to reduce the impact of what would otherwise have been awesome size. The complex rises from a tightly gridded site plan that helps to define an otherwise amorphous location behind a highway strip shopping center. Drawing from early-twentieth-century vernacular tradition, the ensemble seeks to convey dignity as well as humility.

Intentionally bold and brash, Murphy/Jahn's 1985 State of Illinois Center in Chicago makes a sweeping curve that steps back as the building rises from the street. The glass-enclosed structure dramatically changes color and form as one takes different viewpoints, challenging traditional notions about the composure of civic buildings. Containing rental office space and a shopping mall that share the public atrium, the building was among the first government buildings to be developed with revenue in mind.

The Linda Vista Library in California, completed in 1988 to the designs of Rob Wellington Quigley, is fragmented into strikingly dissimilar component parts. Using explicitly cheap and commonplace materials, the architect rejects permanence and monumentality in favor of exuberance, cheer, and friendliness.

The public purpose of the 1992 Washington State Labor and Industries Building (figures 185, 186) in Tumwater, Washington, is proclaimed by an asymmetrical glass-and-aluminum entry, whose conical shape symbolizes the building's importance in the timber industry. Designed by The Leonard Parker Associates, the building is broken into three separate but linked segments to reduce its scale, with aluminum and cast stone employed in a variety of finishes to heighten its informality.

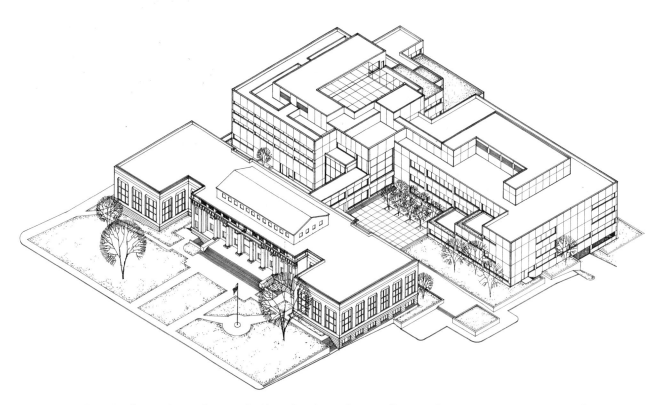

178, 179 Douglas County Justice Services Building; Roseburg, Oregon, Zimmer, Gunsul, Frasca Partnership, 1976. *Photo: Ed Hershberger.*

[AXONOMETRIC] Maintaining a modest profile, the addition combines new and expanded court, enforcement, and correction functions.

[EXTERIOR] Setbacks and the variety of window configurations reduce the building's scale, impact, and formality.

180 Mecklenburg County Courthouse; Mecklenburg, North Carolina. Wolf Associates, 1977. *Photo: © David Franzen/ Esto.* Defining a new public plaza, the glass-fronted courthouse also serves as a circulation spine that links a parking garage and government office building.

181, 182 Federal Building-U.S. Courthouse; Jacksonville, Florida. William Morgan, 1975–79. *Photo: Dan Forer.*

[EXTERIOR] Exposed for their full height at the opened corner, the tall concrete columns advertise the building's civic purpose without imposing a bulky presence.

[SECTION] Articulating the component parts, the interlocking system of reinforced concrete columns, beams, and slabs helps to minimize the building's scale.

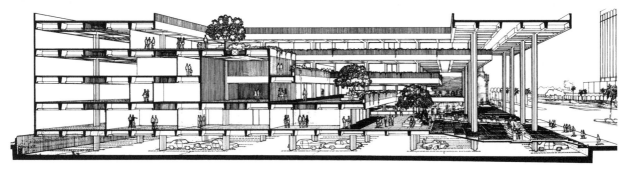

183 Tallahassee City Hall; Tallahassee, Florida. Heery & Heery, 1983. *Photo: Timothy Hursley.* The building is user-friendly by virtue of its small scale and lively facade.

184 Orlando Park Village Center; Orlando Park, Illinois. Perkins & Will, 1989. *Photo: Nick Merrick/Hedrich-Blessing.* The complex encompasses village hall, civic center, and recreation facility in three separate buildings. Rather than having a common shape, each component differs by virtue of the activity contained within.

85, 186 Washington State Labor and Industries Building; Tumwater, Washington. The Leonard Parker Associates, 1990–92. *Photo: Michael Ian Shopenn.*

[EXTERIOR] The informally composed section at the left accommodates social activity, while the office section at the right is factorylike in configuration, humanized by color and texture. Pivoting between them, the glazed entrance rotunda (center) is an ad hoc shape that takes its cue from nearby evergreens.

[SITE PLAN] To minimize the negative effects of large parking areas, the architects divided them into intimate roomlike spaces.

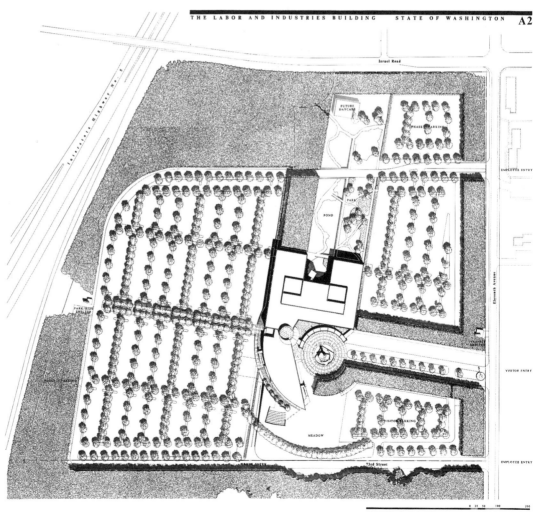

THE LABOR AND INDUSTRIES BUILDING   STATE OF WASHINGTON   A2

SITE PLAN   N

POSTMODERNIST CLASSIC

While one tendency of the closing decades of the twentieth century steered away from classicism, another approached it anew—but it rejected universality in favor of the particular, personal, and unique. Struggling to serve up both contemporaneity and tradition, some architects tried to eat their cake—and frost it, too.

"My building is threatening," observed Michael Graves of his 1980–82 Portland Public Services Building (figure 187), in Oregon, "because it attempts to make classical classifications." Graves claimed an artist's freedom to search broadly for inspiration, emphasizing pictorial qualities rather than tectonic or structural values. "Architecture is not a 'problem,'" stated Graves, intent on broadening the Modernist approach to provide "solutions" that don't only respond to logic. Portland's bulky square plan explodes Classic scale and proportions, while giant Classic motifs are appended to the facade like so many magnets on a refrigerator. By contrast, Allan Greenberg's Judicial District of Hartford Courthouse of 1978–80, in Manchester, Connecticut, portrays a very literal classicism. A scholarly revamping of a former supermarket as a small-town courthouse, the building achieves dignity with a boldly articulated entrance and impressive stone quoins at the corners.

As classicism has welcomed modernism into its tradition, the opposite is also true. The Modernist firm of Edward Larrabee Barnes and John M.Y. Lee & Partners has acknowledged the insistent influence of the District of Columbia's classical setting in their Federal Judiciary Building of 1992. The main facade speaks the language of the nearby landmark Union Station, with its rhythm of arches, heavy masonry, deep shadows, and ornamental vocabulary. Less constrained by context, the opposite facade celebrates a frank minimalism. By contrast, Chicago's Harold Washington Library (figures 188, 189) by Hammond, Beeby & Babka (1988–91) adventures into an exuberant Beaux-Arts classicism. Occupying an entire city block, the ten-story building is at heroic scale, with exaggeratedly thick brownstone sheathing, expressively deep window and door reveals, and florid gable ornamentation. A tall atrium at the top level provides an indoor ceremonial space very welcome in Chicago's harsh climate.

The eighties and nineties revived the regional and vernacular versions of classicism that flourished in mid-nineteenth-century America. A style that one might call Carpenter Classic is manifest at the Salisbury Town Hall (1988) designed by R. M. Kliment and Frances Halsband in a small historic town in Connecticut. Answering the residents' nostalgia for an earlier town hall destroyed by fire, the architects employed white clapboards and a cupola, then designed an imaginative portico and whimsical shedlike additions to indicate contemporaneity. California's Pleasant Hill City Hall of 1991 (figures 190, 191), by Charles W. Moore with Urban Innovations Group and Fisher-Friedman Associates, was designed in an intense collaboration with the community, producing apparently casual free-style arrangements of archways and loggia, pediments and moldings, chimneys and rooflines. Moore also toyed with classicism in collaboration with Urban Innova-tions Group in two other civic centers around the same time, one in Beverly Hills and another in Oceanside, California.

187 Portland Public Services Building; Portland, Oregon. Michael Graves, 1980–82. *Photo: Proto Acme Photo/Paschal Taylor.* Graves employs ornament and color boldly in representing a low-budget municipal building as a Classic composition.

188, 189 Harold Washington Library; Chicago, Illinois. Hammond, Beeby & Babka, 1988–91. *Photos: © Judith Bromley.*

[EXTERIOR] The three-part classical composition is broken into an exceedingly strong base, a thick middle opened by large windows, and a florid entablature.

[INTERIOR] The Winter Garden doorway takes great liberties with classical forms and proportions.

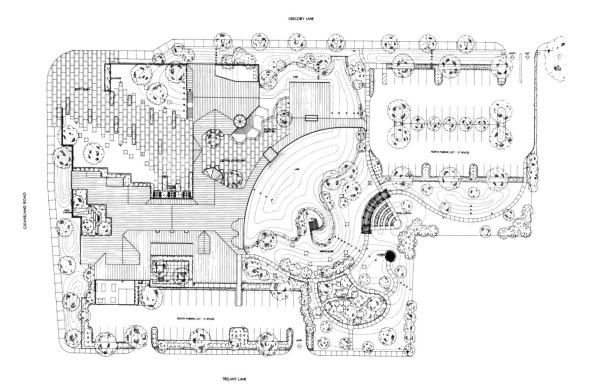

190, 191 Pleasant Hill City Hall; Pleasant Hill, California. Charles W. Moore with Urban Innovations Group and Fisher-Friedman Associates, 1991. *Photo: Charles W. Callister, Jr.*

[SITE PLAN] Designed to create a focus for a suburbanized community, the complex orients to both interior pedestrian plazas and perimeter parking.

[EXTERIOR] The loggia entrance is a whimsical interpretation of a Classic stoa. Answering the community's ecological concerns, the scenic lake also provides the water used in the air-conditioning system.

HISTORIC PRESERVATION

Historic preservation's evolution from an emotional citizens' protest movement to governmental "standard operating procedure" can be bracketed by the dates 1978, when Jacqueline Kennedy Onassis led an Amtrak crusade to Washington to lobby the Supreme Court on behalf of saving New York's Grand Central Terminal, and 1994, when First Lady Hillary Rodham Clinton presented awards for government projects that overwhelmingly favored rehabilitation over new construction. The rapid destruction of historic post offices, town and city halls, libraries, and courthouses that occurred in the fifties, sixties, and early seventies slowed to a halt. Since the mid-seventies, local, state, and federal entities have been increasingly diligent in seeking new or continued use for older government buildings and the adaptive use of nongovernmental buildings to serve a public function.

The revitalization of declining small-city downtowns was a central focus of the historic preservation movement. One example is Madison, Wisconsin, where city fathers planned a new downtown cultural and civic center to put new uses into an empty Montgomery Ward Department Store (1941) and an historic movie theater (1928), which had great importance as downtown anchors. In designing the Madison Civic Center (figures 192, 193), completed in 1980, Hardy Holzman Pfeiffer Associates wove the older buildings together into a single facility that serves as a museum, art center, several theaters, and public meeting spaces.

Learning to appreciate the grandiose and highly memorable Victorian buildings that modernism had spurned, activists of the seventies and eighties created ingenious mechanisms for saving them. The preservation of the Old Post Office (figure 194), an 1899 Romanesque Revival monument in Washington's Federal Triangle, required a reversal of the federal government's initial decision to demolish the structure, creation of an entirely new policy allowing joint public-private use, and entrepreneurial savvy in creating a fast-food and boutique operation. The adaptive use was designed by Arthur Cotton Moore Associates and completed in 1983, creating an entirely new focus of eateries and boutiques on three levels and an expanded and newly covered central courtyard.

Increasing sophistication in design, engineering, and construction materials has enhanced the practicality of preservation. An example of a very large building that was adapted for modern use is Chicago's twenty-story Burnham Building (Burnham Brothers, 1923). For some years an antiquated relic, it was adapted in 1991 to modern courthouse and office use as the State Judicial and Office Complex (figures 195, 196) by Holabird & Root. Capturing the space of the former courtyard, the architects resolved such physical constraints as floor areas too small for the requirements of the courtrooms and ceiling heights too low to accommodate modern-day air-conditioning, sprinklers, and lighting systems. In the case of San Francisco's U.S. Court of Appeals, an extremely fragile building was preserved. The imposing Beaux-Arts landmark had survived the earthquake of 1906 only to be severely damaged by the one of 1989. In saving the building, Skidmore, Owings & Merrill undertook a seismic retrofit, jacking up the entire structure to place a sliding platform under it that would deflect the force of any future earthquake.

The era's deepening respect for the commonplace human values and experience embedded in historic buildings is evident in the redevelopment of a complex such as the Showers Center (figures 197), a very big, but very plain mid-nineteenth-century red brick furniture factory in Bloomington, Indiana. The redesign (1990–95) by the Odle McGuire & Shook Corporation prepared the facility for use as not only a city hall but a corporate headquarters and a university-related research facility—an intensity of use that contributes to the vitality of the downtown. A modest nod at Classic tradition, while also a confident affirmation of Modernist functionalism, the project supports the conclusion that American architectural tradition is moving forward even as it remembers the past.

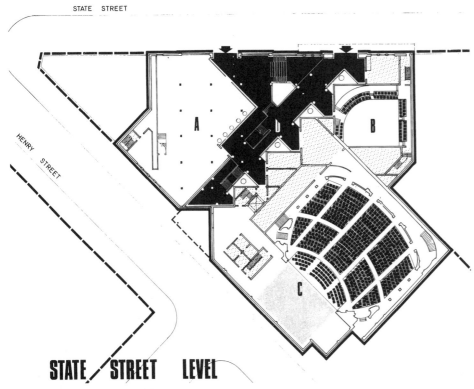

STATE STREET

HENRY STREET

A

B

C

STATE STREET LEVEL

192, 193 Madison Civic Center; Madison, Wisconsin. Hardy Holzman Pfeiffer Associates, 1980. *Photo: © Norman McGrath.*

[SITE PLAN] The heart of the new Civic Center is a diagonal ''crossroads'' that creates both a place for indoor rendezvous and a convenient through-block passageway.

[EXTERIOR] Entrances to a former department store and theater now open to the new Civic Center, thereby preserving the historic appearance of State Street. Infill added on both sides of the older buildings provides additional space for the new complex.

194 Old Post Office; Washington, D.C. Arthur Cotton Moore Associates, 1983. *Photo: Hoachlander Photography Associates.* The adaptive use of the historic post office required a cut into the main-floor level to create a three-level atrium for a shopping and dining mall.

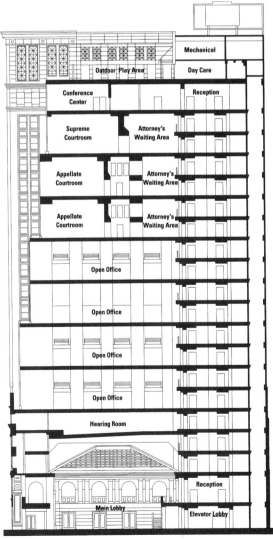

Stacking Diagram Looking South

195, 196   State Judicial and Office Complex (formerly Burnham Building); Chicago, Illinois. Holabird & Root, 1991. *Photo: Russel E. Phillips Photography.*

[EXTERIOR] The renovation incorporates the former courtyard into new courtroom spaces. Detailed in sympathy with the original design, the penthouse addition houses modern mechanical systems as well as a day-care center and rooftop play area.

[SECTION] Interior spaces had to be refitted and reconfigured in order to satisfy contemporary requirements for security, communication, comfort, and operations.

197 Showers Center; Bloomington, Indiana. The Odle McGuire & Shook Corp., 1990–95. *Photo: Timothy Hursley.* Sharing the facility with educational and commercial tenants, the City Hall's railroad canopy entrance signals the new civic function. Interior spaces were reconfigured to increase the level of natural light and to create double-height court spaces.

4

ART
MUSEUMS

ART MUSEUMS

In earlier times, art belonged to priests and kings, intimately bound with religious rites and the assertion of power, glory, and privilege. The eighteenth-century Enlightenment and the egalitarian spirit of the French Revolution gave the art collections at the royal palace of the Louvre to the common people. Swelled by Napoleon's war booty, the national collection had a professional director, specially built skylit galleries, labels on the walls, ample open hours for the public, and special visiting times for artists. A magnificent palace in Vienna renovated for the display of the imperial collection was open at regularly scheduled hours to "anyone with clean shoes." The nineteenth century saw grand, classically styled public museums, such as the Altes Museum in Berlin and the British Museum in London, dedicated to indoctrinating common people with the notion that fine art was "one of the most important branches of human civilization." Amid rapid social changes resulting from urbanization and industrialization, the art museum gained importance as a place where the elite could teach good manners to the working class.

The brash, exuberant commercialism of the nineteenth century burdened the American museum with an added responsibility—to civilize a society that had little sense of its own cultural tradition. "America is more concerned with being rich and strong than with art that implies civilization," complained James Jackson Jarves in his book *The Art Idea* (1864). Wanting to teach good taste, morality, and ci-

vility to ordinary people, Jarves placed his Old Master art collection on display at public institutions. "We cannot make the world more beautiful without making it better morally and socially," he declared.

If commercial values reigned supreme, civic leaders in many cities remained sufficiently committed to the moral and educational benefits of art that they established museums even before there was any art to hang on the walls. In 1870 the founders of the Metropolitan Museum of Art conspired to take advantage of "redundant wealth" to scoop up European and Asian masterpieces at bargain prices. Within the decade, Philadelphia, Chicago, and Cincinnati had major museums of their own. Gilded Age millionaires such as Benjamin Altman, Henry Clay Frick, J. P. Morgan, and Horace Havemeyer continued to acquire overseas collections, enjoying the triumph of the successful hunt and the glory of seeing their names appended to museum walls, establishing a pattern of generous philanthropy that continues to this very day. By 1914, there were sixty art museums nationwide; by 1938, almost four hundred.

A populist approach to art appreciation gathered force in the twenties and thirties, inspired by such museologists as Joseph Cotton Dana, director of the Newark Museum, who advocated the establishment of branch museums, school loan programs, the integration of art into the public school curriculum, and patronage of contemporary art.

THE DEMOCRATIC MUSEUM

Postwar America's growing commitment to modernism coincided with a deepening confidence in the museum as a force for social change, as a powerful educational tool, and as a weapon against elitism. Modernists such as Walter Gropius insisted that art, music, and theater could counter the isolation and alienation endemic in industrialized societies.

Forward-thinking museums championed the unity of all the arts, not just historic "high art," but also contemporary avant-garde art, folk and ethnic art, photography, industrial design, graphic and performance art. New York's Museum of Modern Art, Hartford's Athenaeum, the Oakland Museum, and others encouraged the growth of art audiences by aggressive advertising campaigns and outreach programs such as traveling exhibits, lectures, tours, and film and dance performances. Besides viewing art in the galleries, visitors came to buy the museum shop's art reproductions, craft items, T-shirts, books, catalogs, and postcards.

A growing presence in our society, the museum is a focus for continuing education, leisure-time diversion, acculturation, social activity, personal growth, and individual creativity—university, cathedral, shopping mall, country club, and community center, all wrapped in one. To broaden and demystify the art experience, the museum supplies labeling, books, catalogs, videodisks, self-guided and docent-guided tours, and exhibit-related reading rooms. Hosting a variety of community events in ample reception rooms, the museum gains importance as a locale for public ceremony.

"The American art museum can be described only in the superlative degree," wrote Karl Meyer in his sweeping survey of American museums, published in 1979. "There is no parallel in history for the accumulation of so much art by so few for the pleasure of so many," he said, reporting on the expenditure of more than 561 million dollars in the creation of 123 art museums and over 10 million square feet of space in the 1950–80 period. "The concept of limits of growth does not apply very much to museum directors or trustees," art chronicler Calvin Tompkins noted trenchantly in 1980. Each new museum develops new and larger audiences. The completion of the National Gallery's East Wing in the early eighties, for example, added four or five million visitors to the two million that the museum had averaged annually since the forties. By the late eighties, Americans were making more than a half-billion visits to art museums each year. In 1988 more than 75 million Americans participated in the ritual of viewing art at some seventeen hundred art museums and satellite galleries. More people now go to art events than sport events.

Today's museums are highly professional enterprises, carrying out traditional responsibilities for collecting, preserving, studying, exhibiting, and interpreting collections with consummate skill. Increasingly conscious of their role as guardians of societal values and beliefs, museums have begun to address museological practices that have tended to make certain groups and individuals feel like outsiders. A broader and more complex sense of mission now dictates that museums serve society's larger goals, specifically addressing local communities, women, gays, blacks, ethnic groups, the elderly, and the handicapped. Museums have become increasingly active patrons and advocates for contemporary art, commissioning art that might otherwise find no buyers, advising collectors, and offering encouragement to up-and-coming artists.

SUPPORT FOR THE ART MUSEUM

Shaking off the often suspicious attitude toward the arts that prevailed during the fifties, the Kennedys made culture glitter. The Johnson administration established support for the arts as public policy. The Nixon and Carter governments ballooned funding for arts through the National Endowment for the Arts, the Institute for Museum Services, and state arts councils. The practice of leveraging private funds with public seed money was so well established by the eighties that declining federal support for art could be countered by funding from other levels of government, from philanthropies, and from tax-deductible business and personal gifts. These decades saw the extraordinary involvement of ordinary people who join museums, pay higher attendance fees, contribute to annual appeals, attend special events, donate art, volunteer time, and use their power of persuasion to involve others. In our times, regular folks became powerful patrons.

The economic benefits of cultural tourism have long been recognized in cities such as New York, Chicago, and Boston. Pragmatic civic leaders in forward Sun Belt cities such as Miami, Houston, Raleigh, and Los Angeles now also understand that a good museum focuses public pride, builds a city's reputation, and stimulates economic activity. City fathers strategized that the Dallas Museum of Fine Arts could spark an entire sixty-acre cultural district in a revitalized downtown. Atlanta's High Museum of Art was to be a badge of the city's cultural coming-of-age.

Nevertheless, financial concerns have kept museums off-balance. "Business prospers where culture flourishes," exulted the corporate head of Philip Morris. Soaring exhibit expenses encourage museums to permit sponsors to blur the thin line that separates enlightened philanthropy from blatant self-promotion. Chronic shortages of funds compel museums to be exceedingly aggressive entrepreneurs, operating high-pressure boutiques, bookstores, and restaurants, licensing cheap copies of objects on display, and exploiting media hype with "blockbuster" exhibits. Some critics claim that waiting lines, crowding, and insistent commercialism profoundly diminish the quality of the encounter with art. Others argue that the intimacy between art consumerism and commercial consumerism is the inevitable result of the extraordinary accessibility that art now enjoys.

ARCHITECTURE

There's no standard imagery nor any replicable formula for the design of the contemporary art museum. Each is the unique product of history, collecting, and educational philosophy, of the idiosyncrasies of funding agencies, trustees, administrators, local sponsors, and audiences.

Local self-image rides on the design of an important, or even a not-so-important, art museum. Trustees like to award the commission to a celebrated architect with a national reputation in hopes that the architect's fame will ease fund-raising. Yesterday's Medici prince or rising industrialist is today's corporation head, city council member, or trustee.

The architect regards a museum commission as a signal opportunity for recognition and visibility, to shape a building type very special to our time and our culture, and, most of all, to enrich the lives of ordinary people. "Whatever the architect's ethics, philosophy, or formal options, a museum will always be judged by what it is," said museum director Marie-Claud Beaud. It is a "space that sets up an encounter between an architect's creation and artists' creations, between the work of art and its visitors, between the contemplation of art and its intelligibility, between the works of art and the space that contains them."

One's experience in the museum relates first to how one moves through it. Although no museum type is pure, three paradigms are basic: the loft, with open gallery spaces that encourage self-directed movement; the path, whose very form controls the visitor's travels; the palace, with a sequence of corridors and rooms, of circulation spaces and viewing spaces, that determines diverse experiences. The use of light, the nature of materials, the detailing—all these act on the visitor, too, to permit an intense, personal, refreshing, and enlightening experience. If our society no longer acts out its faith in cathedrals, at least it has its art museums.

LOFT

The "loft" paradigm originated in the grand department stores and exposition halls of the late nineteenth and early twentieth century—true people's palaces whose expansive interior spaces permitted unprecedented mass displays to mass audiences. The loft moved into modernity when it married an aesthetic that values free, universal space and simple, lean construction. It became a neutral, boxlike volume—a kind of warehouse for art. Moveable partitions allow curators to create the setting most suitable for a particular exhibit and encourage visitors to enjoy self-determined, casual movement. Artificial lighting, minimal framing, and spare hanging serve to highlight, isolate, and dramatize the art object.

New York City's Museum of Modern Art (figures 198, 199) heralded the new future for the museum. The first section of MOMA was completed in 1939 to a design by Philip Goodwin and Edward Durrell Stone, its radical modernity based on the museum's own 1932 exhibit on the International Style. Without having to mount an impressive stairway, the visitor enters directly from the street through a simple entry that seems more like one of a commercial office building than of a civic monument. The lobby orients the visitor to galleries, bookstore, theater, lounge, classrooms, and administrative spaces. Minimal divisions between galleries, flat wall surfaces, shadowless illumination, sophisticated air-conditioning—all were intended as explicit statements on modernity.

The open loft plan made the modern museum a place for the "enjoyment, not the interment of art," said Mies van der Rohe,

imagining a small museum in a sculpture garden so as to "eliminate the barrier between the work of art and the living community." Mies's Cullinan Hall (1958) at the Museum of Fine Arts in Houston, Texas, as well as Skidmore, Owings & Merrill's Albright-Knox Art Gallery (1962) in Buffalo, New York, are both elegant, efficient loft configurations appended to older Beaux-Arts buildings. The open plan makes architectural space a "defining rather than a confining space," affirmed Mies, who was encouraged by technological advances that permitted greater spans of unencumbered open space, more sophisticated lighting with spotlights and track lighting, and improved methods of installation and display.

In contrast to MOMA's efficient, neutral setting, the 1951–53 Yale Art Gallery (figure 200), in New Haven, Connecticut, designed by Louis I. Kahn, creates a deepened emotional experience. The commission that made Kahn famous, it synthesized influences from the Beaux-Arts, Wright, Le Corbusier, and the International Style. Kahn searched for the "spiritual quality inherent in a structure which conveys the feeling of eternity." While he admired the structural perfection, clarity of form, and logical scale of ancient buildings, Kahn's Modernist stance also stimulated the frank display of newness, advanced technology and mechanical services, and the innovative use of materials. "I think an architectural space is one in which it is evident how it is made," said Kahn. Experiencing the space, the visitor must also respond to the power of the structure.

In the fifties, many American architects were attracted by the forcefulness of Le Corbusier's

Notre-Dame-du-Haut chapel at Ronchamp. A profound source of influence closer to home was his 1964 Carpenter Center for the Visual Arts in Cambridge, Massachusetts, compelling for its bold sculptural form and roughly finished concrete, which material—in French, béton brut—generated the term Brutalism. This approach was popularized in America by Marcel Breuer, among others. The Whitney Museum of American Art (figures 201, 202), which Breuer designed with Hamilton Smith in 1964–66, is an imposing sculptural form, faced in a brooding dark gray granite. The base of the museum sits back from the sidewalk line to open a belowground sculpture court (now a restaurant), while the upper floors step forward at successive heights to create galleries of different sizes and heights. To one side of the galleries, the stairway is a heroic form, dramatizing the character of the materials and how they are joined. No polite background building, this is an assertively individualistic monument.

The art boom of the sixties and seventies caused serious space shortages in older museums and great controversies about how to expand them. Issues of appropriate style, scale, and spatial relationships are confronted head-on in the 1976 Allen Memorial Art Gallery at Oberlin College (figures 203, 204, 205) in Ohio, by Venturi, Rauch & Scott Brown. Intending the addition to pointedly contrast with the existing museum—a 1917 structure in an early Renaissance style by Cass Gilbert—the architects designed the new gallery for traveling exhibits to function as a modern loft, making it distinctly overscaled in proportion to the older building. "We liked jamming an independent new pavilion onto the old pavilion," said Postmodernist Robert Venturi, marking the emphatic juxtaposition with pointed symbolism. Venturi's book *Learning from Las Vegas* (1972) excited architectural circles with the notion that an appliqué of decorative motifs enriches the symbolic mean-

ings of bland modern buildings. Venturi described the Oberlin complex as "a succession of forms and symbols, juxtaposed and receding: a Quattrocento monument, a decorated shed, and then an enhanced loft."

While Venturi's work at Oberlin involved improvised symbolism, that of Kevin Roche John Dinkeloo and Associates at New York City's Metropolitan Museum of Art (figures 206, 207) exploited traditional formality, grand scale, and large masonry expanses. The additions built during the decade of the eighties, following the architects' overall master plan, have a monumentality that makes them as imposing as the museum's Victorian and Beaux-Arts wings. Housing the Egyptian Temple of Dendur, as well as the collections of European art of Robert Lehman and of African and Oceanic art of Michael Rockefeller, the new space is developed as a series of rigorously simplified geometric volumes appended, almost shedlike, to the back and sides of the older museum. "Because one's beliefs when working on a design are intensely held, one wants to make a statement as intense as possible so that it is clear and understandable," says Roche. Abundant daylight supplements artificial light in the spacious galleries where visitors feel free to roam. Interior garden courts built to link new structures to the older ones provide the visitor with some moments of relief from the intensity of the museum experience.

The nineties witnessed functionalist discipline yield to intense, highly personal experiments with form. The dynamic shape of the 1994 Kemper Museum of Contemporary Art and Design (figures 208, 209) in Kansas City, Missouri, makes it resemble a bird in motion. Designed by Gunnar Birkerts & Associates, the museum is articulated into three sharply angled wings, the gallery spaces dramatized by steeply pitched rooflines. The 1993 Frederick R. Weisman Art and Teaching Museum of the University of Minnesota (figures 210, 211), by Frank O. Gehry and Associates, declares the museum itself as a work of art. This building is alive to the conditions of the site and the potential to arouse the museum visitor to greater concentration and feeling. As if energized by the rapid motion of the adjacent river, one facade is composed of an exuberant piling up of waving sculpted shapes, sheathed in shiny stainless steel. In contrast, the sides facing the campus are of the plain red brick typically used in local college buildings.

The nineties have paid serious attention to issues of urbanism. An enhanced presence on a characterless highway strip is achieved for the Phoenix Art Museum (figures 212, 213) in a 1994–96 expansion by Tod Williams Billie Tsien & Associates. Two imposing wings of desert-colored concrete extend the original 1960s museum out to the sidewalk line, creating a formal pedestrian entry on the street and improved auto access on the side.

198, 199 Museum of Modern Art; New York, New York. Edward Durrell Stone and Philip Goodwin, 1939; Addition (right), Philip Johnson, 1964; Museum Tower (left), Cesar Pelli & Associates, 1982. *Photos: Adam Bartos, © Museum of Modern Art [exterior]; © Museum of Modern Art [interior].*

[EXTERIOR] As originally conceived, the museum's modest scale, simplicity, absence of a formal entry, and unpretentious side-street location were a welcome to popular audiences. Dramatically modern compared to the highly ornamented buildings that neighbored it at the time of its construction, the museum was also announcing itself as a champion of avant-garde art.

[INTERIOR] The original galleries were designed as a series of neutral, low-ceilinged spaces similar in scale to a comfortable living room; later galleries were taller and grander.

200 Yale Art Gallery; New Haven, Connecticut. Louis I. Kahn, 1951–53. *Photo: © Grant Mudford.* Architecture exerts its presence in the powerful form of the round stairwell and the deep trusses that integrate structure with lighting and ventilation.

201, 202 Whitney Museum of American Art; New York, New York. Marcel Breuer and Hamilton Smith, 1964–66. *Photos: Ezra Stoller, © Esto.*

[EXTERIOR] The facility is distinguished by the palpable weight and mass of poured concrete, extravagant articulation, varied floor heights, and eccentric window openings.

[INTERIOR] The open grid ceiling accommodates partitioning and lighting, facilitating the reconfiguration of gallery spaces. Window openings are intended to orient the visitor, since the works of art are artificially lit.

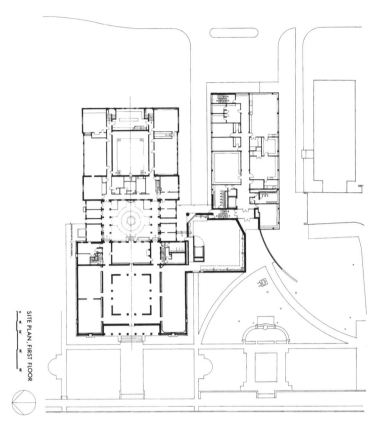

SITE PLAN, FIRST FLOOR

203, 204, 205 Allen Memorial Art Museum, Oberlin College; Oberlin, Ohio. Venturi, Rauch & Scott Brown, 1974–76. *Photos: © Tom Bernard.*

[PLAN] At bottom, the 1917 museum; center, the new gallery with a reoriented main entry; top right, library and classroom space. Set back and to the side of the existing building, the additions are intended to look like additions.

[EXTERIOR] In a tongue-in-cheek rejection of classicism, the new addition is sheathed in a checkerboard of pink granite and red sandstone panels that echo the color, but definitely not the spirit, of the original. The flat surface and minimal metal-framed industrial window openings playfully rebuke historic ornament.

[INTERIOR] The blank walls of the gallery are broken by clerestory lighting that relieves the largely artificial light, and a window opening that provides an out-of-doors view of a stubby Ionic column that seems to spoof Classic tradition.

206, 207   Metropolitan Museum of Art additions; New York, New York. Kevin Roche John Dinkeloo and Associates, 1970–c. 1980. *Photos: Kevin Roche John Dinkeloo and Associates.*

[EXTERIOR] The recent additions to the nineteenth- and early-twentieth-century museum extend the complex into Central Park at the sides and rear. Slanted glass walls allow daylighting of the galleries.

[INTERIOR] The abstract space of the loft presents the objects in isolation from their cultural context.

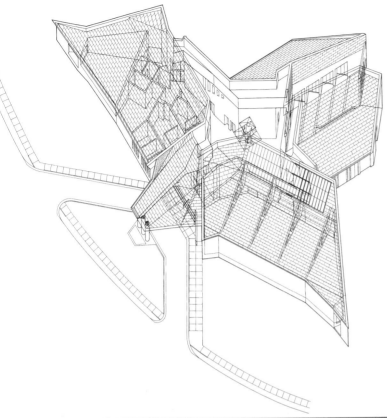

208, 209 Kemper Museum of Contemporary Art and Design, Kansas City Art Institute; Kansas City, Missouri. Gunnar Birkerts & Associates, 1994. *Photo: Timothy Hursley.*

[AXONOMETRIC] The plan is eccentrically shaped and sharply angled to yield an active, assertive presence. The visitor enters through the columned portico at the left center, passes through the irregularly shaped atrium space, and turns to the right to enter the main gallery. One can see that a significant proportion of the facility is taken up by administrative offices, conference area, café, and bookstore, which occupy the other wings.

[INTERIOR] The gallery space is enlivened by dramatic trusses.

210, 211 Frederick R. Weisman Art and Teaching Museum, University of Minnesota; Minneapolis, Minnesota. Frank O. Gehry and Associates, 1993.
Photos: © Don F. Wong.

[INTERIOR] Sculptured wall and ceiling forms and active skylight illumination profoundly affect the dynamics of the space and how one views the art.

[RIVER FACADE] Perceptions of the building are influenced by the sense that the action of the river has somehow been translated into form and light.

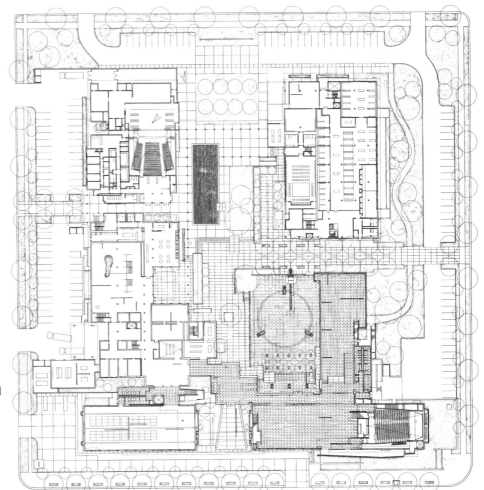

212, 213 Phoenix Art Museum; Phoenix, Arizona. Tod Williams Billie Tsien & Associates, 1994–96. *Photo: Bill Timmerman.*

[SITE PLAN] The 1996 additions extend the complex to the sidewalk line and create a monumental new entrance.

[GALLERY] Loftlike galleries enjoy subtle details, finishes, and lighting effects to heighten the perception of objects on display.

PATH

The first art museums—the colonnaded *gallerias* of Renaissance Italy—were conceived as indoor streets where strolling visitors took in the display and greeted their friends. The assertive architecture of contemporary museums greatly intensifies that experience of the museum as "path," inventing choreography and creating a kinesthetic adventure through space and time. Compared to the neutral space of the loft that sets art to reign supreme, the dynamic space of the path involves visitor, art, and structure in a complex relationship that not infrequently places art in competition with architecture.

The insistent concentration on spiraling motion at the Solomon R. Guggenheim Museum (figures 214, 215) represents the fullest realization of Frank Lloyd Wright's principles of Organic architecture. Designed in the 1940s to house the donor's collection of mainly abstract European art, the museum's construction was stalled by the war and was completed only in 1959, the year of Wright's death. Braced by the walls of side bays where the art is displayed, the structure is essentially a self-supporting concrete ramp, spiraling upward to enclose a vast open atrium—achieving Wright's long-sought-for "continuity" between space and structure, as well as providing distant vistas of the art. Light from the glazed central dome energizes the seven-story-high space and the sculptural forms of the ramp. Illumination for the art, because of the failure of Wright's clerestory lighting, is principally artificial. One sees art only as the architect will permit, close up in its bay or in a distant vista across the atrium.

Wright's influence on museum design has been profound, if not always obvious at first glance. Architects Mario Ciampi & Associates applied the ramp principle at the University Art Museum at the University of California in Berkeley (1964–70). Built of strongly textured concrete, the museum has five cantilevered terraces that fan out in an arc around a central lobby. Casting vigorous patterns of light and shade, skylighting accentuates the architectural features of the museum. The spiral paradigm translates to a square configuration at the Everson Museum (1968) at Syracuse University, in New York. I. M. Pei's design cantilevers four two-story-high, blank-walled concrete blocks in an interlocking pattern around a large, glazed sculpture court. From ground level, one ascends a spiraling stairway that broadens into interconnecting galleries, bridges, and balconies, experiencing a changing mix of artificial light as one moves away from the source of natural light in the center. At the Walker Art Center in Minneapolis, Minnesota, as originally built in 1971, the visitor follows a carefully measured spiral path through loftlike galleries of various sizes and proportions that broaden out from the elevator and stair occupying the off-center core. "I was dedicated to the idea of anonymous white spaces," said the architect, Edward Larrabee Barnes. "The question was how to arrange these spaces so that the galleries themselves would become a procession."

Like the Everson and the Walker, the 1967–74 Hirshhorn Museum and Sculpture Garden (figures 216, 217) on the mall in Washington, D.C., presents an imposing, blank-walled presence to public view. But the Hirshhorn is cylindrical in form, essentially a four-story doughnut around a sculpture garden in the center hole. The visitor follows a neat circular path through each level, an interior ring for sculpture lit from the central court, an outside ring for paintings artificially illuminated. The museum was designed by Skidmore, Owings & Merrill to provide a permanent home for the donor's collection of contemporary art as well as space for traveling exhibits.

The collection of Impressionist, Postimpressionist, and American paintings at the Scaife Gallery (1974) of the Carnegie Institute in Pittsburgh created expectations for an intimate, quiet experience. Edward Larrabee Barnes's design, a restrained Modernist addition to a florid Beaux-Arts museum, creates interlocking U-shaped galleries that are loftlike in their spareness, but configured in size and proportion so that the visitor enjoys a close relationship to the art on the walls. A careful blend of natural and artificial light brings out the changing character of the paintings under varying conditions of weather and time of day. "People want to see art in the daylight, the way it was painted," said the architect.

Altogether another kind of experience is the excitement of seeing crowds of visitors move through an exploded atrium space at the East Wing of Washington's National Gallery of Art (figures 218, 219). Designed by I. M. Pei & Partners (1971–78), the museum deliberately contrasts with the sedate original museum (see page 175 and figures 227 and 228). "To capture the spirit is more important than to satisfy the function," declared the architect, whose design mandate was to make the museum attractive for public receptions and to families who might be tempted by the nearby National Air and Space Museum. The design capitalizes on the trapezoidal geometry of the site to create dynamic pathways through and around the spectacular overscaled atrium, which is enlivened with patterns of shadows created by a huge glazed skylight. A belowground diagonal moving belt connects visitors to food service, book stalls, souvenir shops, and exhibit space. The East and West Wings serve as anchors, as at a shopping mall. "Architecture has to perform its function as the theater of life," said Pei. The "museum should be a fun place to visit, a pleasant place for people to linger and return."

Local civic leaders expected the design of the High Museum of Art (figures 220, 221), a young institution with a small collection, to "make a statement" about Atlanta's coming-of-age culturally. The precise, white metal-sheathed museum, completed in 1983 to a design by Richard Meier & Partners, is a bright Modernist retort to Wright's Guggenheim. The museum is essentially L-shaped around an expansive central atrium separated by screens from the galleries that face it. The interior, brilliantly daylit by the skylights and glass walls, has a switchback ramp with windows that take in views of the city as visitors ascend to galleries on four levels. "The circulation, lighting, installation, and spatial qualities of the design are intended to encourage people to experience the art of architecture as well as the art displayed," said Meier.

Enigma substitutes for clarity and ambiguity for order at the 1983–89 Wexner Center for the Visual Arts of Ohio State University (figures 222, 223) in Columbus, Ohio. Eisenman/Trott's design explores the layering of history on the site over time, configuring the complex along a diagonal pathway that incorporates the uncovered foundations of an old armory, the remains of brick chimney stacks, and a buried structure covered by a slanted roof. Framed by a white steel scaffoldlike structure that leads from the campus entrance to the arts center itself, the pathway becomes the central spine of the complex, supporting a variety of spaces for exhibits, performances, teaching, and back-of-the house activity.

A return to civic imagery distinguishes the

pointedly sedate limestone facade of the 1991 Seattle Art Museum (figures 224, 225, 226) by Venturi, Scott Brown & Associates. A grand ceremonial stairway parades the visitor into the museum's soaring lobby space and to a broad interior staircase that also serves as a gallery. On the second floor, the path continues as a central hall, with galleries to either side of it, expanding on the third floor to a double rank of galleries.

214, 215 Solomon R. Guggenheim Museum; New York, New York. Frank Lloyd Wright, 1944–59; addition, renovation, and restoration, Gwathmey Siegel & Associates, 1992. *Photos: © Jeff Goldberg/Esto [exterior]; Ezra Stoller, © Esto [interior].*

[EXTERIOR] The expansive rounded form represents Wright's revenge on the city's tight rectangular grid plan. Conceived by Wright as a "temple for adult education," the spiraling form portends the ritual of viewing art that will be enacted on the interior.

[INTERIOR] Upon entry one is able to grasp Wright's notions of the unity of space and structure. The boldness of the ramp and the soaring space of the atrium dramatize the visitor's experience, even if they compete with the art for attention.

216, 217 Hirshhorn Museum and Sculpture Garden; Washington, D.C. Skidmore, Owings & Merrill, 1967–74. *Photos: Ezra Stoller, © Esto.*

[INTERIOR] Separate circular pathways on each exhibit floor create a highly logical, if sedate, visitor experience.

[EXTERIOR] The cylindrical museum and the rectangular sculpture court build a design totality.

218, 219 East Building, National Gallery of Art; Washington, D.C. I. M. Pei & Associates, 1971–78. *Photos: Ezra Stoller, © Esto.*

[EXTERIOR] Grandiose in size, extravagant in shape, and entirely lacking ornament that gives it scale, the marble-sheathed museum provides a baroque punctuation point to the line of sober classical monuments along the Mall.

[INTERIOR] Bridges, balconies, and a striking sculptural stairway link the atrium to a varied assortment of nontraditional gallery spaces on four levels that somewhat uncomfortably house the large traveling exhibits that the museum was mainly designed for.

220, 221   High Museum of Art; Atlanta, Georgia. Richard Meier & Partners, 1980–83. *Photos: Ezra Stoller, © Esto.*

[EXTERIOR] The diagonal ramp from the street to the atrium dramatizes the ceremony of entry.

[INTERIOR] The atrium emphasizes the experience of architecture; the art is viewed in intimately scaled galleries apart from the central space.

222, 223 Wexner Center for the Visual Arts, Ohio State University; Columbus, Ohio. Eisenman/ Trott, 1983–89. *Photo: © Jeff Goldberg/Esto.*

[EXTERIOR] The Center is an assemblage of disparate elements.

[AXONOMETRIC] The gridded skeleton defines a strong diagonal processional through the scattered complex.

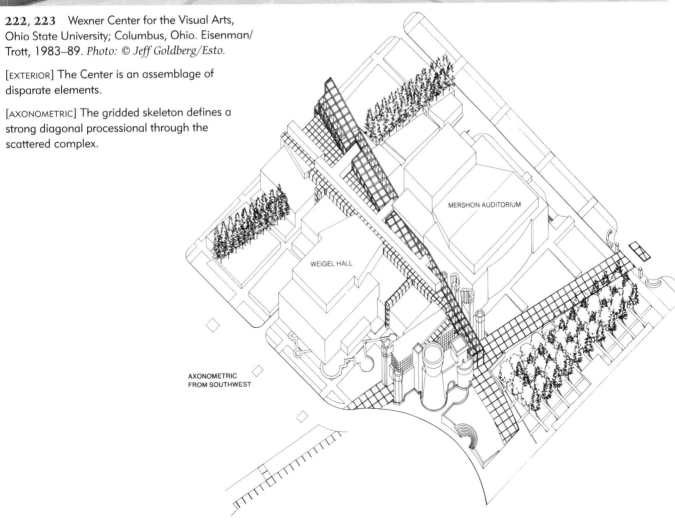

AXONOMETRIC
FROM SOUTHWEST

WEIGEL HALL

MERSHON AUDITORIUM

224, 225, 226 Seattle Art Museum; Seattle, Washington. Venturi, Scott Brown & Associates, 1991. *Photos: Susan Dirk [exterior]; VSBA [interior].*

[EXTERIOR] The overscaled fluting and incised museum name announce civic purpose. The stairway provides ceremonial entry to the museum from the off-street public plaza.

[AXONOMETRIC] The main level holds visitor services: a bookstore, checkroom, auditorium, and classrooms. An interior stairway paralleling the exterior one leads through gallery spaces on upper floors.

[INTERIOR] The strong sense of progression continues through the galleries, which are generic loft spaces.

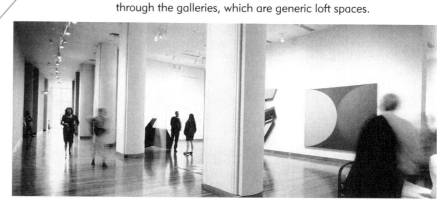

PALACE

The "palace" paradigm derives from the great late-nineteenth- and early-twentieth-century museums of the American Renaissance. These Beaux-Arts monuments had Classic facades to impress the public, axial and cross-axial corridors to allow diverse routes, a hierarchy of gallery spaces to suit different types of art, and furnishings and detailing that gave an architectural context for the art on display. Scorned by modernism until the recent past, the palace model is coming back into favor again, influenced by the return to history and the requirements of mass audiences.

The last major art museum to resist modernism, the National Gallery of Art (figures 227, 228) is a grand City Beautiful monument that houses the outstanding collection of Old Master paintings and sculpture donated to the nation by the financier Andrew Mellon. Completed on the Mall in Washington, D.C., in 1941 to the design of John Russell Pope, the museum encompasses grand ceremonial spaces and salon-like galleries, fine materials and rich finishes, all bathed in soft skylighting. It invites the visitor to participate in the solemn ritual of contemplating artistic masterpieces—and, as well, to pay homage to the man rich enough to give them away.

The interest and variety of the palace plan were quickly grasped by Philip Johnson as he began to distance himself from orthodox modernism. Johnson's Amon Carter Museum (1961) in Fort Worth, Texas, takes advantage of it in one way, the 1963 Sheldon Memorial Art Gallery (figures 229, 230) in Lincoln, Nebraska, in another. "Architecture is surely *not* the design of space, certainly not the massing or organizing of volumes," Johnson wrote in the mid-sixties, insisting that the main point of architecture is the organization of procession. "Architecture exists only in *time*," he declared, emphasizing the viewing of art as a ceremonial experience.

Notwithstanding the weakening grasp of modernism in the seventies, the revived traditionalism of the J. Paul Getty Museum (figure 231) was something of a shock. But if the design had no immediate progeny, it certainly opened the door to revivalism. Built in 1970–74 in Malibu, California, the museum was designed by Langdon & Wilson following the philanthropist's insistence that the setting not only had to make a popular audience feel right at home, but also had to make his collection of Classic antiquities look good. Based on a first-century Pompeian model, this museum is no awesome temple, but a gracious suburban villa. Comfortably scaled reception rooms, an open atrium, beautiful gardens, and a splendidly landscaped natural site are all in the spirit of sunny, suburban California.

Louis Kahn's museums seem to have roots in still more ancient history. "Let us go back in time to the building of the pyramids . . . there prevails the feeling of Silence in which is felt man's desire to express," he said in 1970, in one of those lectures that enthralled an entire architectural generation. Kahn's search for the elemental *and* the modern, the emotional *and* the rational, underlies the design of the Kimbell Art Museum (figures 232, 233, 234) in Fort Worth, Texas, built in 1974. Incorporating open porticos and courtyards, the serene concrete composition consists of a series of low vaulted spaces. The unobstructed floor space of the galleries divides into discrete roomlike zones that can be variously arranged for different exhibits. "A visitor to an art museum ought to be charmed; otherwise why expect him to come?" asked the museum's director, who wanted to make people feel "as if they are in somebody's great big house." Kahn's lighting effects, however, transcend domesticity. "I sense light as the giver of all presence," he said. "Structure is design in light."

The fugue that Kahn composed—gentle but formal enclosure, dignified procession, form-giving light—reverberated through museum design. Kahn's Center for British Art at Yale University (1969–77) in New Haven, Connecticut, completed after the architect's death in 1974, emphasizes urbanistic considerations, with a windowed street facade and retail stores built right up to the building line. Once inside, the visitor's wonderment at the domed, skylit court confirms the high purpose of the museum. Galleries occupy three upper floors, where sophisticated handling of concrete, stainless steel, and oak produces the elegant, salonlike atmosphere of the classic City Beautiful museum. Memories of the Beaux-Arts similarly humanize Edward Larrabee Barnes's Dallas Museum of Fine Arts (1983, since altered) in Texas. Exploiting a subtle combination of natural and artificial light, each gallery is proportioned for the type of art it displays. Museum design is an "architectural composition involving time," stated Barnes, emphasizing the sense of entrance, logical sequence, climax, and return.

In the eighties, a renewed appreciation for the continuity of tradition sent many architects in search of methods of detailing and systems of ornament that would relate the new building to place, past, and present. "History," said Hugh Hardy, "is like a giant trunk that you loot to serve your purposes on a given day." In the 1982 additions to the Currier Gallery of Art (figures 235, 236, 237) in Manchester, New

Hampshire, Hardy Holzman Pfeiffer Associates reinterpreted the 1920s classicism of the original structure in simple, forthright, and economical fashion. The expanded spaces are sympathetic with both the style of the older museum and the character of the surrounding residential neighborhood.

In fact, urbanistic values grew increasingly influential in the eighties and nineties, both in for new facilities and renovations. With the street presence of a Renaissance palazzo, the Charles Shipman Payson Building (1978–83) of the Portland Museum of Art, in Maine, adds dignity to the old port city. Designed by I. M. Pei & Partners, it also picks up the local vernacular with a brick and granite facade that helps to define the facing public square. The museum progressively steps down in height and narrows in width toward the rear of the lot, containing an arrangement of different-size galleries and clear circulation paths that ease the visitor experience. In the case of the Dayton Art Institute (figures 238, 239) in Ohio, renovated by Levin, Porter in 1982, a new addition preserves the existing street facade for pedestrians, transforming the back of the facility into a gracious entrance for visitors arriving by car. Once inside, a series of circular rotundas connecting various passageways help the visitor to orient to various points in the museum complex.

The Beaux-Arts principles of the palace plan have helped to bring visual order and an improved visitor experience to ad hoc constructions accumulated over time. The tasks of accommodating very diverse collections, facilitating school-group visits, and imparting a sense of coherence were central to the Newark Museum's (figures 240, 241) master renovation plan and the execution of the first several phases by Michael Graves (1982–89). The scheme links four existing structures by means of skylit courts and passageways. "The way to show objects has to do with putting them in rooms, not spaces,'' Graves insisted. ''One should create an ambience around the object that encourages associations with the object.'' A similar set of challenges shaped a 1992 master plan for New York City's Brooklyn Museum (figures 242, 243) by Polshek & Partners with Arata Isozaki & Associates. Intended to carry an incomplete Beaux-Arts scheme into the next century, the project would restore the muse-um's civic presence on the public street while creating a new entry oriented to the park and parking lot at the rear. The gently Modernist new structures that have already been built will, eventually, be climaxed by a tall truncated obelisk that will boast of the great Egyptian treasures within. Frankly admired tradition, a rigorously functional approach, and the constraints of budget and existing facilities rule the future of this museum.

227, 228   West Building, National Gallery of Art; Washington, D.C. John Russell Pope, 1941. *Photos: Courtesy National Gallery of Art.*

[EXTERIOR] The view of the roof reveals the organization of interior space. A strong axis begins at the ceremonial stairway leading to the entry foyer and rotunda. The visitor is then reoriented to a cross axis, a long corridor lined with roomlike galleries on both sides. The side wings create secondary axes.

[INTERIOR] The rotunda and corridor are impressive reception and circulation spaces, while the galleries are closer to human scale to enhance the experience of the art.

229, 230 Sheldon Memorial Art Gallery; Lincoln, Nebraska. Philip Johnson, 1963. *Photos: Ezra Stoller, © Esto.*

[EXTERIOR] The organization of the limestone facade, from the low plinth to the strong cornice line, is a clear reference to a Classic temple. The tone of the visitor experience is set by the formality of the approach.

[INTERIOR] The glass-walled entrance hall focuses on the dramatic switchback stair that will start the tour. The galleries, of various dimensions, are artificially lit.

231 The J. Paul Getty Museum; Malibu, California. Langdon & Wilson, 1970–74 (since altered). *Photo: Leland Y. Lee.* The comfortable scale and abundant landscaping welcome the visitor. Galleries are on two floors, with technical services and a parking garage occupying a lower position on the hillside site.

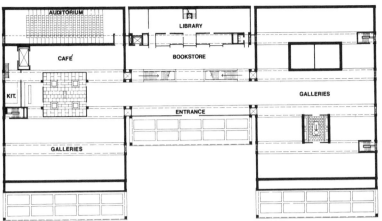

232, 233, 234 Kimbell Art Museum; Fort Worth, Texas. Louis I. Kahn, 1974. *Photos: © Robert Shaw [exterior]; © Grant Mudford [gallery].*

[PLAN] A formal, three-part plan that evokes the Beaux-Arts. The gallery space at the right of the central entry hall holds temporary exhibits; the space to the left of it, the permanent collection. The floor plan suggests the openness of loft space, but the ceiling vaults and the channels between them (indicated by dotted lines on the plan) actually seem to shape the galleries into roomlike spaces.

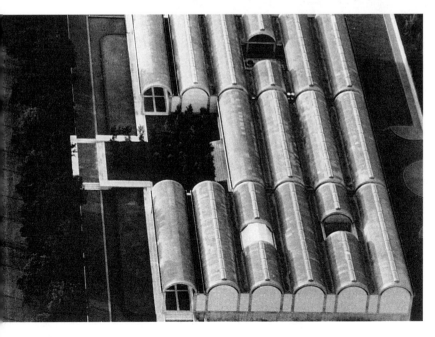

[GALLERY] The space provides loftiness as well as intimacy. The innovative light diffusers, acting together with natural skylighting, create subtle lighting effects.

[EXTERIOR] Attracting rather than awing the visitor, the approach to the museum is softened by a ninety-degree turn and passage through a grove of trees.

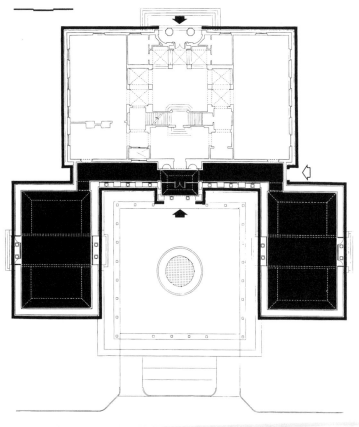

235, 236, 237 Currier Gallery of Art; Manchester, New Hampshire. Hardy Holzman Pfeiffer Associates, 1982. *Photos: © Cervin Robinson.*

[PLAN] Taking a cue from the proportions, scale, and formality of the 1920s museum (top), additional space is added as symmetrical wings to the rear, around an open court. The loggia ties all these elements together, creating a new, accessible entrance.

[EXTERIOR] Simplified Classic orders and plain brick reflect a modern aesthetic as well as contemporary cost constraints.

[GALLERY] Diminishing the apparent height of the galleries, the shaped roof contributes to a more intimate atmosphere for the viewing of art. Translucent skylights diffuse daylight.

238, 239 Dayton Art Institute Propylaeum; Dayton, Ohio. Levin, Porter, 1982. *Photos: Gregory Glass/Dan Ingersoll [exterior]; Glen Calvin Moon [interior].*

[EXTERIOR] A curving wall embellished with an outscale classical fragment advertises the entry point like a billboard.

[INTERIOR] The rotunda is a pivot point for pedestrian circulation.

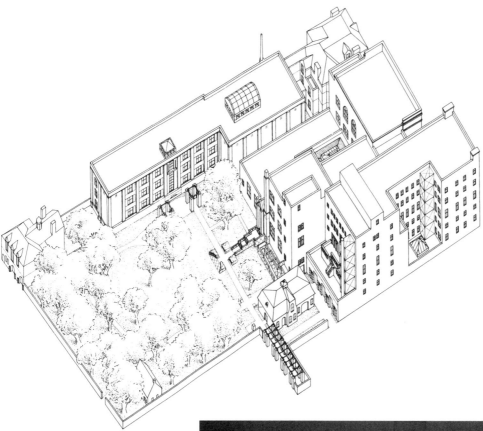

240, 241 The Newark Museum; Newark, New Jersey. Michael Graves, 1982–89. *Photo: © Steven Brooke Studios.*

[AXONOMETRIC] The new classically inspired rear entry orients cars and school buses while preserving the traditional appearance of the older buildings on the public street.

[GALLERY] Severely simplified, the roomlike spaces have thick walls and classical proportioning.

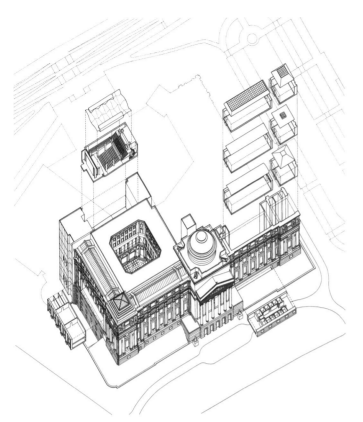

242, 243 The Brooklyn Museum; Brooklyn, New York. Polshek & Partners with Arata Isozaki & Associates, 1992. *Photo: Pat Bazelon.*

[AXONOMETRIC] The master plan achieves rationalized circulation, a formal vehicular entry, and new gallery space.

[GALLERY] Spare details, such as the arched ceiling and limestone door surround, enhance the roomlike ambience of the galleries.

5

RELIGIOUS BUILDINGS

RELIGIOUS BUILDINGS

Founded on the principle of religious freedom, dedicated to Judeo-Christian values, this nation has generally acted on the belief that its destiny is a special concern of Divine Providence. "Seest thou not God's purpose from the first?" Walt Whitman rhapsodized in "Passage to India." America is "the Israel of our time," Herman Melville exhorted in *White-Jacket*. America regards religious affiliation as a defining feature, key to one's heritage, family ties, and social standing.

In the mid-twentieth century, no matter the proliferation of denominations nor their diversity of practice, Americans generally shared the belief that church or synagogue membership builds character and makes good citizens. In 1956 Congress adopted "In God We Trust" as the national motto and in 1954 added the words "under God" to the Pledge of Allegiance. The Reverend Norman Vincent Peale was cited that year as one of the "twelve best salesmen of the year."

If fears of "Godless Communism," atomic war, and rampant materialism contributed to the desire for religious affiliation that swept over America, so did gratitude for the end of depression and war, and optimism that a new era was dawning. Creating a religious-building boom, new young suburban families looked to church and synagogue not only for spiritual support, but for a sense of belonging, social activity, and educational programs for the children. Religious institutions enjoyed a prosperity heretofore unknown, *Fortune* magazine reported, noting collection plates that "do not tinkle with coppers but rustle with bills."

The revolutionary spirit of the sixties fired church activism in social and societal causes. "Peace" and "Love" banners waving, radicalized ministries invited communal planning, turning to "relevant" issues, and closing the gap between sacred and profane. More space in the religious building was given over to missionary service to the community in the form of day care, nursery schools, after-school recreation programs, drug and alcohol counseling, homeless shelters, job training, and golden-age groups. The Catholic Church disavowed "triumphalism"—the use of architecture to exalt its own power and glory. As liturgical reform had already affected Protestants, the Second Vatican Council (1962–65) encouraged Catholics to follow the communal practices of the early Christian Church, with more active lay participation in liturgy and greater closeness between congregant and clergy.

By the end of the sixties, however, pessimism had supplanted optimism, despair had replaced hope. "Is this the monster our religion, our arts have spawned?" asked architect and social visionary Percival Goodman, mourning the deteriorating fabric of American society. "If it is, do I not have the duty to say both art and religion are irrelevant?" While a 1957 survey had revealed that sixty-nine percent of all Americans viewed religion to be on the rise, a sounding taken ten years later—as youth gravitated toward hippiedom, drugs, and mysticism—

189

showed that almost the same number believed that religion was of diminishing significance in society. Falling church attendance and rising costs stalled church construction. "What is absolutely basic for our use? And what is not?" asked one church leader, calling for the most rigorous standards of utility and economy. "If the people won't come to the church, let the Church go to them," declared another, pointing to "marketplace ministries" and shopping-center chapels.

The seventies produced the growing influence of Islam, charismatic and Pentecostal movements, New Age beliefs, televangelist ministries, and loosening denominational affiliation. Religious activity exploded, with 140 million Americans and 300,000 clerics, representing at least eighty separate denominations, attending more than 344,000 churches and synagogues. Declining older congregations in northeastern and midwestern cities struggled with aged and redundant buildings, while burgeoning exurban and Sun Belt metropolises faced heavy pressures for new building with scarce resources. In his 1985 State of the Union address, President Reagan spoke proudly of religious renewal in America and the "rediscovery of the values of faith, freedom, family," urging Congress to approve school prayer and legislate against abortion.

Preaching a return to the spiritual values of early-nineteenth-century Christian America, fundamentalism grew increasingly powerful in the eighties and nineties and, in its attempt to place private morality on the public agenda, increasingly went head-to-head with liberal factions, both secular and religious. Nondenominational evangelical ministries, such as those led by Jerry Falwell and Robert Schuller, were the most rapidly growing sector of organized religion in America. One result of this development was the megachurch, of which at least four hundred have thus far been built.

Holding thousands of worshippers at a time for hymnal, country, and rock music services, they combine entertainment with worship, serving as arena, theater, and auditorium all in one.

THE POWER OF TRADITION

Organized religion, which is conservative by its very nature, is intimately bound with one's life passages—birth, coming-of-age, marriage, death—and the customs and beliefs of one's family and clan. The evolution of religious buildings over the centuries has maintained the continuity of tradition, providing many commonly understood forms and symbols: height demands humility; the tower calls to worship; the cupola bestows status; art and rich materials inspire awe; the cross and Star of David identify church and synagogue.

The religious building should foster spirituality, meditation, renewal. To Catholics, followers of Eastern Orthodoxy, and some Episcopalians the sanctuary (the immediate area around the altar) is a sacred place. Its focus is the sacrament of the Eucharist, the miraculous transubstantiation of bread and wine into the body and blood of Christ and their consumption by the congregation. Ranging from the more ritualistic Presbyterians to the more word-based Reformed groups, most Protestants, on the other hand, regard the church as more of a meeting place, where the emphasis is on the sermon, communal bible reading, prayer, music, song, and meditation. Similarly, Jews do not regard the synagogue as a holy place, but as a place of study and prayer. Every denomination must provide for a wide range of secular activity, including administration, social service, fellowship, and study.

Beyond religious requirements and attributes, styles of religious buildings relate to culture generally. The American heritage encompasses the Spanish Baroque, which lives on in the missions of the southwest; Neoclassical styles from Georgian to Greek Revival on the eastern seaboard and west to the Mississippi; and the pointed-arch Gothic Revival and round-arched Romanesque Revival that flourished in the revivalism of the nineteenth century. Prairie School, Arts and Crafts, and eclectic choices distinguished pre-World War I America from coast to coast. Right up to the present time, the churches of rural congregations and those with strong ethnic identity hold fast to their heritage. A simple tower or pointed-arch motif allows the vernacular structure to partake of Georgian or Gothic tradition; multiple gable fronts and onion domes relate to Russian Orthodox tradition; elaborate stonework may be sympathetic to an Italian-American congregation; spartan buildings suggest a Lutheran congregation; a building like a meeting hall or lodge may reflect an African-American congregation.

THE CALL OF MODERNITY

Is modern religious design bound to fail human needs because our "culture is in pursuit of self-development rather than a faith transcending the self" as Richard Sennett charged in *The Conscience of the Eye*? Or, will new forms generated by modern investigations of space, light, and structure prove useful to future generations rededicated to transcendent values? Walter Gropius is supposed to have refused to design a religious building because he felt it beyond his talent as a modern architect. But Le Corbusier's search to create a true "center of meaning . . . a vessel of intense concentration and meditation" at the pilgrimage church of Notre Dame du Haut (1953) at Ronchamp, France, stood architecture on its head.

The notion that free, flowing space is an es-

sential condition of modernity—with light its corollary—paralleled the ideas of the highly influential Protestant theologian Paul Tillich, who emphasized "holy emptiness" and "majestic simplicity." Some architects struggled with innovation for its own sake, attempting to create entirely new forms for traditional practice. Some may have exaggerated height or shape in the effort to evoke religious feelings. Others went back to tradition in treating the church building itself as a symbolic form. Barry Byrne's St. Francis church of 1951 in Kansas City, Missouri, is in the shape of a fish, an early Christian symbol. Mario Ciampi's church of St. Peter, in Del Mar, California, of 1962, is modeled on the crown of thorns.

Religious buildings comprised a high proportion of the postwar era's most advanced designs. " 'Modern' or 'contemporary' design has taken hold," the *Saturday Evening Post* reported in 1958, stating that half of all new churches were modern in design, up from twenty-five percent four years previously. "Some of these buildings have caused people to say, 'But they don't look like churches,' " declared the weekly. "In turn, one might ask, 'What is a church?' "

Reexamining the relationships among architecture, devotion, and spiritual experience, some denominations were more audacious than others. The Benedictines have been among the boldest Catholic patrons, welcoming cutting-edge designs by Pietro Belluschi, Marcel Breuer, and Stanley Tigerman. Possibly the Protestant sponsor most dedicated to modernism has been the Missouri Synod of the Lutheran Church, which emphasizes simplicity in religious ritual. Secular colleges and universities have been progressive clients, frequently selecting architects of great stature, such as Paul Rudolph, Mies van der Rohe, Richard Neutra, Frank Lloyd Wright, and Eero Saarinen.

The unity of all the arts in religious building enjoys long tradition. Catholic and Eastern Orthodox churches invest great significance in liturgical objects, including the altar, vestments, crucifix, chalice, candlesticks, sanctuary lamp, baptismal font, and Stations of the Cross. Church furnishings are fewer and less important in Protestant worship, whose heritage generally dictates plainness and simplicity. Jewish congregations observe biblical strictures against graven images, employing abstract designs for the ark (where the Torah is stored), Torah ornaments, bimah (reading table), and eternal light.

The combination of vigorous building activity and eager innovation over the last half century has produced an extraordinary panoply of religious buildings. Innumerable differences and variations make categorization difficult, but, nevertheless, it is possible to consider two sets of criteria in combination. One regards orientation, which is generally axial for liturgy-oriented congregations and centralized for evangelical or word-based congregations. The second is stylistic tendency, which generally divides into traditionalist, abstract, or expressionist modes.

AXIAL PLAN

Following the rectangular form of the basilica that early Christians borrowed from the Romans, the longitudinal plan produces the strong axial orientation that dramatizes the Eucharistic liturgy. One enters through a narthex (a vestibule on a short side of the rectangle), passing the holy-water font, which symbolizes the rite of baptism as the means of entering the membership of the church. The long nave, the main body of the church, culminates at the altar or communion table. A pulpit (lectern) used for sermons and readings is to one side. There may be aisles as well as chapels, either at the sides of the nave or in transepts (arms that cross the nave). The size and location of the choir depends on the importance the congregation gives to singing.

Liturgical reforms of the fifties and sixties prescribed greater closeness between parishioners and priests, encouraging congregations to seek a middle ground between axial and centralized orientations. This produced experiments with square and diagonally oriented plans that continued through the early eighties, when there began a return to the traditional long axis of the nave church.

TRADITIONALIST

It was a slow turn to modernism in the forties and early fifties, churchgoers usually expecting a church to "look like a church." In most places, this implied some kind of revival style: in San Francisco, an ensemble of stucco and Spanish tile; in Boston, one of brick with Georgian windows. Miami and Los Angeles were among a few cities that were quick to accept modern architecture into vernacular tradition.

Certainly, Our Lady of Victory Church (figures 244, 245) in Manhattan, designed by Eggers & Higgins and completed in 1945, conforms both to the New York City streetscape and to traditional expectations for religious character. Commanding a corner location, the church portrays importance and permanence. On the interior, the monumental arched opening of the apse (the niche behind the altar), dramatically lit and elevated several steps above the level of the nave, gives visual and emotional prominence to the altar and crucifix above it. Classic detailing—a prominent cornice, niches holding statues of saints at either side of the apse, a coffered ceiling—convey the power and venerability of the church. Exploiting the spiritual associations of Gothic imagery, the Cathedral of St. Joseph (1962) in Hartford, Connecticut, was designed by Eggers & Higgins of reinforced concrete framing and structural stained glass. Of exceedingly tall, narrow, and long proportions, the nave reaches a dramatic climax at the altar, surmounted by a high aluminum canopy. Down lights and spotlights add theatrical intensity to the natural light entering through the stained glass in the side walls.

244, 245   Our Lady of Victory; New York, New York. Eggers & Higgins, 1945. *Photos: Gottscho–Schleisner Collection, Library of Congress.*

[EXTERIOR] The massive arch and elaborately pedimented gable identify the church with the style of the Georgian Baroque.

[INTERIOR] Architectural ornament and illumination create a dramatic focus for the altar.

ABSTRACT MODERNIST

Certain Protestant denominations, searching for the purity and spirituality of early Christian practice, embraced the avant-garde's foray into abstraction. If the austere minimalism of Mies van der Rohe's chapel at the Illinois Institute of Technology in Chicago raised doubts among some that divinity could be expressed "in the details," the warmer atmosphere of religious buildings produced under the influence of the Finnish Modernist Alvar Aalto and of the midwestern Prairie School provided proof that modernism was, nevertheless, capable of satisfying spiritual and emotional needs.

At Christ Church Lutheran (figures 246, 247) of 1949–50 in Minneapolis, Minnesota, Eliel Saarinen and Eero Saarinen's rigorous abstractions achieve a quiet spirituality. Drawn by sophisticated lighting effects, the viewer's attention is riveted by the exceedingly simple communion table and the plain cross on the brick wall behind it. Tilted, curved, and textured, the brick walls and ceiling achieve subtle spatial effects as well as good acoustics. Domestic in scale, as befits its residential neighborhood, the church complex also encompasses a freestanding bell tower, community space, and classrooms grouped around a courtyard. A related example is the brick-and-concrete Church of the Good Shepherd (1967–68) in Moorehead, Minnesota, by Sovik, Mathre & Madison, whose nave is enclosed by stark brick walls and a gently sloping wooden ceiling.

By contrast, the steeply pitched shedlike forms of the 1963–65 Central United Protestant Church (figures 248, 249) in Richland, Washington, by Durham Anderson Freed, create a dynamic impression. The nave and sanctuary are conceived as a single space, the communion table and pulpit occupying a freestanding platform brilliantly lit from a setback clerestory window. The extremely simplified planar surfaces of the interior carry through to the exterior. Related in execution is the brick Wertz United Methodist Church of 1972, in Columbus, Indiana, by the McGuire & Shook Corporation, whose spire is an elaborate rising twist. The communitylike grouping of pitched-roof forms of the Church of St. Jude of 1969, in San Francisco, by Patrick J. Quinn and Dennis J. Shanagher, reflects the post-Vatican II tendency to give greater visual importance to the secular components of the church complex. This is seen in the broadened nave, which approaches a square, and the forward position of the altar, which is surrounded by seating on three sides.

246, 247 Christ Church Lutheran; Minneapolis, Minnesota. Eliel Saarinen and Eero Saarinen, 1949–50. *Photos: Ray Gierke.*

[INTERIOR] Strong side light emanating from a concealed source imparts a sense of mystery to the chancel area. A railing sets off the communion table in the center, and the pulpit rises on the right side.

[EXTERIOR] Bell tower and nave are simplified cubic volumes enlivened by the texture of materials and carefully developed light and shadow patterns.

248, 249 Central United Protestant Church; Richland, Washington. Durham Anderson Freed, 1963–65.

[INTERIOR] The angled ceiling lends drama to the austerely simple chancel end.

[EXTERIOR] The assymetrical, sharply pitched roofline and the elevated crucifix reveal this as a religious building.

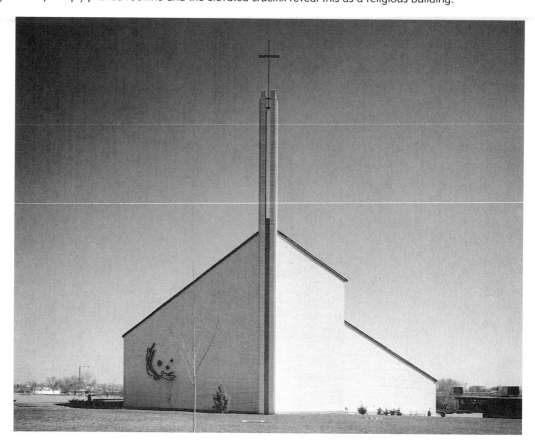

EXPRESSIONIST

Modernism dramatized nature even as it exalted the machine. Lloyd Wright, the highly regarded son of his more famous father, evoked a pantheistic relationship with the out-of-doors on the rugged coastal strip that is the site of the Swedenborgian Wayfarer's Chapel (1951) in Palos Verdes, California. Embodying the congregation's belief in the intimacy of the world of nature and the world of the spirit, the small glass-walled chapel is constructed of a rank of treelike wood trusses that carry one's gaze past the altar into the depths of the wooded landscape. By contrast, it is a dramatic cliffside site in the stark desert landscape of Sedona, Arizona, that holds the Chapel of the Holy Cross (figures 250, 251) of 1956. Designed by Anshen & Allen, the bare reinforced concrete shell is windowless on the two long sides and almost completely glazed on the two short sides. The glass wall behind the altar opens the interior to a vast desert panorama.

Engineering feats that evoke extreme spirituality had their heyday in some fifties and sixties religious buildings whose emotional quality surely rivals that of the Gothic era. As that historic epoch exploited stone ribs and buttresses to create heaven-seeking verticality, our modern times have conveyed spirituality by means of reinforced concrete, stone and metal trusses, and structural glass. Praised at its dedication "as a symbol for the world to know that the U.S. is truly a nation under God," the 1956–62 Air Force Academy Cadet Chapel (figure 252) in Colorado Springs, Colorado, was designed by Skidmore, Owings & Merrill. On a long, narrow rectangular plan, the structure is constructed of a dramatic space frame of aluminum tetrahedrons filled in with jewellike colored glass. St. Paul's Lutheran Church in Sarasota, Florida, designed by Victor Lundy, is an adventure in catenary-arch construction. The roof is suspended by cables hanging from a beam held by the side walls, so that the act of construction seems like an act of devotion. "The inescapable truth is that great architecture is creative architecture . . . involved inextricably with truth, with love, with the full passion of being," said Lundy.

The intense spirituality associated with great height and breadth is expressed with eloquence at St. Francis de Sales (figures 253, 254, 255) of 1961–67 in Muskegon, Michigan, designed by Marcel Breuer and Herbert Beckhard with a cavernous nave some seventy-five feet high. The apse, dramatized by the convergence of a daring system of concrete planes and rigid arches, is illuminated by cut-in skylights that direct intense natural light from above. Heroic in aspiration and evoking the Gothic in spirit, Breuer sought the courage "to defeat gravity and to lift the material to great heights, over great spans—to render the enclosed space a part of infinite space."

Heralded by a bold freestanding belfry, the thirty-foot-high cast-concrete enclosure of the 1962 St. Patrick's Church (figures 256, 257) in Oklahoma City establishes a powerful sense of separation from the outside world. Designed by Murray Jones Murray, the church is roofed by hyperbolic-paraboloid concrete "umbrellas" that emphasize breadth and transparency rather than height and mass. The glass-walled nave is enclosed within a cloisterlike inner ambulatory lined by cast-concrete panels that depict a parade of angels. Designed by Joseph Albers, they seem to offer the congregant a vision of the world beyond.

By contrast, the solidity of materials—the compelling physical presence of walls and roof—deepen the sense of spirituality at Tuskegee Chapel (figures 258, 259) of 1968–69 in Tuskegee, Alabama, used as a concert hall for the famed Tuskegee Institute choir. Designed by Paul Rudolph, its form reflects the original intention to build a tour de force of concrete construction, but it was actually built using more conventional steel framing and brick walls. Elevated above the broad nave, the spacious choir and canopy-covered pulpit at the fan-shaped end of the chapel awaken a sense of anticipation. Intense spotlighting as well as the natural light from concealed clerestory openings add theatricality to this space for song and celebration.

250, 251 Chapel of the Holy Cross; Sedona, Arizona. Anshen & Allen, 1956. *Photos: Julius Shulman.*

[EXTERIOR] The view from the rear dominates the approach road.

[INTERIOR] The cross motif at the apse end of the church is applied over a window wall that opens the wild, rocky terrain to view.

252 Air Force Academy Cadet Chapel; Colorado Springs, Colorado. Skidmore, Owings & Merrill, 1956–62. *Photo: Balthazar Korab.* Creating an emotional experience by means of aluminum and stained glass, the chapel was branded as "Air Age Gothic."

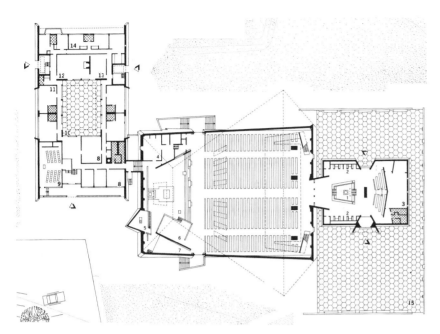

253, 254, 255 St. Francis de Sales; Muskegon, Michigan. Marcel Breuer and Herbert Beckhard, 1961–67. *Photos: Bill Hedrich/Hedrich-Blessing.*

[PLAN] The sanctuary is the center of a composition that includes offices (left) and baptistery (right).

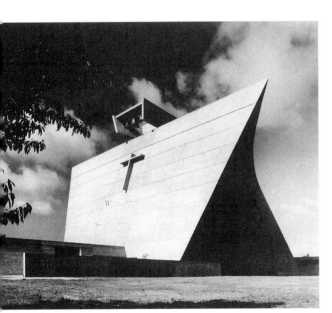

[EXTERIOR] Composed as a hyperbolic paraboloid, the side walls of the nave describe a double curve. The concrete surfaces reveal the imprint of the architectural forms used for their construction.

[INTERIOR] Dramatic height and expressed structure create the emotional quality of the space.

256, 257   St. Patrick's Church; Oklahoma City, Oklahoma. Murray Jones Murray, 1962. *Photos: Julius Shulman [exterior]; Bob Hawks [interior].*

[EXTERIOR] Cast concrete creates decorative surface effects.

[INTERIOR] Glass walls open to accommodate additional parishioners on important holidays.

258, 259 Tuskegee Chapel; Tuskegee, Alabama. Paul Rudolph, 1968–69. *Photos: Ezra Stoller, © Esto.*

[INTERIOR] The tilted planes and emphatic asymmetry of the walls and ceiling not only improve the quality of the acoustics, but also symbolize the importance of song.

[EXTERIOR] Active massing portrays various functions: at the rear the chapel (topped by a cross), for meditation; in the center an entry to the music school; at the front the steps leading to the chapel.

CENTRALIZED PLAN

Embodying the spirit of the Protestant Reformation, the Colonial meeting house represented an alternative to the nave church, its form emphasizing congregate seating and responsive services, with greater importance on the pulpit than on the altar. All denominations had a revived interest in this configuration in postwar America and investigated various circular, square, hexagonal, and cross-axial plans in an effort to encourage individual commitment, a sense of community, and more active participation in religious practice.

With an emphasis on preaching, singing, and responsive reading over Eucharist-based liturgical rites, Baptist, Methodist, and other word-based evangelical churches usually prefer plans that highlight the pulpit. The services of Jewish congregations revolve around communal prayer and bible study. Unitarians, disavowing a priesthood, prefer nonhierarchical buildings that encourage individuals to gather in fellowship, following personal belief in the nature of God and the universe.

The seventies, a time preoccupied with the secular mission, produced the concept of the "nonchurch," a flexible space having no fixed liturgical elements in order to permit easy conversion from community use to religious observance. "We do not necessarily manage the encounter with God by establishing a place for it," declared Edward Sovik, architect of many religious buildings in the Midwest.

ABSTRACT MODERNIST

"We have tried to portray the ancient and primitive meaning of Christian worship," the parishioners explained. "In being more modern . . . we are actually more primitive and more ancient." Designed by Olav Hammarstrom, the Chapel of St. James the Fisherman (figures 260, 261) of 1957 in Wellfleet, Massachusetts, was constructed by local carpenters using beams, rafters, and shingles fabricated by hand right on the site. Following a square plan with aisles that form the shape of a cross, the pews are arranged to face the chancel in the center, lit by the skylight above it.

Focusing on fundamentals, congregants discovered the practicality and economy permitted by cool modernism. Designed by Howard R. Meyer and Max M. Sandfield with William W. Wurster, Temple Emanuel (figures 262, 263) of 1955–56 in suburban Dallas, Texas, is a highly functional composition of simple brick volumes. The form of each element refers to its use. The curved wall of the domed sanctuary determines an arrangement of benches that bends around the ark and bimah. In Marietta, Georgia, spare form and local materials create a gentle, regional modernism at John Knox Presbyterian Church (figures 264, 265) of 1965–66, designed by Toombs, Amisano & Wells. Built of granite rubble stone, the church rises on a square plan to a pyramidal roof pierced by a square tower. One enters the church under a choir loft to face a central chancel three steps up from the level of the nave, set off by four square wooden posts that support the tower. A strong focus, simplicity, and economy of means create an atmosphere of quiet contemplation.

By contrast, a modified cruciform plan that can flexibly accommodate worship and secular activity is employed at the 1974 St. Patrick's Catholic Church (figures 266, 267, 268) in the resort town of Robertsdale, Alabama, where the congregation expands and contracts with the seasons. The design by Blitch Architects, inspired by local barns, sheds, and silos, employed slanting rooflines to individualize the separate areas. On a busy street in midtown Manhattan the requirements of an urban ministry at St. Peter's Church (Lutheran) include ample office space for social services and a sanctuary that provides good acoustics for musical services and theatrical performances. Designed by Hugh Stubbins & Associates, the pitched-roof church of 1971–78 is five-sided, with benches around a raised chancel facing a glass wall that opens to a view of the city beyond. (See figure 351 for street view.) "I meant to provide an environment that is evocative of another place, a place of the mind, a place of the senses," explained the sculptor Louise Nevelson, who designed the interior in collaboration with Massimo and Lelia Vignelli.

260, 261 Chapel of St. James the Fisherman; Wellfleet, Massachusetts. Olav Hammarstrom, 1957. *Photos: Joseph Molitor.*

[EXTERIOR] The structure is exceedingly spare in form, finish, and materials. The pyramidal tower provides visibility within the community and to offshore sailors.

[INTERIOR] From the entry, one proceeds past the baptismal font toward the sanctuary, following the progression from baptism to communion. Pews face the communion table in the center, which is highlighted by the suspended crucifix.

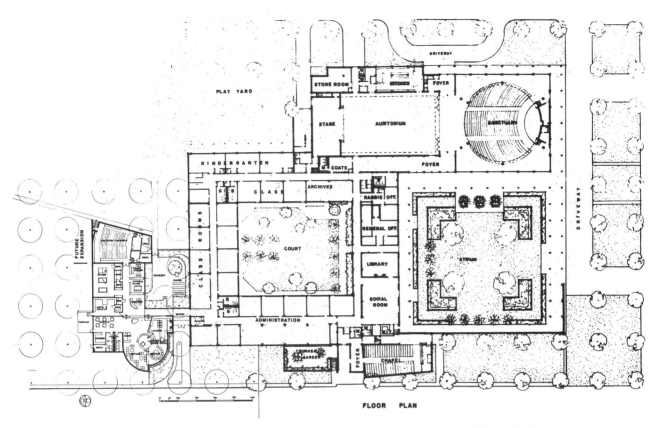

262, 263 Temple Emanuel; Dallas, Texas. Howard R. Meyer and Max M. Sandfield with William W. Wurster, 1955–56. *Photo: Ulrich Meisel.*

[PLAN] An orderly, villagelike configuration. Classrooms and administrative space surround one landscaped court; a covered pergola defines another; and a rectangular auditorium opens up to the circular space of the sanctuary.

[EXTERIOR] The sanctuary is located in the tall cylindrical volume.

264, 265   John Knox Presbyterian Church; Marietta, Georgia. Toombs, Amisano & Wells, 1965–66.

[EXTERIOR] The church occupies a walled precinct, with an open-air courtyard that provides the transition from the worldly to the spiritual.

[INTERIOR] The open skylight, expressed structure, and concentric seating arrangement create a highly focused interior space.

266, 267, 268 St. Patrick's Catholic Church; Robertsdale, Alabama. Blitch Architects, 1974. *Photos: Frank Lotz Miller.*

[PLAN] The sanctuary at the center can be opened up to expand the social spaces.

[INTERIOR] The communion table is highlighted by the lower height of the ceiling.

[EXTERIOR] The forms of the church evoke the rural vernacular.

EXPRESSIONIST

Within the bounds of modernism, the search to portray mass and bulk provided one promising avenue toward emotionality and spirituality. The cylindrically shaped chapel at M.I.T. (figures 269, 270) of 1953–55 in Cambridge, Massachusetts, designed by Eero Saarinen & Associates with Anderson, Beckwith & Haible, seems timeless, encouraging contemplation of the unknown. Hovering almost mysteriously above a water-filled moat, the chapel is blank and windowless, except for arched openings in the base. Encircled by textured, undulating brick walls, the congregation faces a freestanding altar dramatized by the brilliantly lit shower of metal pieces in the screen designed by sculptor Harry Bertoia. Continuing the exploration of the centralized plan a decade later at the North Christian Church in Columbus, Indiana, Saarinen sited the windowless, hexagonal structure in an earth berm. Dramatic illumination from the skylight encircling the soaring spire rivets attention on the altar table in the center.

The emotional power conveyed by complex and enigmatic spatial configurations is apparent in Louis Kahn's 1959–63 First Unitarian Church and School (figures 271, 272) in Rochester, New York. "Architecture is the thoughtful making of spaces," said Kahn, striving to make each space convey a feeling particular to its use. A shadowy, emotionally charged space, the sanctuary was conceived as "a square center on which I placed a question mark," according to Kahn. A hovering shape in the form of a Greek cross, the roof seems to protect against the brightness and openness that emanates from the square light towers at the four corners. The classrooms off the surrounding ambulatory, by contrast, are evenly lit and cheerful.

The emotionality, energy, and optimism of synagogue architecture in the immediate post–World War II years surely represented a rebound from the Holocaust. "Judaism repudiates pessimism," explained the rabbi Ben Zion Bookser, emphasizing Jewish belief that goodness ultimately triumphs over evil. With its obvious reference to a biblical tent, the centralized plan is a hallmark of the Jewish house of assembly, although it is by no means exclusive to synagogue architecture, nor are synagogue plans always centralized. Eric Mendelsohn, an important leader of the expressionistic approach and a pioneering European exponent of modernism, designed the dome-shaped concrete structure of the Cleveland Synagogue and Community Center (1946–52) in Ohio a few years after he emigrated to America. Exalting the elastic potential of steel and concrete, Mendelsohn strove to produce "structural and architectural expression entirely different from anything ever known before." Frank Lloyd Wright, who had influenced Mendelsohn in his youth, served as an evangelist of expressionism at Elkins Park, outside of Philadelphia, Pennsylvania, where Wright's Temple Beth Sholom of 1959 was designed to be "the kind of building that makes people . . . feel as if they were resting in the very hands of God." An equilateral triangle in plan, the structure rises as a hexagon in elevation, supported on powerful concrete beams. Sloping translucent glass walls

212

slide into the glass roof to form a kind of tent. Wright imagined the synagogue as "a mountain of light."

The firm of Kivett & Myers designed the 1967 B'Nai Jehudah (figures 273, 274), in Kansas City, Missouri, an energetically massed form that spirals up around a concrete post some eight stories high. Hand-hammered concrete inside and out reveals the mark of the worker, evoking the energy and effort of construction. One of the many Christian religious buildings that demonstrate expressionist eloquence is the 1968–69 Christ Episcopal Church in Tacoma, Washington, by Paul Thiry. Almost square in plan, the concrete structure, which is entered on the diagonal, is composed as a series of tilted and intersecting wall planes brilliantly lit from a set-back skylight.

The drama of transformed form, space, and light is a major theme in the work of Pietro Belluschi, one of the most prolific designers of religious buildings in the postwar era. A landmark on the city skyline, St. Mary's Cathedral of 1963–70 in San Francisco, California, is a vaulted concrete structure that soars almost twenty stories high. The engineering, a tour de force of thin shell concrete construction, was the work of Pier Luigi Nervi. What might Michelangelo have thought of the cathedral? "He could not have thought of it," said Nervi. "This design comes from geometric theories not then proven. It could only have been conceived today." Seating some 1,200 worshippers in column-free space on three sides of the projecting chancel, the church was one of the first to be planned according to the principles of the Second Vatican Council. If the church is "to endure as a symbol of our faith," said Belluschi, "it must consist of elemental forms, handled with the kind of simplicity that becomes both structure and symbol, to be looked at and remembered."

By contrast, an emotional response to architecture is encouraged in a synagogue that is almost domestic in scale, the 1988 Gates of Grove Synagogue (figure 275) in East Hampton, New York, designed by Norman Jaffe. The energy of the building results from the active massing of a series of forcefully interlocking pitched-roof volumes whose intersection is marked by sloping clerestory windows. A glass wall behind the ark projects the interior into the grove of trees that surrounds the sanctuary, creating brilliant daylight effects.

In Garden Grove, California, one of the first of the megachurches was the 1980 Crystal Cathedral (figures 276, 277), designed by Philip Johnson and John Burgee. It is certainly spectacular, rising on a four-sided, star-shaped plan as an extravagant glass volume, with hundreds of facets supported on triangular white metal trusses. It has been estimated that as a tourist attraction in Orange County, it is second only to Disneyland. Most commonly, however, megachurches are plain-Jane structures that resemble utilitarian warehouses or junior colleges rather than buildings of high design.

269, 270 Chapel, Massachusetts Institute of Technology; Cambridge, Massachusetts. Eero Saarinen & Associates, 1953–55. *Photos: Ezra Stoller, © Esto.*

[EXTERIOR] The structure is a stern presence in the campus setting.

[INTERIOR] The variety of lighting effects create an emotional impact: direct natural light from the skylight, strong spotlighting, and reflected light on the lower walls from the water in the moat.

271, 272 First Unitarian Church and School; Rochester, New York. Louis I. Kahn, 1959–63. *Photos: © Grant Mudford.*

[INTERIOR] Contrasting to the dark, contained character of the center of the space, the corners seem to dissolve in brightness, heightening the emotional intensity of the atmosphere.

[EXTERIOR] A vigorous composition, with window and door openings recessed deeply within projecting piers and abruptly rising light towers.

273, 274 Congregation B'Nai Jehudah; Kansas City, Missouri. Kivett & Myers, 1967. *Photos: Paul S. Kivett.*

[EXTERIOR] The energetic massing of the roof—a conical helix in shape—distinguishes the sanctuary from the adjacent classroom and social spaces.

[INTERIOR] The synagogue experience is charged by the sense of expanding space, dynamic structure, and dramatic lighting effects.

275 Gates of Grove Synagogue; East Hampton, New York. Norman Jaffe, 1988. *Photo: © Norman McGrath.* The combination of artificial and natural light throws the active forms of the synagogue into dramatic relief.

276, 277 The Crystal Cathedral; Garden Grove, California. Philip Johnson and John Burgee, 1980. *Photos: Gordon Schenk.*

[EXTERIOR] Sheathed in reflecting glass, the ample, hovering volume of the church fits into the California landscape. Almost the only details are the deep portals that welcome the visitor.

[INTERIOR] The visitor is immediately struck by the sheer amplitude of the Crystal Cathedral's interior space.

REGIONAL/POSTMODERNIST

Traditional imagery joins with modern construction techniques at Pietro Belluschi's Trinity Episcopal Church (figure 278) of 1959–63 in Concord, Massachusetts, designed in association with Anderson, Beckwith & Haible. Its exposed laminated wood arches—an entirely modern material—seem to rival the structural expressiveness of the Gothic cathedral's pointed-arch stone ribs. Belluschi's borrowings from historical design vocabulary here also include vernacular fieldstone walls, gabled roof, pointed arches, and stained glass.

The return to traditional architectural themes grew more compelling as the saucy eclecticism that developed in the late seventies combined with the growing interest in producing churches that "look like churches." At the 1978 St. Cecilia Catholic Church (figures 279, 280, 281) in Houston, Texas, architect Charles Tapley borrowed a Carolingian apse and a Romanesque tower from distant history. But the plan is innovative, creating a processional link between the barrel-vaulted main body of the church and a separate chapel/baptistery on the opposite side of a garden entry. This configuration preserves the focus and intimacy of a centralized plan, while achieving the formality and ceremony of an axial plan.

Located in Pacific Palisades, California, and designed by Moore Ruble Yudell, St. Matthew's Parish Church of 1979–83 is based on a rectangular plan turned on its side to produce a short central aisle and a seating arrangement that closely rings the altar. The congregation, heavily involved in the design, influenced the inclusion of such traditional motifs as cross gables, wood board-and-batten sheathing, exposed trusses, a rose window, and a gigantic cross. The design of Robert A. M. Stern Architects responds to the context of a Brooklyn, New York, neighborhood in the facade of Kol Israel Congregation (1988), while also drawing upon the imagery of a fourteenth-century synagogue in Toledo, Spain. The interior, instead, recalls a thirteenth-century synagogue in Prague.

At first glance, the board-and-batten St. Andrew Presbyterian Church (figures 282, 283, 284) of 1990–92 in Sonoma, California, may seem like a nineteenth-century barn complex, so at home is it in its rural landscape. The cross atop the broad tower reveals the religious purpose of the building, designed by William Turnbull Associates, which is also an up-to-date community facility. Intensely urban, by contrast, is Grace Place Episcopal Church and Community Center (figure 285), an industrial loft in downtown Chicago, Illinois, rehabilitated as a religious building in 1985 by Booth/Hansen & Associates. The renovation put the brick facade in a good state of repair, with a parish hall on the ground floor, and the sanctuary, enclosed within an elliptical screen wall, one floor up. Surmounted by a crucifix affixed to a rough wooden post and beam, the altar is freestanding on a circular platform, dramatically skylit to create a powerful central focus. Imbued with modernism, the design also conveys the spirituality of primitive religious practice.

278 Trinity Episcopal Church; Concord, Massachusetts. Pietro Belluschi; associated architects, Anderson, Beckwith & Haible; 1959–63. *Photo: Joseph Molitor.* The church is built on a longitudinally oriented nave plan, but its centrality is enhanced by wide transcepts, the projection of the chancel into the crossing, and the broad triangle of the stained-glass window in the apse, designed by Gyorgy Kepes.

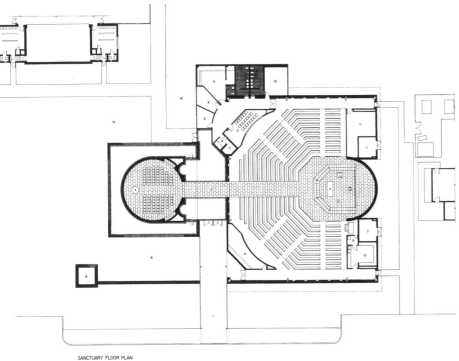

SANCTUARY FLOOR PLAN

N

279, 280, 281 St. Cecilia Catholic Church; Houston, Texas. Charles Tapley, 1978. *Photos: Richard Payne/FAIA.*

[PLAN] From the parking lot (at the bottom of the plan), one proceeds to the covered entry and turns left to a small chapel, or right to the main sanctuary, where a shallow, circular seating arrangement establishes an intimate relationship to the altar.

[EXTERIOR] The bold circular openings of the belfry and the curve of the sanctuary's roof sound a clear call to worship.

[INTERIOR] Set off by the curved apse, the communion table dominates the church interior.

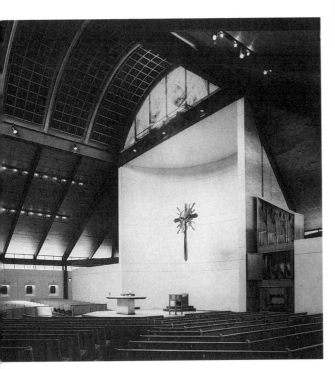

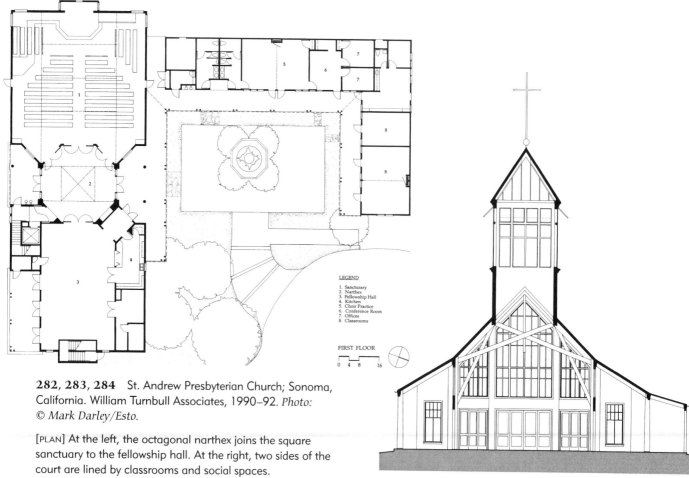

LEGEND

1. Sanctuary
2. Narthex
3. Fellowship Hall
4. Kitchen
5. Choir Practice
6. Conference Room
7. Offices
8. Classrooms

FIRST FLOOR

0 4 8   16

SECTI

0 2 4

282, 283, 284   St. Andrew Presbyterian Church; Sonoma, California. William Turnbull Associates, 1990–92. *Photo: © Mark Darley/Esto.*

[PLAN] At the left, the octagonal narthex joins the square sanctuary to the fellowship hall. At the right, two sides of the court are lined by classrooms and social spaces.

[SECTION] Exposed trusses allude to the mid-nineteenth-century Carpenter Gothic style.

[EXTERIOR] Barnlike, the structure fits comfortably into the rural setting. The open tower illuminates the narthex beneath it.

285 Grace Place Episcopal Church and Community Center; Chicago, Illinois. Booth/Hansen & Associates, 1985.
Photo: Timothy Hursley. The encompassing curve of the screen wall and the benches rivet one's focus on the circular platform in the center.

6

EDUCATIONAL BUILDINGS

EDUCATIONAL BUILDINGS

"Education alone cannot heal the world's wounds. But it can help. A basic principle of American democracy is the more education, the better," *Life* magazine editorialized in 1948, bestowing kudos on the recently enacted G.I. Bill of Rights. Free college tuition not only gave World War II veterans a warm thank-you for their service, but also endowed colleges and universities with massive federal subsidies. Higher education would become one of the single most powerful agents of change in American society.

The Supreme Court's bans in 1950 on racial segregation in colleges and in 1954 on all segregated education began a slow but sure rollback of the discriminatory practices that had kept African-Americans at the bottom of the social and economic ladder. Fueling fears that America was losing the Cold War, the Soviet Union's leap into space in 1957 highlighted the importance of education in a technological age. The federal government, traditionally reluctant to interfere in state and local matters, got behind the teaching of science, math, and languages. The American Dream took on the Technicolor brightness of equal, high-quality, advanced education—and the school building rose as the physical embodiment of that dream.

"The college man makes more money," a 1952 survey reported gleefully—a bonus that grew greater and greater as the clean-scrubbed and buttoned-down youth of the fifties were reinvented as long-haired, ragged wanderers in the sixties and seventies, and bright-eyed yuppies in the eighties and nineties. For all America, education became the lever that shifts the worker from farm and factory to office and laboratory. As never before in history and as in no other nation on earth, America came to depend on higher education to nourish intellectuals, shelter social activists, encourage artists, and stimulate business management, health science, and information technology.

In numbers that swelled with each passing decade, women, minorities, immigrants, second-careerists, retirees, and the handicapped depended on the educational establishment for skills, self-fulfillment, and economic survival. Between 1950 and 1990 the proportion of teens who graduated from high school jumped from thirty-five to eighty percent; that of college graduates leaped from six to twenty-one percent. Community colleges opened new horizons to those who might otherwise have terminated education with high school. Elite universities, dropping class, race, gender, and ethnic barriers, offered skyrocketing options for advanced study and research. The Great Society programs of the sixties expanded educational opportunities from cradle to grave: instruction in one's native language, compensatory education, job training for the unemployed, access for the handicapped, enrichment for the gifted, new realms for retirees. All remain the hard substance of the American Dream—despite growing difficulties in paying the price.

SCHOOL AS SYMBOL

The helter-skelter growth of nineteenth-century cities respected the school building as a proud and enduring monument. "We want the people . . . to understand that this is a noble institution of learning . . . a structure of which the son of the wealthy man need not be ashamed, and that the son of a poor man may feel proud to enter," a dignitary announced in 1854. Impressive volume, solid brick and stone, a prominent site, an imposing front door—such features portrayed the institution's importance to the community, the municipality, and society at large.

In standardized, hygienic, well-lit classrooms, formally arranged on both sides of a central corridor, children sat at fixed desks in rigid rows, facing a single teacher at the head of the class. Recitation, repetition, and rote taught reading, writing, and 'rithmetic.

The revolution in education ushered in by the early-twentieth-century progressive theories of John Dewey and others demanded a setting suitable for child-centered, independent, activity-based learning. "No such thing as imposition of truth from without is possible," said Dewey. Students were to learn from experience rather than instruction; small groups had to be free to roam from activity to activity, from classrooms with movable tables and chairs to corridors lined with display cases and activity areas for music, plays, shop, and art.

Progressive innovations found a natural home in the blend of laboratory and home achieved by the Modernist school, pioneered in the 1930s by such leading lights as Richard Neutra and Howe & Lescaze in the suburbs of Los Angeles, New York, and Philadelphia. Enjoying a heyday in the twenties and thirties and a revival in the sixties and early seventies, progressivism failed to revolutionize education because teachers found it too challenging to manage, and parents and taxpayers considered it too unstructured to trust. Nevertheless, as we shall see, its spirit of innovation had a profound and enduring influence on the design of educational buildings.

CAMPUS AS TRADITION

The American college or university campus is a uniquely American creation. "A world in itself, a temporary paradise, a gracious stage of life," marveled Le Corbusier, touring here in the late 1930s. To impressionable youth, the campus itself is an educational experience, a setting whose physical form embodies community values, loyalty, and intellectual inquiry.

The special character of the American college setting was apparent from the very beginning, largely because of the marked difference between its spatial expansiveness and the tight urban spaces of European universities. Harvard, for example, enjoyed a pleasant situation "at the end of a spacious plain, more like a bowling green than a wilderness," as one seventeenth-century traveler described it. The word "campus" was first used in the 1770s to refer to the rural setting of Princeton University, a site selected for its distance from the "corruption" of the city. By contrast, Yale's was an urban setting, but its neat row of academic buildings faced right on the spacious town green. Thomas Jefferson's classically inspired "academical village" at the University of Virginia opened a handsome architectural ensemble to the rural countryside.

In the late nineteenth century, the landscape planner Frederick Law Olmsted was enormously influential in the design of land-grant colleges such as Cornell and the University of Michigan, where he translated Romanticism's taste for the picturesque into informal ensembles of buildings, irregular topography, and scenic vistas. The turn toward formality at the turn of the century produced an image of the university as a picture-perfect Neoclassical "city of learning," as at the Berkeley campus of the University of California. Ralph Adams Cram, master planner for Princeton University in the twenties, envisioned the school as a city walled "against materialism and all its works," idealizing a suggestive monastic setting with Neo-Gothic or Neo-Georgian quadrangles.

It is the totality of the campus setting, more than any single structure, that resonates for the alumni and the college community. "An institutional metaphor," as planner Richard Dober reminds us, the campus landscape encompasses very particular relationships among buildings, fences, seating, vistas, paths, greenery, memorials, ceremonial spaces, playing fields, and other features. "A campus without landscape is as likely as a circle without a circumference, an arch without a keystone, an ocean without water," said Dober.

ORDER

1940–1960

ELEMENTARY AND SECONDARY SCHOOLS

After World War II, Modernist design flourished even as progressivism waned. The new generation of schools, wrote Lewis Mumford in 1952 in *The New Yorker*, were distinguished by humane scale, flexible spaces, and dynamic cross-axial plans; no self-important WPA "barracks" but "schools for human beings."

The polarities of Traditionalist and Modernist design may be illuminated by a single pair of school buildings. William Bryant High School Addition (figure 286) of 1939 in Queens, New York, designed by the staff of the New York City Board of Education stands close by the sidewalk, bulky, boxy, strict, factorylike. The formal, stripped-down Georgian style of the Depression era asserts the civic importance of the school, while its plainness insists on no-nonsense productivity.

By contrast, the Winnetka, Illinois, Crow Island School (figures 287, 288, 289) of 1940 is "a place of joy," the architectural expression of an educational philosophy that encourages creativity and self-expression as well as mastery of basic skills. By Perkins & Will with Eliel and Eero Saarinen, the design focuses on the individual classroom as an extension of the home, with an atmosphere conducive to nonregimented, activity-based learning.

The school-building binge of the family-oriented postwar decades was fed by young suburbanites who rejected noisy and nuisance-ridden city streets for green and spacious landscapes. Most of them far too cautious to adventure into Modernist design for their homes,

they accepted it willingly for their children's schools. It stood for progress, it provided flexibility, and it was economical to build.

The new suburban school emphatically broke away from a boxy plan and a heavy masonry look. The 1952 West Columbia Elementary School in Texas, by Donald Barthelme, exploited climate and landscape in a plan based on "neighborhoods" of glass-fronted classroom wings around a series of open-air courtyards. John Lyon Reed's Hillsdale High School of 1955–56, in San Mateo, California, employed a modular plan and movable panels to permit the reconfiguration of interior spaces to suit changing needs. With skylighting, even inside rooms received adequate illumination. Exposed steel-joist construction and colorful infill panels created a bright and airy appearance. The spare modernism of the 1957 James Monroe Junior High School (figure 290) in Tulsa, Oklahoma, designed by Murray Jones Murray, was softened by the rolling, green twenty-acre site, which was planned to accommodate additional school facilities over time.

The spirit of innovation also encouraged new ways of developing urban sites. On a constricted plot in a congested New Orleans neighborhood, Curtis & Davis raised a classroom wing of the Thomy Lafon School (1953) to create a covered play area beneath it. Exterior stairways minimized the need for indoor corridors. The first public school built in Brooklyn, New York, since the beginning of the war, Wingate High School (figure 291) of 1954 designed by Gruzen & Partners, exploited a functional banjo-shaped plan that reduced the otherwise imposing bulk of the building and helped cut down the distances that students have to travel between classes.

COLLEGES AND UNIVERSITY CAMPUSES

The self-conscious sense of place that distinguishes the spacious landscaped campus may also characterize the constricted urban campus. This can be noted in the 1939 limestone-fronted Hunter College (figure 292) designed by Shreve, Lamb & Harmon for an East Side Manhattan block. A striking addition to an earlier twentieth-century structure, the stylish International Style facility is based on functionalist planning that stacks a full range of academic and social activities nineteen stories high.

The forties coupled ambitious expectations with bold new principles. The projected university at the visionary mile-square Broadacre City that Frank Lloyd Wright described in *When Democracy Builds* (1945) reflected the architect's hope for education as the "very lifeline of democracy." Wright imagined quiet retreats for reflection and concentration where university students could study organic principles of nature under the tutelage of scientists, philosophers, artists, and architects. The architect's design for Florida Southern College (figure 293) of 1938–59, on the site of a former citrus grove in Lakeland, Florida, set out to control the haphazard development that usually resulted from the start-and-stop largesse of politicians and philanthropists. Planned for organic growth and flexibility, Wright's is a gardenlike setting that assigns highly individualistic glass-walled buildings to key nodes along covered esplanades.

A profoundly influential educator, Walter Gropius challenged the weight of tradition in a 1948–50 design for Harvard University's Graduate Center (figure 294). How can we "expect our students to become bold and fearless in thought and action if we encase them in sentimental shrines feigning a culture that has long since disappeared?" queried the founder of the Bauhaus, then head of Harvard's Graduate School of Design. Inveighing against any "static conception of the world," Gropius insisted that change and growth—not permanence—are the essential conditions of modernity. Working as a partner of The Architects Collaborative, Gropius designed the Graduate Center to be a low, hovering series of concrete-framed buildings that loosely define a series of interlocking spaces connected by covered walkways. There could be no more explicit denial of Harvard's traditional tight red-brick quadrangles.

Education has to concentrate on the promise of modern technology, insisted Ludwig Mies van der Rohe, an emigré from the Bauhaus to Chicago in 1938, where he took up the campus design for the new Illinois Institute of Technology (figure 295) which was largely executed between 1939 and the mid-fifties. Insisting that architecture has to create "order out of the desperate confusion of our time," Mies reinterpreted the urban college campus as a linear network of open and built space entirely freed from the usual constraints of the city block or the college quadrangle. Rigorous geometric discipline and hierarchical organization were also applied in the spectacular Colorado Springs, Colorado, setting of the United States Air Force Academy. Designed by Skidmore, Owings & Merrill in 1958–62, the campus was intended to be a metaphor for military training itself. The industrial imagery of its architecture, claimed Nathaniel Owings, was as "styleless as the most modern guided missile."

Modernism's continued evolution on the college campus reflected broad and diverse influences. Moore & Hutchins's campus design for Goucher College (figure 296) in Towson, Maryland, was inspired both by the architects' Beaux-Arts training and Wright's Organic principles. Continuing from 1938 into the 1950s, the first building phase was developed along a central spine that permitted orderly additions on several cross axes. By contrast, the design of Foothill College (1959–62) in Los Altos Hills, California, by Ernest Kump with Masten & Hurd is a Modernist approach accommodated to California climate, the native landscape, a suburban outlook, and a taste for the Japanese. Based on a spacious grid, it incorporated some forty redwood-and-concrete pavilions into a series of outdoor rooms.

286 William Bryant High School Addition; Queens, New York. New York City Board of Education, 1939. *Photo: New York Landmarks Conservancy.* The formal composition represents the discipline and order within.

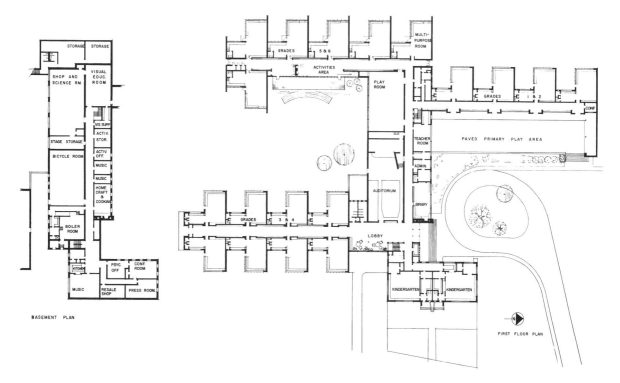

BASEMENT PLAN

FIRST FLOOR PLAN

287, 288, 289 Crow Island School; Winnetka, Illinois. Perkins & Will with Eliel Saarinen and Eero Saarinen, 1940. *Photos: Hedrich-Blessing.*

[PLAN] Fingers into the suburban landscape, separate wings accommodate different age groups. The central spine houses offices, lobby, auditorium, and playroom.

[EXTERIOR] The school seems friendly and informal by reason of its staggered massing and low profile; the clock tower adds symbolism and memorability.

[CLASSROOM EXTERIOR] Each L-shaped classroom is connected to an individual outdoor space.

290 James Monroe Junior High School; Tulsa, Oklahoma. Murray Jones Murray, 1957. *Photo: Ben Newby.* The crisp steel frame, brick curtain wall, and modular window panels express the modernity of the school.

291 Wingate High School; Brooklyn, New York. Gruzen & Partners, 1954. *Photo: Ben Schnall.* The geometry of the elevation expresses the functionalism of the plan, which has a rectangular wing for shop and science facilities, and a curving wing for cafeteria, auditorium, and skylit art studios.

292 Hunter College; New York, New York. Shreve, Lamb & Harmon with Harrison & Fouilhoux, 1939. *Photo: New York Landmarks Conservancy.* The severe facade distinguishes the college from nearby apartment buildings.

293 Florida Southern College; Lakeland, Florida. Frank Lloyd Wright, 1938–59. *Photo: Ezra Stoller, © Esto.* Covered pathways unite Wright's highly individualistic buildings into a total landscape setting.

294 Graduate Center, Harvard University; Cambridge, Massachusetts. The Architects Collaborative, 1950. *Photo: Courtesy of the Frances Loeb Library, Graduate School of Design, Harvard University.* Asymmetrically massed and lightly poised on the ground, Gropius's buildings challenge traditional notions of monumentality and permanence.

295 Illinois Institute of Technology; Chicago, Illinois. Mies van der Rohe, 1939–52 (and later). *Photo: Office of Public Relations, Illinois Institute of Technology.* Mies's uncompromisingly precise steel-framed buildings (seen in the right foreground) are designed on a strict twenty-four-foot module, projecting the campus's two-dimensional, right-angled plan into the third dimension.

296 Goucher College; Towson, Maryland. Moore & Hutchins, 1938–1950s. *Photo: Gottscho–Schleisner Collection, Library of Congress.* U- and L-shaped configurations open the space of the college quadrangle. The Modernist idiom is softened by gently pitched roofs and native rubble stone.

INNOVATION

1960–1975

ELEMENTARY AND SECONDARY SCHOOLS

The commitment to change that characterized the sixties was exuberantly proclaimed by larger, more complex, and more dynamic school buildings. Great Society funding delivered massive federal aid to the children of low-income families and stimulated educational reform generally. The Ford and Carnegie foundations were among those who spurred new curricula and innovative methodologies, such as team teaching, multimedia instruction, flexible grouping, and other novel ways of using teacher time, the school building, and the school day.

In this expansive spirit, architecture adventured with challenging sites, novel configurations, and new building methods. The Josiah Quincy Community School (figure 297) in Boston, Massachusetts, by The Architects Collaborative responded to all the complexities of an inner-city site serving diverse, self-aware ethnic communities. Completed in 1976, after a dozen years of planning, the facility also encompasses space for community recreation, a clinic, day care, and a neighborhood "city hall." In Columbus, Indiana, Caudill, Rowlett & Scott designed the Fodrea Community School (figure 298) of 1973 as a spirited assemblage of cylinders, cubes, and cutaway volumes—structural innovations emblematic of the commitment to educational change.

Based on the principle that reduced distractions encourage a good atmosphere for learning, the windowless school enjoyed a brief tenure during the sixties. This notion is embod-ied in Heery & Heery's Martin Luther King Jr. Middle School (1972–73) in Atlanta, Georgia. Largely windowless on the exterior, the school has a highly theatrical central commons that is joined to cafeteria and classroom clusters to create a variety of settings for informal learning.

COLLEGES AND UNIVERSITY CAMPUSES

Student demonstrations against military training at Columbia and Berkeley in the late fifties portended the unrest that would shock campuses across the country in the sixties and seventies. An inflamed civil rights movement, educational activism, anti-Vietnam protest, and gay and feminist rights movements played out against a backdrop of permissiveness, reaction, and doubt. Architecture must express the student mood, demanded one group of protesters: "exorbitant, energetic, anxious, frivolous, raw."

Architectural infill: The inevitable result of heady growth in enrollments, new construction sometimes collided violently with existing buildings and open space. In 1962, America's leading architectural historian, Henry-Russell Hitchcock, complained about "buildings just stuck down everywhere that a bit of contiguous land can be acquired, with no thought of their setting or their neighbors."

Certain architects did succeed in straddling the divide that separated tradition from innovation. Respectful of neighboring buildings in

239

materials, scale, and proportion, Harvard's Loeb Drama Center (figure 299) of 1960 by Hugh Stubbins & Associates asserted the commitment to simple geometry, expressed structure, and an open ground plan. The John D. Rockefeller Jr. Library (figure 300) at Brown University in Providence, Rhode Island, completed in 1964 to the designs of Warner Burns Toan Lunde, was a sympathetic, polite, yet definitely contemporary response to the older library adjacent to it.

Fierce architectural individualism was probably more typical of the sixties. Ambitious public educational systems in such states as New York, Illinois, Texas, Massachusetts, and California joined prestigious private universities in awarding important roles to the rising generation of architectural "stars."

The powerful expressionist tendency of the sixties was set in motion by several bravura designs of the late fifties. Eero Saarinen's Ingalls Rink (1958) at Yale University in New Haven, Connecticut, is an idiosyncratic form that rises to a dramatically twisted suspended roof. Louis Kahn's 1958–60 Richards Medical Research Building at the University of Pennsylvania in Philadelphia captured the imagination of a generation eager to enrich modernism's lean functionalism. Sculptural brick-and-concrete towers vigorously differentiate "served" spaces (the classrooms and laboratories) from the "servant" spaces (the mechanical systems and stairways).

The atmosphere became intensely inflamed by Paul Rudolph's 1958–64 School of Art and Architecture (figure 301) at Yale. In a pinwheel configuration, Rudolph's building enlisted the participant in a dynamic encounter with expanding and compressing space, a not always welcome confrontation that was the cause of the major modifications that were made later. A heightened spatial experience was also created at the 1964 College of Environmen-

tal Design at the University of California, Berkeley, a striking assemblage of jutting concrete forms designed by Joseph Esherick with Donald Olsen and Vernon De Mars. At the 1969 Goddard Library at Clark University, in Worcester, Massachusetts, by John Johansen, audacious projections, sharp angles, and exposed ductwork demonstrated the architect's intention to produce a work that proclaimed values of "anti-perfection, anti-masterwork, anti-academic."

Some campus buildings of the sixties may have been built tall as much to bid for attention as to provide needed space. Philip Johnson's muscular seventeen-story Kline Science Center of 1965 at Yale celebrates a hilltop location, its verticality emphasized by glazed-brick ducts that appear like colossal columns on the building's facades. The Health Science Center (figure 302) at the State University of New York at Stony Brook (1968–78), designed by Bertrand Goldberg Associates, breaks free of the ground plane, rising up on stilts to vaunt its idiosyncratic height and shape.

Megastructure: The sixties' fascination with futuristic, self-sufficient environments generated a series of horizontally extended megastructures whose design gave high priority to efficient pedestrian and vehicular circulation. In Oregon, Portland Community College (1967–69) by Wolf-Zimmer-Gunsul-Frasca-Ritter represents a kind of educational shopping mall that encourages students to cruise a two-level central spine that connects four glass-fronted "learning centers" from which they can make a selection. A linear pathway also determined the form of The Art Center College of Design (1974–75) in Pasadena, California, by Craig Ellwood Associates. A dramatic response to a rugged natural setting, the Miesian glass-and-steel bridgelike structure hovers for a length of almost seven hundred feet across a canyon and an approach road. A spectacular linear expanse, too, is the nine-hundred-foot-long Faner Hall (1974), by Geddes Brecher Qualls Cunningham, at Southern Illinois University in Carbondale. The long spine reestablished a sense of orientation and enclosure amid the disarray and inconvenience produced by ad hoc expansion.

One of the most fully realized megastructures of the era evokes the scale of a fair-sized town. The 1974 Ellicot Complex (figure 303) at the State University of New York at Buffalo, the Amherst campus, was designed by Davis, Brody & Associates for a 1200-acre site. The arrangement confines the automobile to underground space and the campus periphery, leaving expansive zones for the pedestrian. Six separate "colleges," each containing housing, classrooms, and social space, are arranged in a pinwheel configuration that asserts the individuality of each within the totality of the campus.

Campus urbanism: A sense of broad horizons freed architects to think boldly in the sixties. The campus would serve as a prototype urban community, a setting that inspires the scientist to search, the artist to create, the entrepreneur to invent, the citizen to participate. In ten or twenty years, or less, some extraordinarily ambitious campus plans were realized almost as originally designed. More, however, succumbed to changes dictated by demographics, the economy, and changing educational and architectural philosophy.

"The art of making may be analogous to the way we were made, to aspire, to be man, to express—Aspiration—Form—Design," said Louis I. Kahn. Inspiration for Kahn's Salk Institute for Biological Studies (figures 304, 305) in La Jolla, California, included both a monastic cloister in Italy and an intense collaboration with the scientist-client, Jonas Salk. Unabashedly elitist, the institute was to thrive as a city of the intellect, a scientific-cultural environment so stimu-

lating that "Picasso might come." The campus is oriented around a central courtyard that brings the visitor into a close encounter with the bold forms of the buildings and the drama of the oceanside site.

By contrast, publicly supported community colleges concentrated on giving a hand up to those starting to climb the educational ladder. And, if many of those colleges aspired to little more than minimal, low-budget design, there were some that did hold high expectations for the educational benefits of quality architecture. One such is in Dallas County, Texas, where the 1972 Richland College (figure 306), a carefully composed Modernist composition, designed by Perkins & Will with The Oglesby Group, creates a memorable setting focused on an artificial lake.

Planned by Skidmore, Owings & Merrill as a campus for inner-city commuters, the intensely urban University of Illinois in Chicago occupies a former urban-renewal site well connected both to mass transit and the highway. Mostly built between 1965 and 1980, the passionately Modernist conception arranged massive concrete buildings according to function rather than, as is typical, by academic discipline. Concentric rings of lecture halls, classrooms, and library facilities were connected by futuristic raised "expressways." A victim of poor maintenance and obsolescence, the campus underwent substantial alteration in the 1990s, which included the demolition of the elevated walkways.

Sensitivity to the natural landscape propelled the design of the University of California system, whose master plan, undertaken by architect John Carl Warnecke in the early 1960s, envisioned a series of university seats on large, scenic land parcels distributed across the state. The concept was that each campus would maintain a sense of the natural terrain while exhibiting a strong architectural character of its own. Each campus in the system was to be divided into a series of smaller college units, whose compactness would permit students to travel from class to class in a ten-minute walk. The Irvine campus, following a master plan developed in 1963 by William Pereira & Associates, followed a formal Beaux-Arts configuration. Centered around the sixteen-acre Greta Park were six radiating quadrangles, one for each of the five divisions of the college and another for a ceremonial entrance. Another take on urbanity is apparent at Kresge College (figures 307, 308) at Santa Cruz (1972–74). Designed by MLTW/Turnbull Associates and Charles W. Moore Associates, this campus shed Beaux-Arts formalism to create a sociable, pedestrianized functionalism. Surrounded by the redwood forest, the college rises on a terrace, with a meandering street at its center and a Postmodernist stage-set assemblage of multi-colored, stucco-covered wood-frame buildings facing onto it.

297 Josiah Quincy Community School; Boston, Massachusetts. The Architects Collaborative, 1976. *Photo: © Steve Rosenthal.* The rising terraces open the complex to the city and the diagonal pathway connects to three different neighborhoods.

298 Fodrea Community School; Columbus, Indiana. Caudill, Rowlett & Scott, 1973. *Photo: Balthazar Korab.* A steel space frame resting on concrete columns produces open, unobstructed areas where students group and regroup for different learning activities.

299 Loeb Drama Center, Harvard University; Cambridge, Massachusetts. Hugh Stubbins & Associates, 1960. *Photo: Joseph Molitor.* The building uses traditional red brick as a nod to the past and concrete framing as a hallmark of modernity. The aluminum grille, decorative as well as functional, is illuminated from the rear to announce performance nights.

300 John D. Rockefeller Jr. Library, Brown University; Providence, Rhode Island. Warner Burns Toan Lunde, 1964. *Photo: Joseph Molitor.* Rejecting the Classic vocabulary of its older neighbor, the new facility (at left) respects it, nevertheless, in massing, scale, proportion, and articulation. The expanded entry level is emblematic of the burgeoning space needs for information services.

301 School of Art and Architecture, Yale University; New Haven, Connecticut. Paul Rudolph, 1958–64. *Photo: Joseph Molitor.* Defying the campus's masonry tradition by the use of roughly textured concrete, the building also flouts historical notions of open and closed, window and wall, structure and space.

302 Health Science Center, State University of New York at Stony Brook; Stony Brook, New York. Bertrand Goldberg Associates, 1968–78. *Photo: Nathaniel Lieberman.* Size, shape, and structure are expressive of diverse functions: at right, a hospital; center, research laboratories; left, science classrooms. Core facilities occupy the common base and rise up through the center of the towers.

303 Ellicot Complex, State University of New York at Buffalo; Amherst, New York. Davis, Brody & Associates, 1974. *Photo: © Norman McGrath.* Modernism's answer to the medieval hill town. Dense and vigorous massing, culminating in a series of ten-story towers, creates a memorable skyline.

304, 305 The Salk Institute for Biological Studies, La Jolla, California. Louis I. Kahn, 1965. (Subsequently enlarged) *Photos: James Cox.*

[AERIAL] Two ranks of loftlike laboratory spaces flank an open courtyard. Separate studies for the scientists are located in the semi-detached wings that project into the court. The architect's plans for housing and social spaces were never executed according to his intentions.

[EXTERIOR] Incisings in the concrete paving point the eye to a vista of the Pacific.

306 Richland College; Dallas, Texas. Perkins & Will with The Oglesby Group, 1972. *Photo: John Rogers.* Form suggests function, with the blank-walled building (at the left) housing large-group instruction and the tower (at the rear) serving as the Campus Center. Extensive landscaping softens hard-edged Modernist forms.

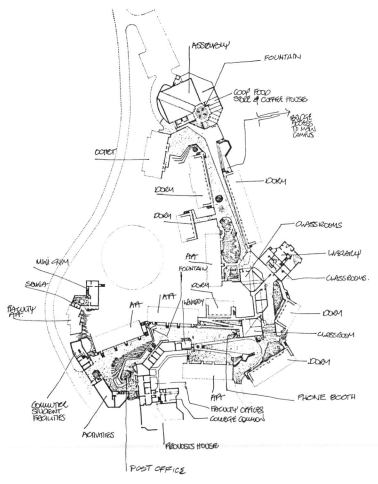

KRESGE COLLEGE
UC SANTA CRUZ

307, 308 Kresge College at Santa Cruz;
Santa Cruz, California. MLTW/Turnbull
Associates and Charles W. Moore Associates,
1972–74. *Photo: © Mark Darley/Esto.*

[SKETCH PLAN] The mix of uses along an
informal axis is designed to give students ample
opportunities for social interaction.

[EXTERIOR] Intended to encourage both
traditional and nontraditional learning modes,
the design of the campus mixes the serious
with the playful.

ACCOMMODATION

1975–1990s

ELEMENTARY AND SECONDARY SCHOOLS

Public school education has drifted between the Scylla of centralized control and bureaucracy and the Charybdis of decentralization and community participation, between the Effective School movement's insistence on standards and progressivism's hopes for self-directed learning, between Americanization and multiculturalism, between the conservative's claim to delivered values and the liberal's devotion to individual differences. In the nineties, demands for economy, individualization, and technologically advanced instruction began to draw the two poles together in the effort to produce an educational system that is both affordable and reasonably free of central control. All this occurred in a period of robust school construction and reconstruction as new immigrants crowded city schools, young families moved to the Sun Belt, and the children of the baby boomers reached school age.

If the exuberance of the sixties and seventies produced no quick solution for the nation's educational problems, it did open many new doors. Although Americans were less confident in the educational establishment by the eighties and nineties, they also saw more potential for closer integration between the school world and life outside. And they were increasingly aware that architecture can only accommodate change over time, not force it.

There's hardly a "standard" school design to be seen. Novel floor plans permit greater access to community groups and more varied learning situations. Lobbies, auditoriums, cafeterias, and corridors, in all manner of shapes and sizes, serve as multiple-purpose spaces, often with the extra height and spatial drama one associates with shopping malls. Classroom plans provide individualized spaces for video- and computer-based learning. In Ohio the 1978 Stow-Munroe Falls High School's L-shaped plan concentrates high-activity space, such as the cafeteria, gym, and auditorium, at the crossing of the L, while spreading the quieter classrooms along a long arc-shaped pathway that closes the L. This design by Richard Fleischman buried the school in an earth berm that saves energy costs and reduces the school's otherwise imposing bulk. The 1986 expansion of the existing Trinity School (figures 309, 310) in Atlanta, Georgia, designed by Lord, Aeck & Sargeant, shunned a single-stroke intervention in favor of a series of add-ons—humanizing the character of the school, improving its function, and maximizing the use of the site.

If floor plans are relentlessly inventive, elevations often flirt with whimsy. Four New York City low-cost school additions from the early 1990s designed by Weintraub & di Domenico, are hardly more than basic metal sheds, enlivened by "paste-on" gabled porticos and appealing postmodern colors. The playful shapes and fanciful colors of Patwin Elementary School (1992) in Davis, California, by The Steinberg Group evoke a game of children's blocks. In schools everywhere, expectations for a high "friendliness ratio" call forth bell towers, clock towers, picturesque rooflines, cheerful colors, and rich textures.

The growing appreciation for the sense of local place and the intimacy of the neighborhood has made a profound impact on school design. The stringent historic-district guidelines of Nantucket, Massachusetts, shaped Earl R. Flansburgh & Associates' 1978 design for the local elementary school (figures 311, 312). The largest structure on the island, the school had to relate to nearby buildings in scale, materials, fenestration, and overall character. In rural Massachusetts, the same architects designed the Sunderland Elementary School (1989) to evoke historic farmlands dotted by tobacco barns, pitched-roof farmhouses, and old-time village centers.

In San Francisco, the 1980 Garfield Elementary School (figure 313) by Esherick, Homsey, Dodge & Davis is a diminutive ten-classroom school whose rooftop houses a greenhouse and outdoor planting area. New York City has welcomed a variety of efforts to create neighborly schools. Richard Dattner's Intermediate School 218 (figures 314, 315) of 1985–92 serves the community with a health center, an after-school community center, and a satellite college for parents. A sympathetic design response to the narrow, winding residential Main Street of Roosevelt Island is clear in Primary/Intermediate School 217 (1992) by Michael Fieldman & Partners, whose plan separates the school into four separate pavilions that come close to the curve of the street in front while opening to take advantage of river views at the rear.

COLLEGES AND UNIVERSITY CAMPUSES

In the sober seventies colleges and universities suffered with leveling enrollment, an economic downturn, and rapidly escalating costs. Growing awareness of constraints kept pace with rising distress over the loss of historic buildings.

By the nineties, vigorous historic preservation initiatives had placed more than six hundred campuses on the National Register of Historic Places. College leadership was forced to use space more efficiently, to accept only incremental change, and to take on the "ticking time bomb" of deferred building maintenance.

The depth of alumni feeling for the college setting could be seen in emotional battles to save such historic buildings as Oberlin's "The Big Five," Eastabrook Hall at the University of Tennessee, and Yale's freshman dormitories. Adaptive use became well-established practice: the concrete-framed stables at Duquesne University were transformed into art studios; a parking garage was converted for the City University of New York's architecture school; a municipal water purification plant was adapted for classrooms at Vincennes University. Surplus military bases, courthouses, churches, office buildings, department stores, and railroad stations—all have been swept into the web of campus life.

The relationship between old buildings and new has been governed by an evolving design philosophy. Through the mid-seventies the handiwork of the architect tended to be insistently contemporary. Gwathmey Siegel & Associates' 1972 repair of the burned-out interior of Princeton's temple-fronted Whig Hall on the Princeton, New Jersey, campus was emblematic of the violence of the fire as well of modernism's revolt against history. An imposing sculptural form occupies the shell of the older building, one wall left open to flaunt the disjuncture. At Cooper Union, in Manhattan, John Hejduk's 1975 dialogue with history brought physical reality to the circular elevator that founder Peter Cooper could only dream of in the mid-nineteenth century. The renovation left the exterior of the Italianate brownstone structure mostly as it was, wrapping the interior space with sleek surfaces and featureless white finishes.

Increasingly, however, careful strategic planning has influenced more subtle transitions between historic and contemporary. Brown University in Providence, Rhode Island, for example, has engaged in a master planning process directed toward the preservation of the historic green at the center of the campus (figures 316, 317). The gracious Faunce House, an early-twentieth-century Neo-Georgian student center designed by McKim, Mead & White, was renovated by Goody, Clancy & Associates in 1989 in a reconfiguration that uses basement space to create underground passageways to nearby buildings, adding a broad front stairway as a sunny place for students to "hang out." Fitting new uses into older campus buildings may have costs as well as benefits, as is seen in the same architects' renovation of nearby Rogers Hall. The alteration of the dwelling to make it serve as an entrance foyer for a substantial rear addition sacrificed the historic interior while it maintained the building's facade as an important presence on the historic green.

Below-grade buildings that remain more or less "invisible" have helped in the preservation of historic campus settings. An early example was the three-story Campus Store (figures 318, 319) of 1970 on the Cornell University campus in Ithaca, New York, designed by Earl R. Flansburgh & Associates. Preserving historic vistas, the structure took advantage of the slope of the site to enclose additional below-grade space. In Cambridge, Massachusetts, Harvard University's historic Harvard Yard is now the site of the underground Nathan Marsh Pusey Library (1976) by Hugh Stubbins & Associates, whose landscaped roof permits walkers to follow traditional cross-campus pathways.

Historic preservation has been used to help remediate the ill effects of rampant growth. The ingenuity that may be required was demonstrated at New York City's Columbia University campus, a McKim, Mead & White "City Beautiful" composition of quadrangles and courts. Assigned an awkward, apparently leftover site, the 1983 Computer Science Building (figures 320, 321) by R. M. Kliment & Frances Halsband wove together several buildings of diverse style and scale, effectively capturing the space between, above, and below three adjacent structures. Designed by Kallmann, McKinnell & Wood, Marx Hall of 1990–93 adds a strong visual focus to the increasingly helter-skelter Princeton University campus. An addition to an 1879 Neo-Tudor-style building, the new construction refers to precedent in its use of brick, limestone trim, and gabled roofline, while it claims modernity in the exposed steel window frames. The 1989 Edward Bennett Williams Law Library (figure 322), by Hartman-Cox, at the District of Columbia's Georgetown University campus, responded to a streetscape shattered by a 1960s Modernist building-in-a-plaza. It employs a design vocabulary that arbitrates between Washington's Stripped Classic and Modernist modes.

Finally, we can see the changing nature of planning itself. The University of Oregon's Science Complex (figures 323, 324, 325) was generated by an incremental, participatory, socially sensitive design process developed by Christopher Alexander and his colleagues and published in *The Oregon Experiment* in 1975. Dating from 1985–89 and designed by Moore Ruble Yudell with the Ratcliff Architects, the meandering Science Walk weaves "rescued" spaces together with new and existing facilities, contributing to the coherence of the entire complex. "When locating buildings, place them in conjunction with other buildings to form small nodes of public life," said Alexander. Campus design is, after all, a communal art form.

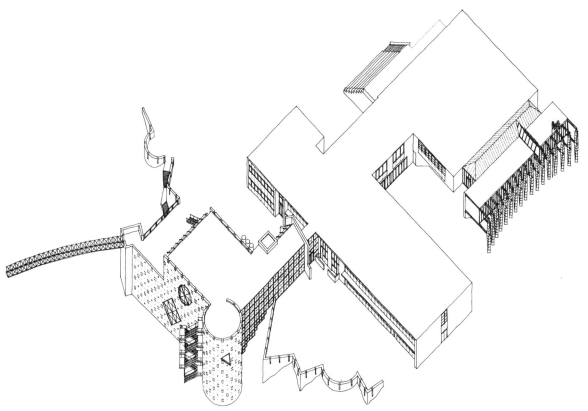

309, 310 Trinity School; Atlanta, Georgia. Lord, Aeck & Sargeant, 1986. *Photo: Jonathan Hillyer/Atlanta.*

[AXONOMETRIC] Additions to the 1960s U-shaped section (center) create a formal new face for a parking lot, a self-sufficient activities center (front), and a playground distant from traffic. The cylindrical tower houses a media center.

[INTERIOR] The informal lobby space is behind a new, colonnaded entrance to the school.

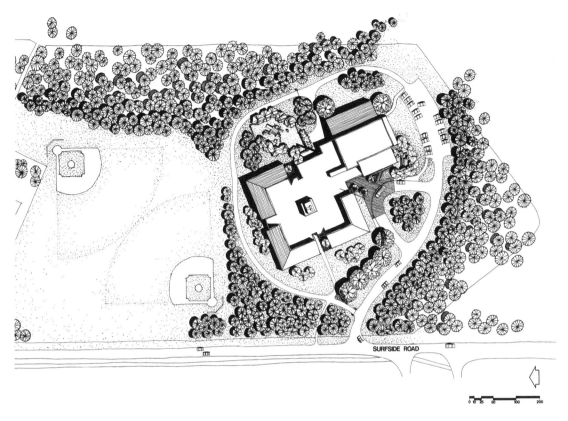

311, 312 Nantucket Elementary School; Nantucket, Massachusetts. Earl R. Flansburgh & Associates, 1978. *Photo: © Peter Vanderwarker.*

[PLAN] Creating an intimate atmosphere while increasing the flexibility of the setting, classes are arranged in three "neighborhood" clusters, each of which consists of an L-shaped arrangement of six classrooms.

[EXTERIOR] Cedar siding, wide trim boards, and varied window treatments connect the design to Nantucket's traditions.

313 Garfield Elementary School; San Francisco, California. Esherick, Homsey, Dodge & Davis, 1980. *Photo: © Peter Aaron/Esto.* The school's small scale, gentle massing, and informal detailing maintain the character of the neighborhood.

I.S. 218
New York, N.Y.

Site Plan
1 Landscaped Courtyard
2 Entrance Court
3 Staff Parking
4 Connecting Walk
5 Amphitheater
6 Running Track
7 Multi-Purpose Court
8 Play Street (School Hours)
9 Rear Yard

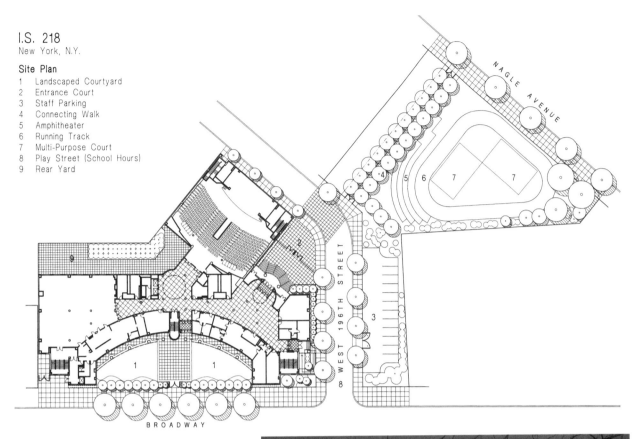

314, 315 Intermediate School 218; New York, New York. Richard Dattner Associates, 1985–92. *Photo: © Norman McGrath.*

[PLAN] The plan facilitates the shared use of the site by three independent institutions at different times of the day.

[EXTERIOR] The school is a stylish building that respects the Art Deco vocabulary of nearby apartment houses. The entry gate, echoing the curve of the school building, combines memorability with informality.

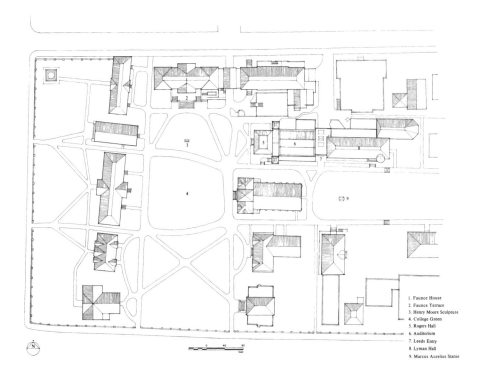

1. Faunce House
2. Faunce Terrace
3. Henry Moore Sculpture
4. College Green
5. Rogers Hall
6. Auditorium
7. Leeds Entry
8. Lyman Hall
9. Marcus Aurelius Statue

316, 317   Brown University; Providence, Rhode Island. Goody, Clancy & Associates, 1989. *Photo: © Steve Rosenthal.*

[PLAN] Faunce House, with its added front steps, is at the top (north) of the historic green. Rogers Hall is on the eastern side, recognized as the foyer for a pair of large auditoriums added to the rear.

[EXTERIOR] Recent changes have made little impact on the campus green.

318, 319 Campus Store, Cornell University; Ithaca, New York. Earl R. Flansburgh & Associates, 1970. *Photo: Louis Reens.*

[EXTERIOR] The underground location preserves aboveground historic vistas and pathways, although it fundamentally alters the sense of the campus landscape.

[SECTION] The use of the slope captures additional interior space.

320, 321 Computer Science Building, Columbia University; New York, New York. R. M. Kliment & Frances Halsband, 1983. *Photo: © Cervin Robinson.*

[EXTERIOR] The courtyard configuration pays homage to Columbia's original plan, while the building itself respects traditional design vocabulary.

[AXONOMETRIC] The computer facility occupies space at several levels in both new and existing buildings.

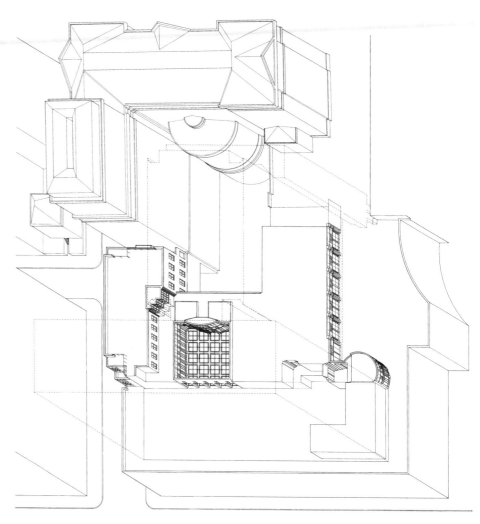

322 Edward Bennett Williams Law Library, Georgetown University; Washington, D.C. Hartman-Cox, 1989. *Photo: © Peter Aaron/Esto.* The library respects urban street tradition in its closeness to the sidewalk and the rhythms of its facade.

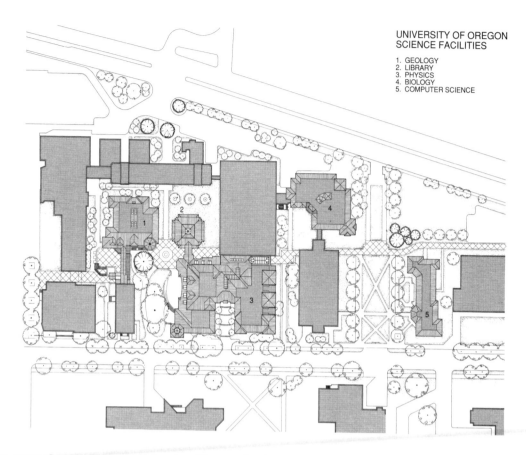

UNIVERSITY OF OREGON
SCIENCE FACILITIES

1. GEOLOGY
2. LIBRARY
3. PHYSICS
4. BIOLOGY
5. COMPUTER SCIENCE

323, 324, 325 Science Complex, University of Oregon; Portland, Oregon. Moore Ruble Yudell with The Ratcliff Architects, 1985–89. *Photos: © Timothy Hursley.*

[SITE PLAN] The addition of four new buildings (indicated by hatching) reinforces the campus's Beaux-Arts pattern of courts and streets. Connections to adjacent buildings are intended to foster interdisciplinary relationships.

[EXTERIOR] Each building incorporates significant social spaces, whether a courtyard with built-in seating, a loggia, or an indoor atrium.

[DETAIL] Dr. Einstein's grimace and other spirited detailing enrich the campus experience.

7

TALL OFFICE BUILDINGS

TALL OFFICE
BUILDINGS

The skyscraper is "America's outstanding contribution to the architecture of the world," boasted Harvey Wiley Corbett, a member of the design team for Rockefeller Center in the 1930s. A soaring symbol of America's wealth, ambition, energy, and efficiency, the post-World War II skyscraper signaled an astoundingly rapid and hugely successful conversion to a white-collar economy. A half-century later, after hundreds of tall buildings had profoundly and forever transformed the face of the nation, critic Ada Louise Huxtable, in *The Tall Building Artistically Reconsidered*, took a more cynical view of its significance. The tall building "romanticizes power and the urban condition," she accused. It "celebrates leverage and cash flow."

We witness the office tower, standing tall, as the best in America. And the worst.

OFFICE INDUSTRY

Since World War II, finance, banking, insurance, advertising, media, law, information services, and education have fueled job growth in America, with managerial professionals demanding larger offices, mechanized procedures, and more workplace luxury. New York City was the first to experience a postwar office boom, witnessing the construction of at least thirty new office towers in the fifties—half of all the office space built in the nation's thirty largest metropolitan areas combined.

Between 1965 and 1970 construction had to keep pace with a growth rate nearly twice that of the previous five-year period. If there was a dismal evidence that many corporations were fleeing to suburban office parks, a growing number of braggadocio office towers seemed to affirm that downtowns would manage to survive. "Signposts in the sky are what these giant buildings are all about," observed the *Chicago Daily News* of the ninety-seven-story John Hancock Building, recognizing office construction as "a branch of outdoor decorating, a subsidiary of the public relations industry."

Cycles of boom and bust are typical of commercial real estate development in America, business downturns usually being more rapid than even the shrewdest speculators can anticipate. Urban skylines thickened and heightened, the 1970s witnessing the construction of thirty-nine new tall buildings in New York City, twenty-one in San Francisco and Chicago, fourteen in Denver and Houston, twelve in Los Angeles and Atlanta, and ten in Miami and Seattle. There was at least one tower of forty stories or more in each of those cities, as well as in Pittsburgh, Dallas, Minneapolis, Miami, and Philadelphia.

Evangelistic politicians preached the gospel of growth. "We need tall buildings," declared San Francisco's mayor Joseph Alioto, "because they give us jobs and taxes." New York City's Ed Koch, Baltimore's William Donald Schaefer, and Pittsburgh's Richard Caliguri were among those mayors who trumpeted high-rise development as the sign and the symbol of a healthy city—with perhaps too little regard for holding on to jobs in manufacturing, shipping, and retailing.

The 1980s saw a doubling of office space in America, a boom having more to do with foreign investment, swollen pension funds, deregulated banks and insurance companies, and tax-advantaged investment than with current or near-future demand. Citizens cried, "Enough!" San Francisco set stringent limits on office development, Seattle established a four-hundred-fifty-foot height limit, and controversies about overbuilding raged in Boston, New York, and Philadelphia.

The real estate bust of the early 1990s raised the specter that the skyscraper might be doomed to obsolescence. Certainly, white-collar employment had been adversely affected by corporate downsizing and the flight of clerical jobs abroad. Future work will be done in virtual offices, office parks, and office rentals. How will our heirs deal with unneeded skyscrapers? wondered engineer Mario Salvadori. Only "posterity will tell whether, like so many other buildings, they will be demolished when they become economically inefficient or whether they will remain as permanent monuments to our dreams and folly." But by the late 1990s, another boom was under way.

THE MODERNIST CITY

"If the skyscraper has developed rapidly," wrote Harvey Wiley Corbett in the thirties, "the practical application of sound theories of city planning can hardly be said to have kept pace." One vision of the city welcomed density—with notions about streets on two levels to separate pedestrians and vehicles, more efficient mass transit, apartments on top of office towers, greenbelts, and waterfront parks. En-

compassing the principles of Le Corbusier's visionary "Radiant City," another philosophy favored thinning out the city—with high-rise towers for living and working stilted above the ground plane in vast, parklike settings crossed by broad roadways. "The city of speed is the city of success," Le Corbusier declared. Indeed, the reconciliation of the automobile and the city still dominated thinking about cities in the fifties and sixties, with solutions ranging from Le Corbusier's vision of streets so wide that there could be no traffic problems, to urban planner Victor Gruen's inclination to banish the car altogether and give streets back to the pedestrian.

Lever House (1952) and the Seagram Building (1958) brought the spread-out notion of urban space right into the city grid, influencing the 1961 New York City zoning provision that encouraged buildings to rise higher if open public space was maintained at street level. In short order, the paradigm was the tower-in-the-park—or, to put it more accurately, the tower-in-the-plaza—with not always desirable results. Denver's Mile High Center banished "messy" retail facilities to basement levels; San Francisco's John Hancock Western Home Office stood aloof from the pedestrian; Boston's State Street Bank had a stark geometric plaza sunk into gloomy below-grade space.

Postwar urban renewal projected huge segments of the older American city in the image of the Radiant City. Large-scale redevelopment for new office buildings and housing seemed to provide a swift, neat cure for obsolete industry, tired transportation systems, and "blighted" housing stock. Pioneering in the use of public appropriations to leverage private investment in downtown redevelopment, Pittsburgh was hailed by *Fortune* magazine as "The City that Quick-changed from Unbelievable Ugliness to Shining Beauty in Less than Half a Generation." Uncle Sam stepped up the incentives. In 1958

Baltimore became the first city to receive substantial federal moneys for what was to become the ambitious Charles Center. A pack of canny real estate developers who saw the profit potential was led by William Zeckendorf of Webb & Knapp—"the great Emperor Penguin of Urban Renewal"—who later launched redevelopment projects in seven cities across the country. The urban-renewal mechanism planted office-building plantations in cities across the country: San Francisco's Embarcadero Center, Philadelphia's Penn Center, Hartford's Constitution Plaza, Denver's Mile High Center, Boston's Government Center, Los Angeles's Bunker Hill. In the late sixties, Detroit's Renaissance City was one of the last, its architect, John Portman, insisting that the most important thing was to create a city-within-a-city "so large that it could stand alone." Visionaries imagined islands of civility, but what was produced, all too often, was alienation and blandness.

THE LIVABLE CITY

The sixties saw furious protests against the rigidity of Modernist planning. Jane Jacobs's *The Death and Life of Great American Cities* (1961) attacked orthodox theory for telling "nothing but lies" about the ways cities work. Cities are not made by planners, Jacobs declared, but by people "loitering on busy corners, hanging around in candy stores and bars and drinking soda pop on stoops. Active use of public space is critical to a vital city," she wrote. "Lowly, unpurposeful and random as they might appear, sidewalk contacts are the small change from which a city's wealth of public life may grow."

In the mid-sixties, New York City's Urban Design Group was among those who pioneered procedures intended to take the human factor into account, revising municipal zoning to en-

courage active, noncommercial uses in tall buildings. Extra height was allowed for the inclusion of theater space at One Astor Plaza, for a museum at the Philip Morris building, for a public atrium and through-the-lobby passageway at Olympic Tower.

Putting urban life under a microscope in the mid-seventies, William H. Whyte's Street Life Project used ingenious time-lapse photography to produce startling evidence of what people expected in the city: to look at other people, informal seating, food vendors, retail shops, warmth, sunlight, closely spaced trees, shelter from wind and rain. "Good places tend to be all of a piece—and the reason can almost always be traced to a human being," Whyte observed.

THE POSTMODERNIST CITY

The back-to-the-city movement of the seventies and eighties gave proof to architect and critic Christian Norberg-Schulz's thesis that the better life would "grow out of human life in a place instead of being imposed from above." By the seventies, for example, civic leaders in Annapolis, Maryland, had persuaded affluent investors to rehabilitate downtown buildings; citizens in Galveston, Texas, had spearheaded historic-district designation, tax incentives, and investment pools for residential and commercial neighborhoods; and the collaboration of arts activists, open-space advocates, social reformers, and historic preservationists in Seattle, Washington, had stimulated substantial state and federal funding for urban conservation.

"What makes a good city?" asked the influential planner Kevin Lynch in *A Theory of Good City Form* (1981), demonstrating that it was critically important for people to find satisfaction in their physical settings. Broadened principles of urban design stressed twenty-four-hour-a-day vitality; active sidewalks with easy links to shops, restaurants, arcades, lobbies, and mass transit; the importance of older buildings, of scale, texture, and memorability. Cities had to be built for people, admittedly fickle in taste, irrational in habit, and unpredictable in behavior.

Into the eighties and nineties, although severely impacted by the often overwhelming scale of new office buildings, some downtown areas profited from incremental improvements at street level. At the Crocker Center in San Francisco, an old alley was transformed into an appealing steel-and-glass arcade. In Chicago's North Loop, an underground Pedway linked mass transit to new office buildings. Downtown Boston's new buildings provided through-lobby shortcuts that encourage strolling. Manhattan's public plazas were required to provide a full measure of public amenity, from snack bars to bicycle racks. In every city, Postmodernist style dictated assertive architectural "features"—entries trimmed with columns and pediments; atrium lobbies enhanced by skylights, waterworks, and landscaping; rooftops that spike the skyline with memorable if idiosyncratic shapes.

IMAGE

The tall building represents a bid for profit, power, and prestige, and its precise form has always addressed those triple imperatives. In the early fifties, the soap-selling giant Lever Brothers' attention-getting, trend-setting world headquarters on Manhattan's Park Avenue made good sense, according to architect Nathaniel Owings, "because the price one pays for soap is ninety-eight percent advertising." In building high-design corporate office buildings, companies such as Seagram, First National City Bank, United States Steel, Equitable, and the Aluminum Company of America not only enjoyed prestige and status but the reward of better rental tenants.

In the sixties, speculative building aimed at mass production, resulting in complaints of shoddiness and sameness. "The only seal of approval I ever want to see on one of my buildings," said one developer, "is a sign out front saying 'no vacancies.' " New York City's rigorously competitive real estate market—honing skills in land assembly, zoning, government approvals, scheduling, financing, and cost control—provided the training ground for the highly efficient real estate development practices that were to spread across the country.

"Architecture must be sold just like any other commodity," wrote Morris Lapidus in *Architecture: A Profession and a Business* (1967). Promoter, image-maker, and supersalesman, the corporate architect had to "excite" and "titillate" the client. The sixties and seventies saw the growth of large, specialized, and highly efficient architectural firms that demonstrated the practice of modern architecture was subject to the same organizational discipline as any other American corporation. In the boom of the 1980s some two hundred and fifty firms each employed more than fifty architects, and many of these firms, like the companies they served—IBM, AT&T, and IDS—were best known by their corporate initials: SOM, KPF, CRS, RTKL, and DMJM.

Coinciding with a growing interest in high design, corporations were undertaking to maximize real estate assets, which, according to a 1983 article in *Harvard Business Review*, represented at least twenty-five percent of the average company's value. "In the IBM company," said president Thomas Watson, Jr., "we think that good design is good business." Supported by aggressive institutional lenders, speculative builders marketed "name brand" architecture, hiring prominent design architects to create the overall image and facade and less famous architects to undertake such basic tasks as floor layout. "Build tall and build beautiful," declared Gerald Hines of Texas, one of the new breed of real estate developers, "and you capture the attention and applause of all the world."

The postwar era's taste for cool Modernist design grew to a voracious appetite for Postmodernist novelty and eye appeal. Clients such as the Reichmann family and George Klein in New York, John Buck in Chicago, and Robert Maguire in Los Angeles gambled on high design as a way to beat out the competition. "Architecturally speaking, buildings are packaged and styled today with uniqueness in mind," taught Gene Phillipps in the *Professional Guide to Real Estate Development*. "Just as automobiles carry the brand name of their makers, so too do many self-consciously made buildings."

ENGINEERING: SKIN AND BONES

A late-nineteenth-century structural innovation, steel skeletal structure, had given license to construct buildings of twenty, thirty stories, and more, eliminating thick masonry support-ing walls that consumed valuable rental space on lower floors. The steel frame carries the weight of the floors (gravity load) down to the ground on columns while retaining enough flexibility to bend—and not break—in response to wind and earthquake stress (lateral load). Additional bracing against wind is provided by diagonal framing elements, usually placed behind the core of elevators and stairways. Steel skeleton construction is based on a structural bay (the space between columns) twenty to thirty feet wide, the columns carrying horizontal girders and beams that hold the floor plates. Enclosing interior space while providing protection from wind and weather, the exterior wall (curtain wall) has to bear only its own weight, not that of the individual floors. In effect, it is little more than a "curtain" hanging on the frame.

In the design of the tall office building, some approaches highlight the "skin," or cladding, of the building. Others emphasize the "bones," or structure. The section that follows focuses on skin and bones, but keeps an eye, as well, on the urban setting, to which the tall building makes such a notable contribution.

CURTAIN WALL

In the immediate postwar years, Modernist architects and pragmatic corporate clients generally shared the view of the turn-of-the-century critic Montgomery Schuyler that tall-building design had to tell "the facts of the case," that is, express the nature of steel frame construction. Stacking white-collar workers one floor above another, office buildings were but modern-day factories, optimally designed for construction economy, efficiency, rentability, and profitability. The introduction of fluorescent lighting and air-conditioning eliminated the need for interior light courts, large windows, and high ceilings, and permitted larger and more flexible working areas.

The many tall Manhattan commercial buildings designed by Emery Roth & Sons basically exploited the same highly successful formula. The architect's aim was not to "create masterpieces," Roth explained, "but to create the best that can be produced within the restrictions that have been placed on us." Completed in 1950 and occupying an entire block-front right to the sidewalk line, Roth's stolid, white-brick-faced ziggurat form at 488 Madison (figures 326, 327) is an exceedingly literal embodiment of the zoning code that required buildings to step back as they rose higher, in order to preserve light and air at the street level. Spare of detail, it is assertively horizontal, insistently functional. Related buildings by the same firm at 505 Park Avenue, 1430 Broadway, and 380, 415, and 575 Madison Avenue were but variations on the theme.

Notwithstanding bottom-line priorities, the tall office building also had to stand for America's corporate hegemony, a condition satisfied—for a short while at least—by the glass-and-metal curtain wall. In Manhattan, the first such treatment of a commercial office building was Lever House (figure 328), designed by Skidmore, Owings & Merrill and completed in 1952. Breaking from the tradition of siting the office building's masonry wall at the sidewalk line, Lever House is composed of two lean glass prisms. One is tall and set perpendicular to the street, the other is low and raised on columns that open to the street, allowing pedestrians to enter an interior plaza. The gleaming minimalism of Lever House spoke to businessmen everywhere. After its completion, designer Gordon Bunshaft could boast that he "never had to sell modernism to anybody."

The prestige of the modern glass curtain wall established, Mies van der Rohe endowed it with an aesthetic derived from the rigor of abstraction and the near-perfection of industrially produced building elements. Mies's design of the 1954–58 Seagram Building (figure 329) in Manhattan, in association with Philip Johnson and Kahn & Jacobs, realized an expressive new language for the curtain wall. Strict grammatical rules governed the manner of joining elements together, of ordering horizontal and vertical members, of proportioning part to part. Beyond precise language, however, it was Mies's use of metaphor, employing "structural" elements as something other than what they appear to be, that achieved real poetry. Mies would be satisfied with nothing less than perfection. "I don't want to be interesting," he insisted, "I want to be good." Precision, eloquence, and excellence describe Mies's continued refinement of the curtain wall: Baltimore's

One Charles Center (1960–63) and Chicago's Federal Center (1961–64) and IBM (1967–70, completed after Mies's death).

Among the firms who carried forward the Miesian legacy was Skidmore, Owings & Merrill, who modified curtain-wall vocabulary to satisfy the changing conditions of the decades. For one example, the need for energy conservation, which grew so important after the oil shortages of the mid-seventies, is represented by the firm's 33 West Monroe (figures 330, 331, 332) in Chicago, completed in 1980. SOM dominated tall building construction in the sixties and seventies, when the firm's offices in Chicago, New York, San Francisco, and Houston shared a strong engineering culture and the capacity to marry high style with structural efficiency and cost economy. In the hands of lesser architects, whose work lacked finesse in proportioning, detailing, joining, or finishing, the Miesian approach proved susceptible to banality, low-budget sterility, and facile decorative effects.

Variations on the curtain wall theme included Harrison & Abramovitz's Alcoa Building (1952–53) in Pittsburgh, which demonstrated ornamental sun-and-shadow effects on stamped aluminum panels. Albert Kahn's National Bank of Detroit (1957–59) employed a marble-and-glass curtain wall for a striking checkerboard look. Denver's Mile High Center (1953–55) by I. M. Pei utilized color coding ("gray for structure, tan for cooling") to create an eye-catching woven texture. Welton Becket's Kaiser Center (1956–58) in Los Angeles took advantage of flashy gold anodized aluminum and precast dolomite panels. "Mies continues to be our conscience," Chicago architect Harry Weese wrote in 1966. "But who listens to his conscience these days?"

As Miesian rationalism lost its authority, the romanticism of sheer height asserted itself, encouraging verticality rather than a gridded ef-fect. In Detroit, Minoru Yamasaki with Smith, Hinchman & Grylls designed the 1961 Michigan Consolidated Gas Company (figure 333) to evoke Gothic perpendicularity. The dark glass of Langdon & Wilson's 1965 First National Bank of Nevada (figure 334) in Reno seemed to dissolve the building into reflections behind a strip of projecting vertical mullions that affirm the ambition for tallness.

In the sixties, a swing of taste away from the precise, mechanical lightness of the glass-and-steel curtain wall produced growing appreciation for plasticity, effects of mass and solidity, and contrasts between light and shadow. This coincided with dramatic improvements in the technology of concrete. One of the first tall buildings to carry precast-concrete curtain walls was the Wachovia National Bank of Charlotte, North Carolina (1955–57), by Harrison & Abramovitz with A. G. Odell, Jr. Installed on a light reinforced-concrete structural frame, the curtain wall is composed of faceted panels containing an exposed aggregate of pebbles and quartz chips that produces decorative surface effects.

The imposing character of the concrete curtain wall was manifest in New York City's fifty-story, steel-framed Pan Am (now MetLife) Building (figure 335) of 1960–63, designed by Walter Gropius as a member of The Architects Collaborative (TAC) with Pietro Belluschi and Emery Roth & Sons. The product of Gropius's search for monumentality and memorability in the urban setting, the building's enormous height and bulk made a huge impact on both the neighborhood of Grand Central Terminal and the city skyline. Avowedly antihistorical in the fifties, by the end of the sixties tall-building design began to consider the character of older buildings and neighborhoods. One example was San Francisco's 1968 Bank of California addition (figure 336), designed by Anshen & Allen. Partially cantilevered over a classically styled bank of 1908, the building's precast-concrete curtain wall echoes the older landmark's sense of weight and monumentality. The design is a far distance from the spare Modernist glass-and-metal paradigm.

326, 327 488 Madison Avenue; New York, New York. Emery Roth & Sons, 1950. *Photos: Adolph Studly.*

[EXTERIOR] Continuous brick facing on the spandrels emphasizes the building's composition as a stack of horizontally extended floors rather than a vertically expressive mass. Ribbon windows are unbroken by mullions (vertical framing elements), suggesting the openness of the floor plan.

[ENTRANCE] Revealing the underlying steel skeleton, freestanding columns permit ground-level space to be given over to glass-fronted storefronts and a setback entry.

328 Lever House; New York, New York. Skidmore, Owings & Merrill, 1950–52. *Photo: Ezra Stoller, © Esto.* Contrasting to the heavy, ornamented masonry masses of nearby buildings, the spareness, lightness, and reflectivity of the precise green-glass curtain wall represented an explicit advertisement for modernity.

329 Seagram Building; New York, New York. Mies van der Rohe with Philip Johnson and Kahn & Jacobs, 1954–58. *Photo: Ezra Stoller, © Esto.* The facade is a grid of amber-tinted glass, bronze spandrel panels, and variously profiled bronze mullions whose composition creates subtle effects of depth, shadow, and scale. The regular rhythm of the vertically aligned elements up the facade serves to emphasize the building's tallness rather than to give a truly accurate expression of the underlying steel grid structure. A similar artfulness explains the treatment of the exposed columns at the base, which are concrete-encased in order to satisfy fireproofing requirements, but are then sheathed in bronze to serve as a reminder of their metal core.

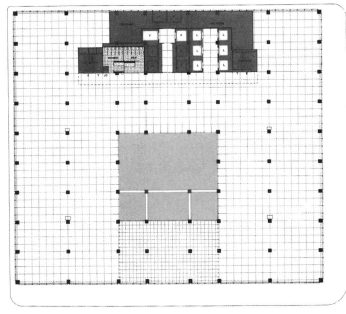

33 WEST MONROE

FLOOR 6

330, 331, 332 33 West Monroe; Chicago, Illinois. Skidmore, Owings & Merrill, 1980. *Photo: Merrick, Hedrich-Blessing.*

[PLAN OF FLOOR 6] The distance between the steel columns establishes the grid expressed on the facade.

[SECTION] Not revealed on the exterior, the multiple atria add variety to interior spaces.

[EXTERIOR] The building achieves energy efficiency through the use of dark glass, insulation in thickened wall panels, and reduced glass surface.

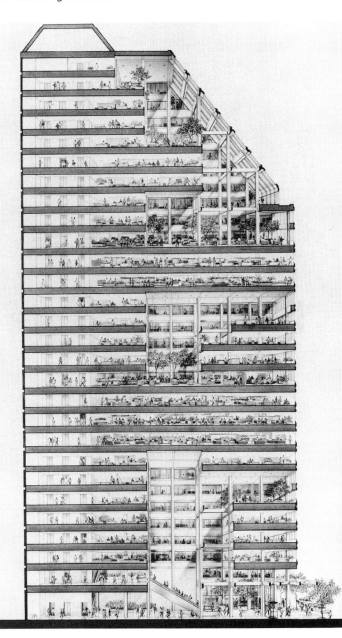

333 Michigan Consolidated Gas Company; Detroit, Michigan. Minoru Yamasaki with Smith, Hinchman & Grylls, 1961. *Photo: Balthazar Korab.* The wall's division into bays corresponds to the module of the skeleton. Although it rises from a bulky square plan, the tower achieves a striking vertical effect with slender window openings and the tracery effect of narrowly spaced steel mullions.

334 First National Bank of Nevada; Reno, Nevada. Langdon & Wilson, 1965. *Photo: Julius Shulman.* The building's vertical dimension is emphasized by the continuous alignment of the steel mullions, which project forward of the glass panels of the curtain wall.

335 Pan Am (now MetLife) Building; New York, New York. The Architects Collaborative with Pietro Belluschi and Emery Roth & Sons, 1960–63. *Photo: Joseph Molitor.* Composed of precast concrete panels with exposed aggregate, the curtain wall is designed to maximize patterns of light and shade.

336 Bank of California Headquarters; San Francisco, California. Anshen & Allen, 1979. *Photo:*
© *Ted Mahieu.* The heaviness of the concrete curtain wall is belied by the lightness and transparency of the
glass-enclosed entrance level of the new tower. Cantilevered over the old bank, the new one uses its
roof as a terrace.

ARTICULATED FRAME

STEEL

"A new era in structural steel design has arrived," trumpeted the trade journal *Engineering News Record* in 1962, praising the use of structural steel with its unprecedented strength, remarkable span, and relative imperviousness to weathering and corrosion. If experiments with the curtain-wall skin had become tired, there was growing excitement about portraying the structural bones. The articulation of structure also satisfied the growing taste for effects of weight, mass, and solidity.

An early sign of the trend was the 1954–58 Inland Steel Building (figures 337, 338), in Chicago, designed by the Chicago office of Skidmore, Owings & Merrill. Earning praise for the kind of structural "honesty" associated with Louis Sullivan and others in the Chicago tradition, the steel structure produced large expanses of column-free interior space. Heralding the beginnings of downtown Chicago's postwar office-building boom, the nineteen-story building was a prestigious logo for the steel company that occupied the top eight floors, as well as a distinguished address for the rental tenants on the remaining floors.

Multiplied to sixty stories, the expressed structural column created a remarkable visual impact at Manhattan's Chase Manhattan Bank (1957–61), designed by the New York City office of SOM. Originally called the Chicago Civic Center, the 1963–66 Richard J. Daley Center (see figure 166), designed by C. F. Murphy Associates with SOM, and Loebl, Schlossman & Bennett, had a record-breaking eighty-seven-foot bay, exploiting the newly developed alloy, Cor-Ten steel, whose very rusting forms a protective surface.

Not just the columns, but the entire horizontal and vertical grid was projected to the exterior at the 1960–62 Business Men's Assurance Company's tower, in Kansas City, Missouri, designed by the New York office of SOM. Dark glass windows set back from the facade add drama to the articulation. Designed by SOM's San Francisco office, the 1962–63 thirty-three-story Tenneco Building in Houston is carried on a steel frame that projects some five feet forward of the window wall, providing protection from the sun as well as a richly textured, almost picturesque surface.

At the 1968–71 First National Bank of Chicago (figures 339, 340) the observer has the impression that the structure is alighting on the ground. Designed by Perkins & Will and C. F. Murphy Associates, the tower tapers on two sides to create a distinctive "bell-bottom" profile. Continuous projecting steel columns set in forty-foot bays and great spandrel girders are eloquent of their load-bearing function.

Investigations of wind bracing, distribution of loads, fireproofing, and construction economy produced a fresh manifestation of the articulated frame in a building such as Manhattan's bulky 1970–72 One Liberty Plaza (figure 341), a showcase for its principal occupant, the United States Steel Corporation, and designed by SOM's New York office. So extensive is the use of steel on the exterior that the usual relationship between solid and void is reversed, making the building seem less a glass enclosure over a skeleton frame than a thick steel wall with deep slots for windows.

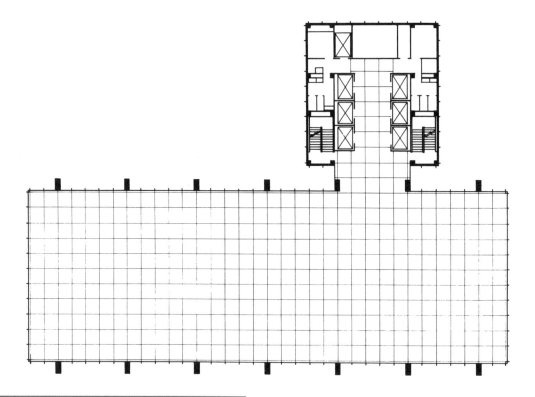

SCALE

337, 338 Inland Steel Building; Chicago, Illinois. Skidmore, Owings & Merrill, 1954–58. *Photo: Howard N. Kaplan, © HNK Architectural Photography.*

[PLAN] The building is composed of a rectangular element containing open office space and a separate square service tower that encloses the elevators, stairs, and mechanical systems.

[EXTERIOR] Not hidden behind curtain walls, widely spaced steel columns run up the facades like giant exposed ribs. The columns support massive fifty-eight-foot-long girders that carry the weight of the floors, eliminating the need for interior columns.

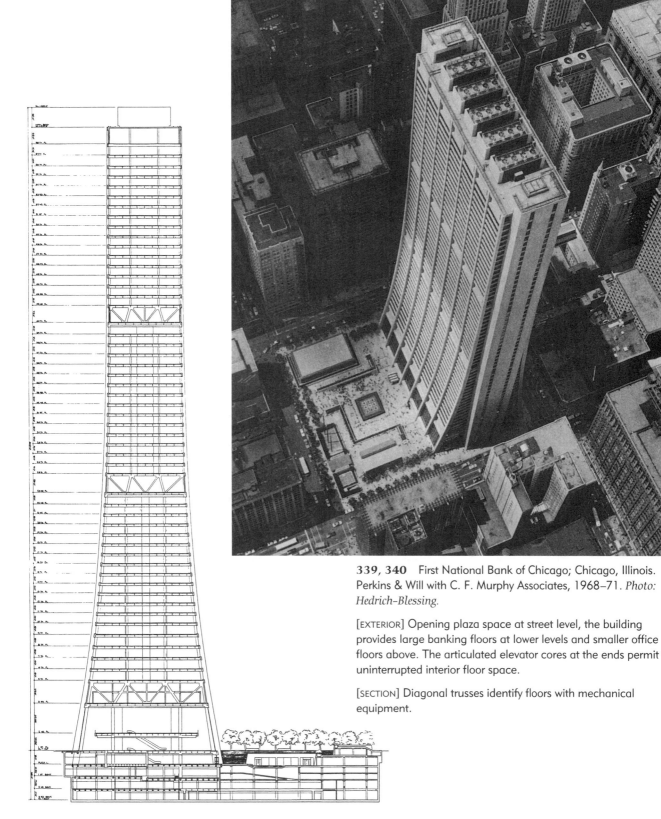

339, 340 First National Bank of Chicago; Chicago, Illinois. Perkins & Will with C. F. Murphy Associates, 1968–71. *Photo: Hedrich-Blessing.*

[EXTERIOR] Opening plaza space at street level, the building provides large banking floors at lower levels and smaller office floors above. The articulated elevator cores at the ends permit uninterrupted interior floor space.

[SECTION] Diagonal trusses identify floors with mechanical equipment.

TRANSVERSE SECTION

341 One Liberty Plaza (United States Steel Building); New York, New York. Skidmore, Owings & Merrill, 1970–72. *Photo: Ezra Stoller, © Esto.* Fifty-foot-long structural bays, six-foot-deep spandrels, and the use of special flame canopies to prevent fire-induced structural failure give the building a sense of mass exceptional for a steel-framed building.

CONCRETE

Improvements in concrete and an increasingly precise knowledge of its structural behavior, economy, construction efficiency, scheduling flexibility, and design freedom combined to increase concrete's competitiveness with steel. A harbinger was the 1959–61 twenty-story Hartford Building (figure 342), a work of the Chicago office of SOM. Composed of narrow vertical members and thin floor slabs, the exposed white concrete frame is pushed forward of the dark glazing by almost five feet to create a compelling visual effect. The 1961 American Cement Corporation headquarters in Los Angeles, by Daniel, Mann, Johnson & Mendenhall, advertised concrete as the focus of the company's business activity in a structure whose two long facades are covered by a latticework of X-shaped precast concrete units.

An entirely new kind of structural system, the structural tube, was employed in Chicago's Brunswick Building (figures 343, 344) of 1962–65. At the Chicago office of SOM, the concept was pioneered by the engineering partner Fazlur Khan, an innovator with a powerful interest in the aesthetic dimensions of engineering. In the Brunswick Building the columns are so closely spaced and so tightly tied together that they act like the side of a rigid box, or tube. In effect, the building's facade is cantilevered from belowground supports. The exterior walls resist lateral loads, and the bracing around the central elevator and utility core carry most of the vertical load, while also acting against wind shear.

Insisting that "structural expression should not overshadow architectural expression," Eero Saarinen was the designer of the 1963–65 Co-lumbia Broadcasting System (CBS) Building (figure 345). An assertive presence in the Manhattan streetscape, the building's form hints at the structural principles at work without actually portraying them in a literal fashion. In this manner, the black-granite-sheathed columns rise directly from the ground, displaying no trace of a base to suggest their load-bearing function.

The emphasis on the underlying bones of these buildings continued in increasingly subtle and sophisticated engineering applications. Designed by the New York office of SOM in association with Harwood K. Smith & Partners, One Main Place (1967–68) in Dallas employed a concrete skeletal frame that tapers back at upper stories to express the diminished load at those levels. Set back some four feet from the facade, window glazing adds to effects of sun, shadow, and reflection. The visual effect of the Cities Service Building (1969–71) in Tulsa, Oklahoma, designed by Stevens & Wilkinson, derives from the powerful Vierendeel truss that composes the rigid concrete-trussed frame, innovative in its exclusion of diagonal members. Post-tensioning (stretching the reinforcing rods to compress the concrete after it has hardened) provides greater wind resistance and reduces the need for interior columns.

The integrity of architecture is "based on what is possible, extracting whatever beauty may be hidden, while doing it in an understated way," said Pietro Belluschi. "Most important, probably, is structure. Not only the way in which a building is put together, or the simplicity of its structural idea, but how this is expressed without striving to make the bones the whole answer," he declared. The three sets of multistory triangular braces located behind the facade of The Boston Company Building (1970) in Boston, designed by Pietro Belluschi and Emery Roth & Sons, are revealed on the facade only by subtle changes in the pattern of fenestration that result from the blockage of the window openings by the framing members.

342 Hartford Building; Chicago, Illinois. Skidmore, Owings & Merrill, 1959–61. *Photo: Ezra Stoller, © Esto.* The spareness of the expressed grid explicitly demonstrates that reinforced concrete needs relatively little mass to accomplish the tasks of carrying gravity load and resisting wind pressure.

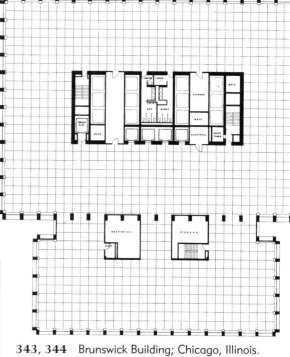

343, 344 Brunswick Building; Chicago, Illinois. Skidmore, Owings & Merrill, 1962–65. *Photo: Philip Turner.*

[PLAN] The closeness of the column spacing is indicative of tube construction. The solid concrete walls of the elevator and stair core are tied into the tube system.

[EXTERIOR] The weight of the concrete structural grid is transferred from upper stories to massive concrete columns at the base by means of a story-high transfer girder. The slimmer dimension of upper framing elements expresses the lighter load at higher stories.

345 CBS Building; New York, New York. Eero Saarinen, 1963–65. *Photo: Joseph Molitor.* The close spacing and forward projection of the columns produce an effect of weight and mass, although the structure is actually highly efficient in its use of material. The setting of the columns on the diagonal makes the building surface appear solid when it is seen from certain angles.

STRUCTURAL AESTHETICS

Beyond simply stating "the facts of the case," the sixties produced an interest in dramatizing, glorifying, even exaggerating the structural principles at work in the tall building. This interest in the aesthetics of engineering tended to encourage closer and more creative collaboration between architect and engineer. One change in the sixties and seventies, explained engineer Paul Weidlinger, was that engineers who "got tired" of telling architects what "won't work" became involved earlier and more intensely in the process, helping the architect to devise complex structural solutions that would work. They were greatly aided by the use of the computer in engineering design, and a building of almost any height, shape, and configuration now became theoretically possible.

The fifty-story, all-concrete 1968–71 One Shell Plaza (figure 346) in Houston allowed Fazlur Khan of SOM to realize his passion for the "direct expression of the structural behavior of the load flow." The design eschews a regularly articulated grid for an arrangement of concrete members that are thickened at certain points to interpret the structural forces at work, creating a facade that appears to undulate. The tallest reinforced concrete building in the world at the time of its construction, the design was based on the tube-within-a-tube concept, the outer concrete tube consisting of closely placed columns and tall spandrel beams and the inner concrete tube comprising shear walls that add stability surrounding the elevator and service core.

By contrast, the 1964–70 World Trade Center (figures 347, 348) in Manhattan exploited a tube structure composed of a closely spaced network of steel trusses, vaunting its sheer size and bulk by the enormous expanse and apparent solidity of its bearing walls. Designed by Minoru Yamasaki & Associates with Emery Roth & Sons, the project encompasses two massive towers one hundred and ten stories high. Their physical presence on the skyline—twinness, height, bulk, solidity, and monumentality—is intended to awe, amaze, overwhelm.

Structural exhibitionism could make the Modernist "shoe box" shape seem decidedly reticent. At the twenty-three-story Knights of Columbus Headquarters building of 1968–70 (figures 349, 350) in New Haven, Connecticut, by Kevin Roche John Dinkeloo and Associates, four massive, brick-faced cylindrical service columns, formed of post-tensioned concrete, boldly extend from the four corners of the building and, together with the service core located within the structure, carry the steel-framed, clear-span floors. The mass and muscularity of the cylinders proclaim the compressive strength and weight-bearing capacity of concrete, while the lacy quality of steel spandrel beams and sun screens, projecting forward of the window wall, emphasizes the flexural strength of steel.

Heroic statements sometimes honor the trumpeter rather than the warrior. For example, Manhattan's seventy-story Citicorp Center of 1971–78 (figure 351) designed by Hugh Stubbins & Associates, flaunts four massive, nine-story-high columns that raise the building some eight stories above ground level to make way for a large open-air plaza. The building's true structural genius, huge diagonal trusses that carry the load down to the corner columns and exposed central core, is hidden behind the slick skin of polished aluminum. Hugh Stubbins & Associates also designed the 1978 steel-framed Federal Reserve Bank of Boston (figure 352), vividly portraying the suspension of the office floors while actually concealing the massive braced trusses in the end service core towers that support them.

The revelation of the steel truss, a skeletal system whose efficiency is improved by the inclusion of diagonal members, produced some of the most memorable structures of the era. Appreciated kinesthetically as well as visually, one of the first of the trussed, or braced, tubes was Chicago's tapered, ninety-seven-story, steel-framed John Hancock Center (figures 353, 354). Dubbed the ''Bourges Cathedral of our time'' by engineering historian Robert Mark, the tapered form has a visual lightness despite its giant size. Dating from 1965 to 1970 to designs by SOM's architect-engineer team, the structural system is based on a massive exoskeleton of diagonal braces that, working together with exterior spandrels and columns, offer wind resistance and eliminate the need for interior shear walls. ''It was as important for us to expose the structure of this mammoth,'' said designer Bruce Graham, as it was to ''perceive the structure of the Eiffel Tower.'' Announcing the trend toward the use of tall buildings for mixed uses, the tapered form creates larger floor plates at lower levels, which can be efficiently divided into office spaces, and smaller floors at the upper stories, producing apartments that command good light and views. At the time of its construction, the tower was second in height only to the Empire State Building, but a more efficient structure because, proportionately, it contains significantly less steel.

The soaring spirit of adventure liberated the design of the braced steel tube at the United States Steel Corporation headquarters of 1968–70, in Pittsburgh, designed by Harrison & Abramovitz and Abbe for a client who appreciated the facility as a giant logo on the skyline. The structure employed a cagelike exoskeleton composed of boldly expressed columns, massive spandrel girders, and cross beams at three-story intervals, all in an imposing, dark, weathering steel.

The principle of joining one tube to another, that is, ''bundling'' them so that the common walls help to support each other, was one of the more sophisticated engineering achievements of the period. A unique and memorable configuration on the Chicago skyline, SOM's Sears Tower of 1968–74 (figures 355, 356, 357) is a cluster of nine black aluminum–clad steel tubes that range in height from fifty to one hundred and ten stories. Close up, one can see the narrow bay of the columns (fifteen feet apart, in this case) that describes the underlying tube structure. Another Chicago landmark project that employed bundled tubes is the pink-granite-clad One Magnificent Mile of 1978–83 (figures 358, 359), designed by SOM. Combining office, residential, and retail uses in a structure composed of three hexagonal reinforced-concrete-framed tubes, the configuration maximizes the use of an awkwardly shaped lot.

In the eighties, the development of hybrid structural systems made it practical to build extremely slender and tall structures that would otherwise have troubled the occupant with unacceptable perceptions of wind sway. The hybrid system employed at SOM's 780 Third Avenue (1982–85) in Manhattan represents the first use of a diagonally braced concrete tube designed with interactions among tube, frame, and shear wall. Sheathed in smooth, dark red granite, the building has a bold diagonal fenestration pattern that proclaims the underlying structure.

346 One Shell Plaza; Houston, Texas. Skidmore, Owings & Merrill, 1968–71. *Photo: Ezra Stoller, © Esto.* Projecting out of the walls, rather than hidden within, thickened structural members eloquently portray the support needed at certain points where the interior tube does not provide it.

347, 348 World Trade Center; New York, New York. Minoru Yamasaki & Associates with Emery Roth & Sons, 1964–70. *Photos: Joseph Molitor [exterior]; © Richard Edelman [detail].*

[EXTERIOR] From a distance, the deep spandrel beams, welded to the columns, make the towers appear to have solid walls. The beams are of steel, encased in fireproofing material and sheathed in aluminum.

[WALL DETAIL] The weight-bearing nature of the perimeter framing is expressed by the high proportion of steel to glass, narrowed window openings, and recessed glazing. The treelike trusses collect upper column loads and direct them to more widely spaced lower columns.

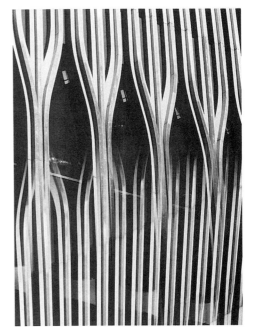

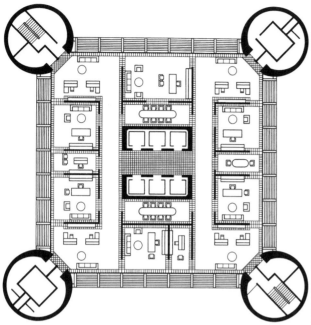

349, 350 Knights of Columbus Headquarters; New Haven, Connecticut. Kevin Roche John Dinkeloo and Associates, 1968–70. *Photo: Kevin Roche John Dinkeloo and Associates.*

[PLAN] Reducing the size of the central core by displacing the mechanical systems and stairs to the exterior corners of the building produced large and unencumbered floor areas.

[VIEW] The weight-bearing nature of the massive concrete service columns is emphasized by dark brick facing.

351 Citicorp Center; New York, New York. Hugh Stubbins & Associates, 1971–78. *Photo: © Edward Jacoby/ APC.* Conceived, but not used, as a means of collecting solar energy, the sloping "shed roof" serves instead as a metaphor for Citicorp's ingenious wind-bracing system, which includes a huge movable concrete mass in the upper stories that counteracts the swaying tendency of lower floors. St. Peter's Church (Lutheran) occupies space on the plaza.

352 Federal Reserve Bank of Boston; Boston, Massachusetts. Hugh Stubbins & Associates, 1978. *Photo: © Edward Jacoby/APC.* Massive three-foot-deep twin trusses transfer column loads for the office floors across the large opening near the tower base.

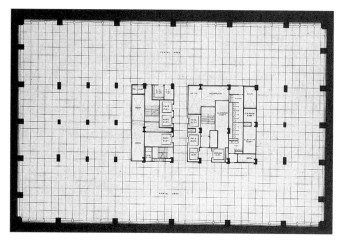

353, 354   John Hancock Center; Chicago, Illinois. Skidmore, Owings & Merrill, 1965–70. *Photo: Ezra Stoller, © Esto.*

[PLAN—38TH TO 41ST FLOORS] The framed tube system, providing peripheral resistance against wind forces, eliminates the need for a shear wall around the central core, which allows the interior to be mainly free of columns and permits the efficient use of smaller floor areas.

[EXTERIOR] Offering less "sail area" against the stronger wind forces prevailing at upper stories, the tapered form is more aerodynamically stable than an equivalent rectangular volume.

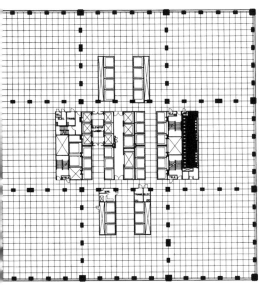

355, 356, 357 Sears Tower; Chicago, Illinois. Skidmore, Owings & Merrill, 1968–74. *Photo: Hedrich–Blessing.*

[PLAN] The base of the building consists of nine column-free squares, which, in elevation, variously terminate at the 50th, 66th, 90th, and 110th floors.

[SECTION] The step-back design permits the large floor areas that Sears required for its own operations while creating smaller floor areas for tenant occupancy on upper stories. A system of double-deck express elevators carries passengers to two "sky lobbies" where they can transfer to single elevators serving individual floors.

[EXTERIOR] The extraordinary height and distinctive profile make the building a good advertisement for corporate tenants.

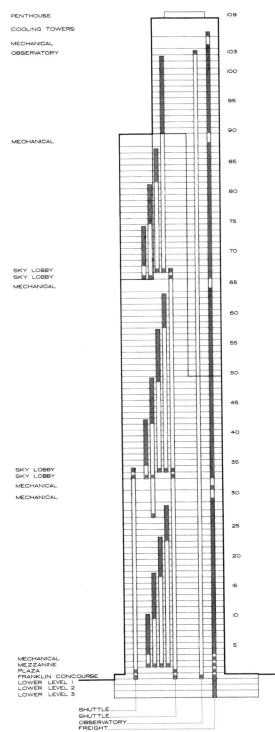

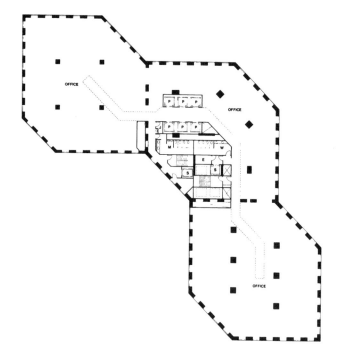

358, 359 One Magnificent Mile; Chicago, Illinois. Skidmore, Owings & Merrill, 1978–83. *Photo: © Gregory Murphey.*

[PLAN] An excellent Michigan Avenue address increased the desirability of the awkward L-shaped site, but it also required a novel structural system in order to achieve sufficient density of uses to make it economically feasible. The free-form shape permits columns to be variously configured for different functional needs.

[EXTERIOR] In the concrete tube system, window openings can be ''punched in'' in any size and location that makes sense for the layout, as long as the basic behavior of the tube effect is maintained.

SLICK SKIN

"Cladding systems have given our builders freedom to create form for form's sake," praised engineer G. Stewart Farnet in a 1986 report to the Council on Tall Buildings, noting an apparently "limitless wardrobe of color, texture, and style." Prodigious improvements in the design, fabrication, and installation of cladding and joints encouraged taut, sleek, and smooth exterior surfaces, although the push of technology to its extreme did also produce some serious skin failures. Creating compelling high-tech logos, the architects of tall buildings exploited glass of larger dimensions, extremely thin cut stone, laminates, reflective solar glass, synthetic sealants, improved gaskets and anchors, and fiber-reinforced concrete. New composite structural systems using combinations of steel and concrete reduced building sway sufficiently to make such thin skins feasible, encouraging all manner of pleated, terraced, and eroded forms. Emphasizing the building skin, these designs tended to deny the underlying structural sophistication that permitted such slice-and-dice manipulations.

Heading the parade of Slick Skin buildings that was to march through the eighties was the I.D.S. tower (figures 360, 361) of 1969–72 in Minneapolis, Minnesota. The fifty-one-story skyscraper, designed by Johnson/Burgee Architects with Edward F. Baker Associates, is part of a complex that includes a hotel and shops and focuses on a grand public atrium. Seven vertical setbacks—"zogs," as Johnson would have it—are set into each of the four corners of the office building, appearing to slice away at its huge physical bulk and adding a range of reflections and shadows that relieve what might otherwise be a mirrored monotony. The dynamic profile also served to increase the proportion of coveted corner office space. A sawtooth configuration was similarly exploited at Chicago's 1980–82 Madison Plaza Office Building (figure 362). Designed by SOM, the steel tube-in-tube structure is clad in bands of silver reflective glass and light gray polished granite. Manhattan's bronze-tinted, all-glass Trump Tower of 1983, designed by Der Scutt with Swanke Hayden Connell, produces an elaborate pleated inset at the corner, hung with a Babylonian garden of plants that sets off its high-tech imagery.

The reflecting quality of the Slick Skin building produces entirely novel effects on the city skyline. The asymmetry and continuity of the pale-green shimmering surface of the 1969–76 One United Nations Plaza (figures 363, 364) seems to dissolve the structure into the Manhattan cityscape. Designed by Kevin Roche John Dinkeloo and Associates, the three-building ensemble takes sharp nips and tucks at various floor levels as it responds to the shape and height of neighboring buildings. At the 1967–76 John Hancock Tower (figure 365) in Boston, Massachusetts, by I. M. Pei & Partners, the design had to mitigate the extreme disparity in size between the tower and surrounding landmarks, most notably historic Trinity Church. Principal designer Henry Cobb sought to bring the two buildings in "close proximity while positioning and shaping the tower in such a way that the church becomes the autonomous center and the tower the contingent satellite in the composition." Presto! The disappearing quality of the mirrored surface transforms a spectacular obelisk into little more than a backdrop. A similar sleight of hand characterizes Manhattan's answer to the Hancock, Edward Larrabee Barnes's IBM tower of 1977–83, whose green-and-gray reflections emanate from a sleekly polished granite and glass skin and whose silhouette changes radically according to one's viewpoint. Inserted into the Chicago cityscape by Kohn Pedersen Fox, 333 South Wacker Drive (1980–83) explicitly responds to the geometries of the site. The broad arch of one reflecting glass window wall echoes the curving Chicago River, while the right-angled masonry facade responds to the grid of the built city.

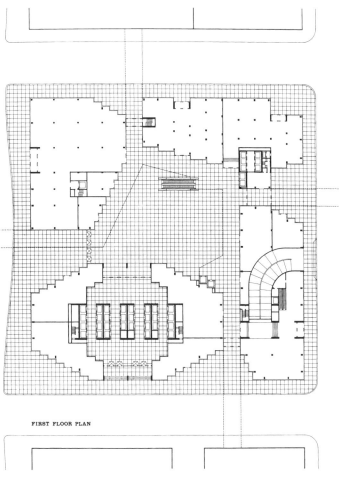

FIRST FLOOR PLAN

360, 361 I.D.S. Center; Minneapolis, Minnesota. Johnson/Burgee Architects with Edward F. Baker Associates, 1969–72. *Photo: © Richard Payne/FAIA.*

[PLAN] Lining up with the traditional street wall, the complex opens a spacious covered public space in the interior.

[EXTERIOR] The greenish blue reflecting glass retains sufficient transparency to reduce the effects of windowlessness and scalelessness that sometimes characterize mirrored glass. The architects designed small panes of glass with slightly projecting framing elements so the building would seem "more of a birdcage than a glass box."

362 Madison Plaza Office Building; Chicago, Illinois. Skidmore, Owings & Merrill, 1980–82. *Photo: © Gregory Murphey.* Mainly reflective glass on the cutaway elevations, the sheathing changes to a preponderance of smooth stone on the flat sides—a change of materials that is visually stimulating as well as energy conserving.

363, 364 One United Nations Plaza; New York, New York. Kevin Roche John Dinkeloo and Associates, 1969–76. *Photos: Kevin Roche John Dinkeloo and Associates.*

[EXTERIOR] Subtle adjustments in the proportion of clear to opaque glass in the uniform aluminum grid reflect the differing heights of office floors (at lower levels) and hotel rooms (at upper levels).

[ENTRANCE DETAIL] The glass skin seems to fold down on itself to create a canopied sidewalk.

365 John Hancock Tower; Boston, Massachusetts. I. M. Pei & Partners, 1967–76. *Photo: George Cserna.* At ground level and on the skyline, the reflecting skyscraper presents a dramatically different face from every vantage point—wedge, broad plane, knifelike sliver.

SIGNATURE STYLE

Stimulated by generous tax incentives, the intense speculative office building boom of the Reagan eighties spurred a feverish search for memorability, marketability, and profitability. Real-estate feasibility formulas most typically produced a tower of 750,000 to one million square feet. It was forty to sixty stories in height, with a square, bulky plan on a five-foot planning module, for a good ratio of inside-to-outside offices. All this was accomplished by using relatively standard structural systems. To exploit odd-shaped sites and to satisfy complex mixed-use programs, designers had to devise innovative composite steel-and-concrete structures. But, no matter the structure, interest in expressing the bones of the building waned as the sharp turn toward Postmodernist eclecticism tempted many to seek decorative surface effects. The tall buildings of the affluent eighties, said architect Helmut Jahn, one of the most prolific designers, "have a lot to do with creating comfort. The buildings try to please, to offend no one." Signature architecture flourished as a skin-deep phenomenon.

Johnson/Burgee Architects' designs for the 1978–84 American Telephone & Telegraph Headquarters (figure 366) in Manhattan entered fantasy and frippery into the discourse. The similarity of the memorable split-pediment top to both a Chippendale highboy chest and the roofline of Robert Venturi's mother's house was noted by critic Martin Filler—such rampant eclecticism helping to divert attention from the building's considerable imposition on the cityscape. The architects ransacked history for the monumentality of Pharaonic Egypt, the dignity of Greece and Rome, and the wit of Mannerist Italy, ultimately creating a design that implies that the building's thin pink granite skin, voluptuously detailed by arches, arcades, and oversized moldings, is actually a loadbearing masonry wall. Rather than bearing down on the ground, the structure actually rises up into the air on giant stilted columns in order to open the ground level for a public space originally open to the sidewalk.

This succès de scandale accomplished, Johnson/Burgee produced a series of office towers with glorified rooflines, including a picturesque Gothic skyline for Pittsburgh Plate Glass (1978–84), a northern Renaissance gable top at Republic Bank (1981–84) in Houston, and a steeply gabled silhouette at 190 La Salle Street (1985–87) that mimicked the 1892 Masonic Temple nearby in Chicago. "Now we're demodernizing," declared Philip Johnson impishly, confident that others would follow the trail—as they did.

As early-twentieth-century eclectics had searched the Classic past for precedents for the tall building, so did late-twentieth-century Postmodernists—but now with new items on the agenda. A pioneering project in this respect was the twenty-six-story Humana Building (1982–86) in Louisville, Kentucky, designed by Michael Graves. The steel-framed, granite-faced tower rises from a massive colonnade at its base, giving the effect of a stone bearing-wall with punched-out window openings at midlevel elevations while enriching the skyline with a vaulted skylight and applied temple forms. An exposed steel truss supports a cantilevered balcony near the roofline—an expression of modern technology, a reminiscence on old Ohio River bridges, and an intentionally provocative use of symbolism.

The firm of Kevin Roche John Dinkeloo and Associates was among others that made an approach to classicism. "Could we, should we, even dare we, try to make a building out of the form of a column?" Roche asked. "I reasoned that since high-rise buildings essentially have nothing to dictate their form, and their structure is essentially very straightforward, they can take on almost any image." Both the 1989 Leo Burnett Building in Chicago and the 1988 60 Wall Street (figures 367, 368) in Manhattan sculpted the skyscraper as if it were a column. Articulated into base, shaft, and capitol, both are tall glass-curtain-wall buildings, one flat-roofed in the Chicago tradition, the other with a shaped roof, as is common in Manhattan. Both are endowed with emphatic colonnades at the base, thickening at the corners, and assertive dark-reflective-glass-and-granite cladding.

The Art Deco imagery of skyscrapers of the twenties and thirties was a second important source for the design vocabulary of the eighties, when architects desired to reduce the visual appearance of bulk by means of stepped setbacks, sculpted crowns, and streamlined ornament.

Certainly, the slender, soaring grandeur of the skyscraper's golden age is hinted at in the set-back silhouette of Murphy/Jahn's sixty-one-story One Liberty Place in Philadelphia (figure 369) of 1984–87. Rising from a three-story masonry-faced podium, the slick blue-glass-and-granite-sheathed tower soars to a grandiloquent crown that pays homage to Manhattan's Chrysler Building. The proportion of masonry to stone diminishes as the building rises, so that the facade becomes all glass at the upper stories. In Manhattan itself, Murphy/Jahn's stylish, stepped-back CitySpire of 1984–89 (figures 370, 371, 372) rises to a domed top that recalls an adjacent Moorish-styled landmark theater. A mixed office-residential project occupying a relatively small midbock midtown site, it rises to an exceed-ingly narrow, seventy-story height by virtue of a bonus of air space transferred from the neighboring theater.

Cesar Pelli & Associates revived Art Deco at the World Financial Center (1980–88) in Manhattan's Battery Park City, a complex of four very bulky towers that step back in several stages to rooftops that sport dome, pyramid and ziggurat shapes. The proportion of glass to masonry on the exceptionally smooth skin of the buildings increases as the buildings rise, so that the facades become all glass at the upper stories. Art Deco motifs are vivid at Pelli's 181 Madison Avenue (1986–90), a fifty-story, steel-framed tower in Chicago. Here Pelli created a three-dimensional woven texture on the facade, setting differing depths for window glazing, granite-faced piers, and painted aluminum mullions. Spiky metal fins at the crown also serve to de-emphasize the building's bulk. The skyscraper as a logo on the city skyline seems to have been Pelli's point of reference at 777 South Figueroa Street in Los Angeles dating from 1987–90. Pelli embroidered the stepped-back silhouette with a sensuous metal-and-glass skin and projecting stone piers that further enrich the facade. "Cities are made up of foreground and background buildings," said Pelli. "Yet no one, whether architect or client, wants to do a background building."

A third major theme of the late eighties and the nineties was urbanism itself. Architecture began to show new respect for the form, materials, and design vocabulary of the existing context, as well as for the comfort and desired civility of increasingly dense and congested downtown areas. Historicism may, at times, have led to hyperbole, as in, for example, 500 Boylston Street in downtown Boston. It is virtually a trade-catalog display of brick and masonry detailing completed in 1989 to the designs of John Burgee Architects with Philip Johnson. But historicism could also be more earnest. One example is Goody, Clancy & Associates' twenty-story 99 Summer Street (figure 373) in Boston, completed in 1987, a gray-granite-clad structure vigorously articulated like older nearby buildings. Distinctive on the skyline because of the stepped-pediment roof dormers executed in terra-cotta-colored enameled steel panels, the project made use of a mid-block site wedged in between several low-rise late-nineteenth-century structures that form a kind of podium for its set-back tower.

Chicago, which witnessed many of the skyscraper's first and finest moments, honored its own late-nineteenth- and early-twentieth-century rationalist tradition during the eighties boom. The strong simplicity of the twenty-six-story 320 North Michigan Avenue (1980–83), by Booth/Hansen & Associates, results from clearly expressed concrete framing and a carefully articulated facade with its traditional tripartite Chicago windows. SOM roamed freely through various epochs—at 225 West Washington (1987) recalling the heavily articulated, masonry-faced forms of the first years of the twentieth century, while at One North Franklin (1991), with its glass corners, setbacks, and rich hues, harking back to the Art Deco.

Issues of urbanism have been the subject of continuing investigations at Kohn Pedersen Fox, an extraordinarily prolific firm that in the span of less than fifteen years produced some fifty major office buildings in twenty-eight states and six foreign countries. In St. Paul, Minnesota, the 1987–91 St. Paul Companies Headquarters (figures 374, 375) was broken into different elements in order to weave the new buildings into the scale, color, and texture of the surrounding city. Affirming that a "large building could be more sensitively scaled to the city if it was made up of distinct parts," William Pedersen explained the firm's intentions "to introduce the complexity of the modern city into the individual building." In Manhattan, KPF's 712 Fifth Avenue (figure 376) of 1985–91 is a fifty-three-story tower. Limestone-clad and intricately detailed in deference to the traditional character of Fifth Avenue, it was set back at the rear of the lot in order to preserve the facades of a low-rise grouping on the avenue that includes an early-twentieth-century landmark storefront. A retail store and public atrium are set behind the restored facades, contributing amenity and vitality to the commercial streetscape. The building stands as a hard-fought compromise between the real estate developer's pro forma and the citizen's quality-of-life concerns—a battle that is sure to continue everywhere.

366 AT&T Headquarters (now SONY); New York, New York. Johnson/Burgee Architects, 1978–84. *Photo: © Peter Mauss/Esto.* A series of tubes are used in combination in order to achieve the desired configuration: two vertical shear tubes in the core on either side of the eight-story lobby space; a cross-braced tube that transfers weight from upper tubes to the stilted columns at the base; a cross-braced tube carrying the weight of the pediment at the top; two partial tubes supporting the narrow end walls. Although it has no structural role, pink granite cladding is heavily detailed to give the appearance that it *is* weight bearing.

367, 368 60 Wall Street; New York, New York. Kevin Roche John Dinkeloo and Associates, 1988. *Photos: Kevin Roche John Dinkeloo and Associates.*

[EXTERIOR] The active articulation of columns, corners, and cornice helps to distract from the building's exceptionally bulky floor plan and forty-eight-story height—the result of "borrowing" air rights from an adjacent historic landmark. Additional upper-story bonus space resulted from the development of certain street-level amenities and a subway connection.

[ENTRANCE DETAIL] The suggestive heaviness of masonry at street level rapidly diminishes as the curtain wall shifts to mainly glass at the upper levels. A monumental presence on the street, the building contains a through-block passageway.

369 One Liberty Place; Philadelphia, Pennsylvania. Murphy/Jahn, 1984–87. *Photo: Lawrence S. Williams, Inc.* The position of the stone on the facade is emblematic of the underlying structure, while the triangular "wedding-cake" top is intended to create a glamorous effect.

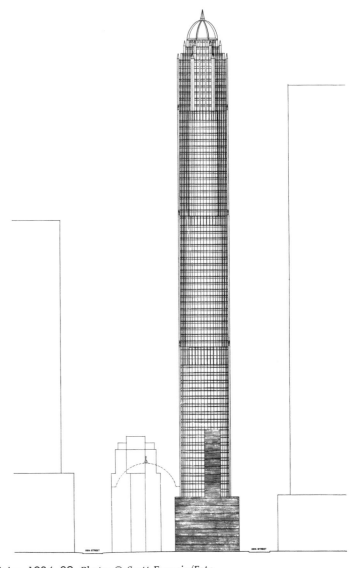

370, 371, 372 CitySpire; New York, New York. Murphy/Jahn, 1984–89. *Photo: © Scott Francis/Esto.*

[EXTERIOR] The concrete tube surrounding the central elevator core is linked to exterior columns through shear walls that are disposed, pinwheel fashion, up the height of the structure. The use of a multilevel diagonal brace on the office floors serves to reduce the number of interior columns needed. In effect, the combination creates nine separate structural systems.

[ELEVATION] Soaring to a height of eight hundred feet on a structural footprint only eighty feet wide, CitySpire has the same slender proportions as the Washington Monument, but it is three hundred feet higher. The lowest tier provides office space; each tier above allows different apartment layouts.

[PLAN] Each floor has a unique plan with a corresponding structural system.

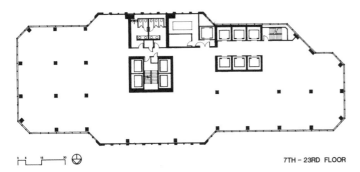

7TH – 23RD FLOOR

46TH – 59TH FLOOR

373 99 Summer Street; Boston, Massachusetts. Goody, Clancy & Associates, 1986–87. *Photo: © Sam Sweezy.*
Moldings built up of several pieces of thin granite at the cornice lines and curved metal window surrounds painted to
look like granite were used to give the facade a surface depth similar to that of older adjacent buildings.

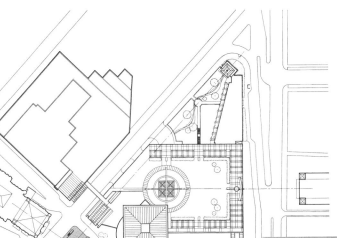

374, 375 St. Paul Companies Headquarters; St. Paul, Minnesota. Kohn Pedersen Fox, 1987–91. *Photo: Don F. Wong.*

[SITE PLAN] Sited on a triangular space that results from a shift in the St. Paul city grid, the complex takes the form of a "community of pieces" rather than a single monolithic structure.

[EXTERIOR] The stone sheathing is detailed and articulated so as to relate to the scale and materials of the surrounding buildings.

376 712 Fifth Avenue; New York, New York. Kohn Pedersen Fox, 1985–91. *Photo: © Cervin Robinson.* This concrete tube structure has sufficient mass incorporated into the cladding to help to dampen the wind-induced vibration that would otherwise be a problem in a structure of such slender proportions.

8

SHOPPING CENTERS

SHOPPING
CENTERS

The artful display of luxury goods in the late-nineteenth-century department store and shopping arcade encouraged the growing middle class to indulge in shopping as a social, leisure-time activity. By the late twentieth century, the American shopping center had practically transformed purchasing into a religious rite. The highway network, the move to suburbia, rising expectations for living standards, easy credit, and the synergy between real estate speculation and mass distribution of consumer goods made it inevitable. "The central sacrament of consumerism is the purchase, its daily ritual is entertainment, and its scripture is advertising," wrote anthropologist Peter Stromberg. As if buying were a proof of individual devotion, today's Americans acquire more goods than any people at any time in history.

Shopping center developers measure distance in driving time, not miles. Just as historic land development was focused on crossroads, canals, and railroad stations, this century's land-use pattern has been determined by a roadscape of limited-access highways that ease sixty-mile-per-hour travel while providing long, uninterrupted views of the shopping center.

Today, with more than ninety percent of households owning at least one car, America has near-total freedom of the road. Shopping centers have spread over farmlands even before housing or industry. "The metropolis is almost everywhere," reported geographer Peirce Lewis. Some 2,900 shopping centers had been built by 1958; 7,100 by 1963; 22,000 by 1980; almost 38,000 by 1990.

THE SHOPPING CENTER INDUSTRY

The rocket-fast takeoff of the shopping center was engineered by sophisticated investment strategies combining market research, finance, design, leasing, and management. The professionalization of the shopping center industry was assisted by its trade association, the Urban Land Institute, and the advice of the practice manual *Shopping Towns U.S.A.* (1960), written by architect and planner Victor Gruen, who practically perfected the concept.

Shopping centers have been based on the simple principle of the symbiosis between "anchors"—typically, the department store that is the shopper's principal destination—and the smaller specialty stores that tempt the shopper to make impulse purchases as he or she walks by. The anchor's good credit rating earns financing (mainly investments from pension funds and insurance companies) for the entire project. The anchors have to pay for advertising and promotion, but they get the right to influence the mix of specialty shops and how the center is operated, and they benefit from favorable rents. Specialty stores add variety to the range of merchandise, and they provide the developer with his or her margin of profit. Though periodic down cycles force developers to keep scrambling, it's also true that shopping center development has been one of the most lucrative, surefire investments ever.

The shopping center developer may be a department store owner, professional land speculator, or institutional investor, but his or her role is the same—to direct a cast of lawyers, surveyors, lobbyists, economists, engineers, investors, bankers, architects, leasing experts, retailers, and managers in the drama of turning cheap raw land into a money mill. "There are men in America who, on perceiving a green field or a meadow, begin to slaver at the gills, and like Uriah Heep, start washing their hands in invisible soap at the contemplation—nay, at the beatific vision—of a glorious development at the site," the English anthropologist Ashley Montagu wrote home in 1967. It's been said that only fifteen developers have built ninety percent of all the regional shopping centers—an accomplishment that surely makes the Simons, Taubmans, and De Bartolos the Caesars, Medicis, and Haussmanns of the age.

The success of chains such as Sears, Roebuck and Co. and A&P in the early decades of the century prophesied big future changes in America's buying habits, but surely not the near-obsolescence of downtown as chain operators began to buy up local department stores and, encouraged by favorable lending terms, move them to suburbia. Specialty shops followed, leaving civic leaders helpless to stem urban decline. By the early seventies, as much as eighty percent of the total corporate sales of retailing giants such as Broadway-Hale, Allied, May, and Federated companies took place in the suburbs.

A highly competitive market has forced retailing's concentration in national corporations whose very survival depends on territorial expansion—not halted by the energy crisis, stricter environmental controls, the overbuilding of the eighties, nor competition from catalog and electronic shopping. Developers are foraying into smaller market niches, new retailing techniques, repositioned older facilities. Shopping is conflated with sports, entertainment, dining, and socializing. There are specialty centers for the high end of the market, discount "power centers" for the budget-conscious, mini-malls for neighborhood conveniences. In league with a dispersing population, shopping center developers are roaming ever farther from established city centers. But they are also coming back downtown again, assisted by sweet deals offered by eager city fathers and hailed as the saviors of the very towns and cities they helped to destroy.

SUBURBS

STRIP

A car-based segment of Main Street displaced to the suburbs, the strip center enjoyed its heyday in the 1950s and 1960s. According to shopping center industry standards, the *neighborhood strip center* ranged from 50,000 to 100,000 square feet in size—typically, comprising a single supermarket anchor and a lineup of some ten to thirty smaller stores for convenience goods and personal services such as dry cleaning and shoe repair. The *community strip center* served several neighborhoods with two to three times that number of stores, typically anchored by a department store as well as a supermarket, on a spread of 150,000 to 400,000 square feet. An optimal parking ratio counted on three to four spaces for each thousand square feet of leased area.

An architecturally unified group of stores built in Baltimore's Roland Park in 1907 was the nation's first planned strip center. Dating from the twenties and thirties, shopping centers in Shaker Heights (Cleveland), Glen Oaks (Long Island), and Greenbelt (Maryland) hinted at an urbane future—perhaps the shopping center could help to focus the amorphous suburb, or encourage walking in the suburbs and not just driving.

By the fifties it was clear, instead, that the shopping center would develop as a stand-alone commercial development without regard to issues of urbanism. One of the more sophisticated designs was the c. 1950 Great Neck, New York, shopping center (figure 377) by Lathrop Douglas. The bold, unified design distinguished it from the usual mix of Main Street shops, projected a progressive image, and was cheap and easy to build.

Enjoying modest prosperity through the sixties and seventies, the strip center started a growth spurt in the eighties and nineties, now dressed in Postmodernist ''style,'' and embellished with landscape amenities—perhaps even including a noncommercial tenant or two, such as a library or day-care center.

377 Great Neck Shopping Center; Great Neck, New York. Lathrop Douglas, c. 1950. *Photo: Gottscho–Schleisner Collection, Library of Congress.* The layout of the strip center encourages impulse buying at the small specialty stores as shoppers head to their department store destination—creating the synergy that has made the shopping center one of the best investments ever. The parking lot itself advertises the availability of convenient parking.

CAMPUS

The concept of an entire freestanding shopping district, pioneered in the early 1920s by Country Club Plaza in Kansas City, Missouri, was developed further in the thirties and forties. In 1950, Northgate, brainchild of the architect John Graham and the nation's first regional center, created a new "Main Street" some twenty miles from downtown Seattle. A close follower was Shoppers' World, by Ketchum, Giná & Sharp, in Framingham, a Boston suburb, notable for the landscaped lawn at its center. The first generation of postwar shopping centers looked to both these trendsetters in developing a concept of the shopping center as a car-free, suburbanized setting, more like a campus than a downtown.

Proliferating with extraordinary rapidity, the *campus shopping center* was regional in scale, occupying from 300,000 to 850,000 square feet, composed of one or two full-line department stores as anchors and a lineup of eighty or more specialty shops offering depth and variety of merchandise. It typically excluded secondhand stores, five-and-tens, liquor stores, movie houses, and restaurants.

Like Northgate and Shoppers' World, most early shopping center campuses have since been razed or remodeled beyond recognition. One landmark shopping center that has survived as "bones" for subsequent redevelopment is the 1954 Northland Shopping Center (figures 378, 379, 380) in suburban Detroit, designed by Victor Gruen Associates. Gruen used a "market town" version of the Main Street paradigm, with a relatively tight cluster of smaller shops around a central department store. Landscaped pedestrian areas evoked plazas, malls, lanes, and arcades that relieved the commercial atmosphere. The model of a landscaped campus also inspired Welton Becket Associates' Century City (1964) in Los Angeles, planned around two anchors surrounded by a grid of smaller stores. It remains largely as it was, except for a food court added in the early 1980s. Designed by the same architects in 1966, but subsequently greatly enlarged, is Fashion Island at Irvine Ranch, Newport Beach, California, which creates a leisurely outdoor experience around a series of staggered courts.

378, 379, 380 Northland
Shopping Center; Detroit, Michigan.
Victor Gruen Associates, 1954.
*Photos: Michael Honos [aerial view];
Photograph House [exterior].*

[AERIAL VIEW] The size of the project
alone assures visibility from the
highway, where easy approach roads
do more to attract the shopper than
storefront displays.

[SITE PLAN] The center consists of a relatively tight cluster of specialty
shops surrounding a large department store. Pedestrian areas evoke
plazas, malls, lanes, and arcades.

[EXTERIOR] The car relegated to the exterior parking lot, the shopper
enjoys a suburbanized pedestrian setting.

MALL

In 1956 President Dwight David Eisenhower won a second term in office, commercial jet travel began, Elvis reigned, and Disneyland opened. That same year saw the inauguration of the nation's first enclosed shopping center, Southdale, in Edina, a Minneapolis suburb. This entirely new North American building type rapidly became known as the "mall"—an irony, to be sure, since the term as coined in eighteenth-century London described a popular grassy strip in the heart of the city.

Designed by Victor Gruen Associates, the Southdale regional shopping center (figures 381, 382) enclosed an unheard-of half-million-square-foot expanse, representing a technological tour de force in terms of construction efficiency and air-handling design. More amazing, perhaps, from the shopper's point of view, was its extraordinarily exuberant setting. Surely drawing on the architect's youthful experience in the theater, the block-long, three-story-high, skylit space was filled with tropical plants, bright color and lights, sparkling fountains, mosaic murals, kinetic sculpture, and eighty canaries in a tall cage. Visitors could entrust the children to supervised play, relax at a European-style café, view exhibits, and enjoy fashion shows and musical performances.

The enclosed shopping mall proliferated even more rapidly than had the shopping campus. The "dumbbell" form, resulting from the narrowing of the central axis between the two department store anchors, was generally around six hundred feet long—the maximum distance the shopper seemed willing to walk from one department store to the next. The aisle had to be narrow enough to allow the customer to view the display of merchandise on both sides, but not so tight as to make the shopper feel constrained. A taller, wider, brighter courtyard space opened up the center and possibly the entrance areas. Banners, art, signage, and plantings softened the spare Modernist interior.

The sixties saw greater size, as much as 850,000 square feet, in designs that bent the dumbbell into zigzags, pinwheels, and X and T configurations, with periodic courts or plazas that seemed to shorten walking distances, relieve the fatigue of shopping, and encourage the shopper to stay longer—and buy more. Completed in 1965 to the design of Harwell & Hamilton five miles north of downtown Dallas, Texas, Northpark Shopping Center (figures 383, 384) is L-shaped, with generous parking-lot landscaping and indoor sculpture that add to its amenity. Introduced in the early sixties at Paramus Park Shopping Center (figure 385) in New Jersey, designed by RTKL, the food court's array of fast-food outlets sharing common tables and chairs became an increasingly important feature of the mall, eventually as powerful a magnet as a department store.

In the seventies the formula stretched to superregional centers of 1.5 million square feet and more. The record-breaking 1971 Woodfield Mall in Schaumburg, Illinois, by Peter M. Tsolinas, Larsen-Wulf, and Charles Luckman encompassed some 2 million square feet, four anchors, and more than two hundred tenant stores. An exuberant central court was shaped by cutaway openings to mezzanine spaces, diagonal ramps, a sunken amphitheater, undulating storefronts, and shaped ceilings.

Cruising the mall is certainly not the same as

strolling on Main Street: broadened sight lines open provocative views of abundant merchandise arrays—and create tantalizing uncertainty about where and how far you'll have to walk. Rich materials, reflective surfaces, and the dynamism of moving elevators and escalators, changing light levels, and the parade of fellow shoppers create an intensely interiorized experience.

Dramatizing what seems to be public space (that is, nonselling space, but still private property, as are all malls), Stratford Square (figures 386, 387, 388) was designed by RTKL and completed in 1981 in Bloomington, Illinois. A lofty court at a midpoint bend of the dumbbell created a grandiose atrium focused on a nineteen-foot-high, seventy-foot-long waterfall. Reflecting the trend to add food and fun to the mix, the mall included ten full-service restaurants, nine specialty food shops, and four cinemas. Malls such as Cherry Creek in Denver, Fox Hills in Los Angeles, and Eastridge in San Jose added variations to the theme. An alternative to dumbbell and centralized plans, the galleria scheme became popular in the eighties. In a farm field at a highway interchange, the 1988 Bridgewater Commons (figure 389) in New Jersey was designed by Anthony Belluschi Associates with a straight and narrow plan that provides clear sight lines down the length and width of the mall.

The eighties and nineties pitched to new and unusual tenant mixes, discount pricing, and tourist and recreational markets, producing a variety of mall hybrids, some giant, others almost dwarf. Totaling 4.2 million square feet with more than eight hundred specialty stores, the Mall of America, completed in 1990 to designs by Hammel Green & Abramson and Korunsky Krank Erickson Architects based on schematics by the Jerde Partnership, forms a square doughnut on four levels with a seven-acre amusement park filling the center. Landscaping, signage, and decor create make-believe places such as South Avenue, West Market, Theater District, and Upper East Side. This is fantasy urbanism in the far-out suburbs—but at the scale of a real city. At the giant Sawgrass Mills (figures 390, 391) the dumbbell seems to explode into multiple segments along a half-mile path. Built in 1990 in Sunrise, Florida, to the high-style designs of Arquitectonica, the mall is fronted by extravagantly styled entrances that hail busloads of tourists from the U.S. and beyond—Asia, South America, and Europe. Main Street has joined the global economy.

381, 382 Southdale Regional Shopping Center; Edina, Minnesota. Victor Gruen Associates, 1956 (partially restored, 1995). *Photos: Chester Freden [exterior]; Warren Reynolds, Infinity, Inc. [interior].*

[EXTERIOR] Virtually blank-faced, the department store anchors assert their bulk and shape in order to be clearly visible to the passing driver. In this center, the underground garage reduces the spread of the parking lot and the distance that shoppers must walk to reach the stores.

[INTERIOR] The central court, located midway between the two department store anchors, forms an interior, two-level "Main Street." Gruen intended the skylights to provide psychological relief from the intensity of the indoor shopping experience.

383, 384 Northpark Shopping Center; Dallas, Texas. Harwell & Hamilton, 1965. *Photos: Ezra Stoller, © Esto.*

[EXTERIOR] Aiding management and security, the limited number of entrances strictly controls the way the shopper circulates through the center.

[INTERIOR] The "public" spaces, organized into courts and plazas of varying widths and heights, are improved by landscaping and a sophisticated mix of natural and artificial light.

385 Paramus Park Shopping Center; Paramus, New Jersey. RTKL, c. 1962. *Photo: Whitcomb/RTKL.* Spatial drama adds to the drawing power of the second-level glass-roofed food court.

386, 387, 388 Stratford Square; Bloomington, Illinois. RTKL, 1981. *Photos: B. Glinn.*

[SITE PLAN] Built on a ninety-six-acre farmland site, the centralized plan intended for an eventual six anchors comprises a series of shortened corridors that join in tall, wide atrium spaces.

[EXTERIOR] Landscaping effects a seamless transition from the shopper's personal automobile to the private world of the mall.

[INTERIOR] A parade of red oak and concrete columns, granite floor tiles, and skylights makes "architecture" out of the plain mall space.

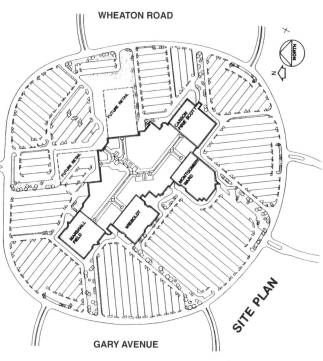

389 Bridgewater Commons; Bridgewater, New Jersey. Anthony Belluschi Associates, 1988. *Photo: Greg Hursley.* To attract specific markets—upscale, popular, and youth—each level of the mall is differentiated by different style, material, and color.

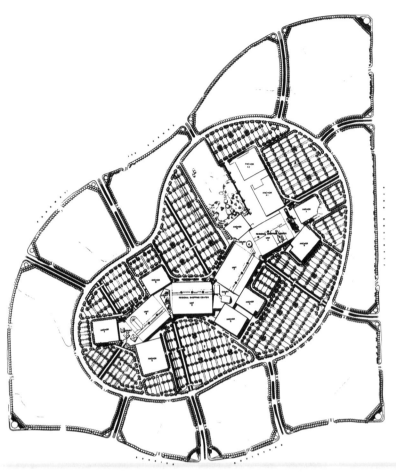

390, 391 Sawgrass Mills; Sunrise, Florida. Arquitectonica, 1990. *Photo: Patricia Fisher.*

[SITE PLAN] Seven (potentially ten) anchors are aligned as a series of dumbbells, each in its own fanciful architectural garb—Modern, Mediterranean, Art Deco, and Caribbean.

[EXTERIOR] Exuberant shapes set the customer's mood.

MUTABLE MALL

Very few malls are to be found in their original condition—a "here today, gone tomorrow" situation inherent to the trend-driven retail industry. So pervasive is the practice of renovation that mall maven William Kowinski, author of *The Malling of America*, speculates that "archeomallology" may become an academic specialty. Surely the trained archeomallologist will observe many layers of history. Cool Modernist tendencies of the fifties and early sixties are visible in bland rectangular geometries, low background lighting, white and primary colors, controlled graphics, simple structural elements, and open store fronts. The emotionality of the later sixties and the seventies is vivid in articulated volumes, diagonal alignments, exploded spaces, dramatic spotlighting, supergraphics, vivid earth colors, and reflective surfaces. The inclusiveness of the eighties and nineties is reflected by high light levels, a lighter color palette, and old-time Main Street imagery.

Changes over time are also to be noted. The mall commonly expanded from a half-million square feet to a million and a half square feet or more, and from one to two to three or four stories. The addition of department store anchors forced a simple, predictable geometry to become irregular and agglomerative. Columbia Mall (figures 392, 393) in Columbia, Maryland,

by Cope Linder Associates, built in 1971 and enlarged in 1981, illustrates this tendency. To the classic dumbbell shape, the second phase added a third major department store at a skewed angle, articulated by a court space whose geometry reflects the additive process.

One vivid example of the relentlessness of change is the transformation of Northgate, the first of the modern regional shopping centers. A single-department-store, open-air center at its inception in 1950, it was enlarged by another department store and covered by a protective sky shield in 1965, expanded by a third department store and fully enclosed in 1975, embellished with a new front facing the highway in 1979, and surrounded by an office park development in the 1980s. Not every change is so total. The 1980s remodeling of the 1960s SmithHaven Mall in Smithtown, Long Island, was handled conservatively enough to retain many original features, preserving the mall's original "meat-and-potatoes" identity. Town Center at Boca Raton, Florida, a classic 1980s three-anchor zigzag dumbbell was virtually doubled in a 1986 expansion that added three anchors and a grander food court. The 1950 Stonetown Mall outside of San Francisco reached a more affluent clientele with a 1990s renovation that turned it into the Stonetown Galleria.

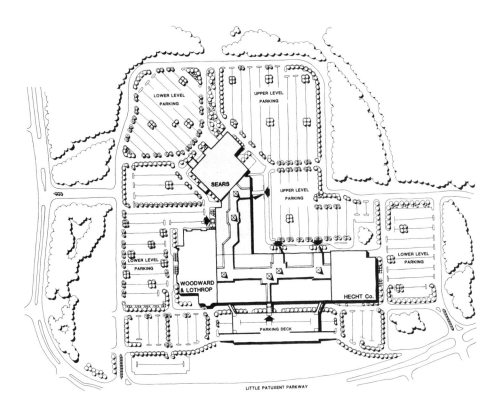

LITTLE PATUXENT PARKWAY

392, 393 Columbia Mall; Columbia, Maryland. Cope Linder Associates, 1971 and 1981. *Photo: © Norman McGrath.*

[SITE PLAN] The additional anchor (the Sears store at the upper left) transforms the predictable geometry of the dumbbell center.

[INTERIOR] The encounter with exploded space, dramatic skylighting, kinetic art, fountains, moving escalators, and the relaxed behavior of fellow visitors puts the visitor into the shopping mode.

TOWNS AND CITIES

FESTIVAL MARKETPLACE

"The meat-and-potatoes of shopping development is still in the suburbs, but the caviar may well be in urban areas," the trade journal *Chain Store Age* predicted in 1967. Undaunted by prevailing pessimism about American cities, some adventurous retailers recognized growing urban markets for luxury goods and products that provide aesthetic appeal and personal satisfaction among sophisticated suburbanites, returning empty-nesters, and "yuppies."

This trend was behind the entirely new kind of festival marketplace that first appeared in the casual, entrepreneurial atmosphere of San Francisco's north end waterfront. Ghirardelli Square by Wurster, Bernardi & Emmons, originally a square-block assortment of motley brick industrial buildings dating from 1865 to 1905, was utterly transformed in 1964 into a fantasy leisure-time environment. Dirty old brick was scraped clean, enticing shoppers to explore the complex's odd nooks, unexpected spaces, and multiple levels, all enlivened by a fountain, plantings, decorative lighting, arty signage, creative restaurants, craft shops, fashion boutiques, innovative displays, and unique product lines. Nearby, The Cannery project (figure 394), completed in 1969 by Esherick, Homsey Dodge & Davis, accomplished a similar transformation of a late-nineteenth-century industrial building into an intriguing setting for leisure-time shopping and socializing.

Salt Lake City's Trolley Square, a festival marketplace in a converted trolley shed, was one among a string of community-backed rehabilitation projects that proved the business sense of heritage tourism. For the developer, federal tax incentives for historic preservation made reusing old buildings profitable. For the entire family, the mixture of shopping and sightseeing provided a taste of nostalgia, the aroma of exotic fast food, and, always, the temptation to spend, spend, spend.

Influenced by the successful practices of Disneyland, developer James Rouse stirred a good measure of management into the mix at Faneuil Hall Marketplace (figures 395, 396). Completed in 1976 on the Boston waterfront to the design of Benjamin Thompson & Associates, the project revitalized the early-nineteenth-century Quincy Hall as a specialty center emphasizing high quality food and craft items. Abundantly decorated with banners, lighting, signs, and attractive displays, it aimed at the festive atmosphere that encourages impulse buying. Creating a pristine and parklike setting enhanced by decorative street furnishings, the project also redeveloped two ranks of flanking warehouses for all manner of luxury shops.

Festival marketplaces grew like boomtowns. "Half-way houses for people from the car culture who are trying to love cities again," according to critic Robert Campbell, some occupied renovated historic industrial buildings, while others were built as new facilities with an old-time flavor. Benjamin Thompson & Associates collaborated with James Rouse on several: Baltimore's Harborplace (1980), New York City's South Street Seaport (1983–85), Jacksonville Landing (1987), and Miami's Bayside Marketplace (1987) (figures 397, 398). The genre proliferated in New Orleans, Chicago, Flint, Battle Creek, Richmond, Toledo, and elsewhere.

Surely, one of the most impressive—if at first improbable—festival marketplaces is the one built into the renovated Union Station (figures 399, 400) in Washington, D.C. A grand 1908 civic monument inspired by ancient Roman baths, it was renovated in 1988 by Benjamin Thompson & Associates and Harry Weese & Associates. Taking advantage of the building's continued use as a train station, the project put restaurants, boutiques, and retail stores wherever foot traffic passes by. A far cry from the dumbbell mall.

394 The Cannery; San Francisco, California. Esherick, Homsey Dodge & Davis, 1969. *Photo: Kathleen Kershaw and Peter Dodge.* A setting that sells history together with housewares, teddy bears, and T-shirts.

395, 396 Faneuil Hall Marketplace; Boston, Massachusetts. Benjamin Thompson & Associates, 1976. *Photo: © Steve Rosenthal.*

[RENDERING] Without the usual department store anchors, the project exploits the historic structures themselves as attractions. Taking the place of shed additions casually added over time, modern glass-enclosed wings provide efficient selling and restaurant space.

[INTERIOR—ROTUNDA] Scraped brick walls and a cut into the upper floor reveal layers of history to today's shopper.

397, 398 Bayside Marketplace; Miami, Florida. Benjamin Thompson & Associates, 1987. *Photo: © Steve Rosenthal.*

[SITE PLAN] Divided into seven different structures, the marketplace is scaled to the waterfront site and the nearby neighborhood.

[ARCADE] The experience of strolling encompasses views of other shoppers, the harbor, the colorful "native" setting, and, most of all—things to buy.

399, 400 Union Station; Washington, D.C. Benjamin Thompson & Associates and Harry Weese & Associates, 1988. *Photo: © Steve Rosenthal.*

[INTERIOR] A celebratory space as well as a through passage to trains, the old main hall of the historic railroad terminal is fitted with a two-level center kiosk providing visitor services and a café.

[SECTION] Left to right: columned entry, main hall, concourse, tracks, and platforms. Sweeping stairways in the concourse connect the main level with a new mezzanine. Below-grade space provides an additional sales area and connects to the D.C. Metro.

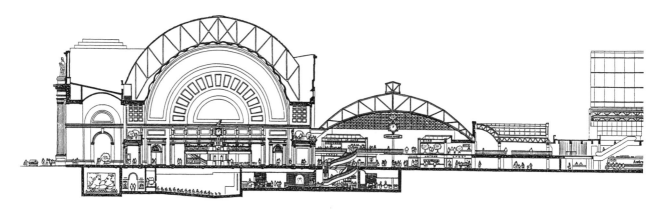

MODIFIED MALL

In the fifties and sixties "location, location, location," determined that the developer would site the shopping center in the suburbs. By the seventies a new set of criteria influenced the choice in favor of a downtown site: ecology, energy, and expense. Availability of vacant urban renewal land parcels and new downtown access roads were additional reasons for bringing the mall back downtown.

Struggling cities such as New Haven, New Rochelle, Buffalo, Sacramento, and San Bernardino were challenged by doubting bankers and department store operators who insisted that downtown malls had to almost duplicate the car-oriented, horizontally spread out, monolithic suburban mall. Plain and bulky, those malls showed scant consideration for the variety of architectural features that enliven the traditional city street wall, nor did they respect the lively sidewalk experience created by varied uses—windows to shop, walkers to observe, and frequent doorways to enter. A late example was Columbus City Center (figure 401) in Ohio built in 1989 to the designs of Brown/McDaniel. This giant takes up almost an entire superblock right in the center of downtown.

By the mid-seventies, rising interest in downtowns encouraged higher land values and taller buildings. One project that anticipated the trend was the 1967–77 ZCMI Center (figures 402, 403) by Victor Gruen Associates. On the main street of Salt Lake City, Utah, it wove a tall office building and a two-story mall into the web of existing buildings. Certain typical configurations have been encouraged by zoning laws, such as those stipulating greater height on wider streets and lower height on narrower streets. Consequently, we see the pairing of tall and low elements at downtown Los Angeles's Broadway Plaza (figure 404), designed by The Luckman Partnership and completed in 1973.

Growing appreciation for urban form has influenced the way the mall meets the city street. A small-town feeling is maintained by the tight configuration of the 1989 Deerpath Plaza Shopping Center (figure 405) in Lake Forest, Illinois. Designed by Nagle, Hartray & Associates, the project is divided into two main buildings, one coming right up to the public sidewalk, the other—with a masonry arcade providing cover for ground-floor shops—set back to create a grassy plaza. Configuring the mall as more urban than suburban, the great arched portal of the 1985 St. Louis Center in Missouri (figures 406, 407), by RTKL, added a strong presence to the streetscape. The multi-block scale of the Embarcadero Center (figure 408) in the Golden Gate Redevelopment parcel in San Francisco is distinctive. Inserted into a modernized and expanded city grid, shops and service establishments occupy the first three floors of four high-rise office towers that are linked to each other and to the hotels that anchor the project by a series of walkways and promenades at the street and upper levels. Designed by John Portman & Associates, the project was substantially built between 1968 and 1981.

The mall-in-the-megastructure reflected new municipal policies intended to encourage a mix of residential, office, hotel, and retail activity. The scheme was welcomed by city movers and shakers who imagined twenty-four-hour-a-day vitality, as well as by real estate developers who anticipated lower risk and higher profit. The landmark project was Water Tower Place (figures 409, 410) of 1976 in Chicago, Illinois, by Loebl, Schlossman, Dart & Hackl with C. F. Murphy Associates, an eight-level mall at the base of a seventy-four-story tower occupying an entire city block. Two department store anchors are interlocked so that each can claim a traditional streetfront entrance on the Michigan Avenue sidewalk, permitting offices, theaters, restaurants, apartments, parking, and hotel to cohabit on the remainder of the site. Like Water Tower Place, Manhattan's Trump Plaza (figure 411), has a dramatic, multistory central atrium at the base of a giant office-residential tower. However, rather than being self-contained, the atrium links the walker to adjacent properties, providing a glamorous alternative to the traditional sidewalk—if possibly threatening to rob it of its vitality.

Fresh appreciation for the scale and texture of the city street is apparent in the latest generation of downtown malls. In Minneapolis, Minnesota, guided by the city's traditional sidewalk alignment, Gaviidae Commons of 1986–89 by Cesar Pelli & Associates encompasses a shopping mall side by side with a department store. The street elevation is enriched by a turreted entrance, wide expanses of windows, intricate masonry details, and an impressive glass-and-bronze entry. The 1988 San Francisco Shopping Center, designed by Whisler-Patri Architects, fits comfortably into the city streetscape. Its eight-story facade is windowed just like old-fashioned department stores, and the top three levels are stepped back to reduce bulk on the street. Fitting the mall to the city, not vice versa, the single department store anchor occupies the top four levels of the mall, served by dramatic spiraling escalators in the central atrium that encourage the vertical movement of shoppers past the specialty stores.

Frequent shop windows visually join the shopping center to the life of the sidewalk at the 1984–87 The Shops at Liberty Place (figure 412) in Philadelphia, occupying a three-story podium of a tower designed by Murphy/Jahn. Like most malls, however, this one has limited direct connections to the sidewalk, confining the shopper to an interiorized experience.

Urbanism itself has become the theme of certain shopping malls. It takes a leap into fantasy at the 1985 Horton Plaza (figures 413, 414), which comprises a six-block district in downtown San Diego, California. Designed by Jerde Partnership, the project encompasses more than one million square feet of retail space, a hotel, offices, cinemas, and, more recently, even an apartment house. Partly walled off from an adjacent nineteenth-century historic district by multilevel parking garages on one side, the shopping center presents a spectacular face to the entering pedestrian on the other.

Other projects respond to the hard realities of climate and culture. Completed in 1990, The Shops at Arizona Center (figures 415, 416) in Phoenix, Arizona, observes the city's block-by-block pattern of development, the tradition of the Spanish plaza, and the heat and aridity of the locale. Designed by ELS/Elbasani & Logan, the center encompasses office buildings and a shopping center around lushly landscaped gardens.

Symbol of the consumer society, the historic glass-enclosed shopping arcade known as the galleria has been yet another source of inspiration. On a four-block site at the heart of Milwaukee, Wisconsin, The Grand Avenue (figures 417, 418, 419) retains an historic arcade as part of a new, 1100-foot-long, three-story spine connecting six buildings, including two older department stores. Completed in 1983 to the designs of ELS/Elbasani & Logan, the project opens to the city's main shopping avenue as well as several cross streets. In the case of Urban Design Group's 1985 Tabor Center (figures 420, 421) in Denver, Colorado, an entirely new galleria was developed. It was designed to reaffirm the continuity of the city's traditional shopping street, which was redeveloped in the eighties to encourage walking and use of public buses.

Cities everywhere have begun to address issues of urbanity, individuality, and identity. Observing the tradition that considers urban density a virtue, RTKL's 1990 Fashion Center at Pentagon City, a stop on the D.C. Metro, wedges a shopping mall, two department store anchors, a hotel, and an office building on a very constricted site. The exterior resembles a typical 1930s department store, while the interior creates an exotic tropical world in a four-story greenhouse space. The 1990 Two Rodeo Drive (figure 422) in Beverly Hills, California, by Kaplan McLaughlin Diaz, attempts to enrich rather than diminish the pedestrian's enjoyment of the street, providing small scale and rich architectural detailing. New amenities enhance the urban setting at the 1991 CambridgeSide Galleria (figure 423) in the small industrial city of Cambridge, Massachusetts. Designed by Arrowstreet Architects to respect the traditional New England streetscape, the project shows a detailed brick-and-stone facade to the public sidewalk. A food court at the rear, opening to a scenic canal view, brings the shopper into contact with the out-of-doors.

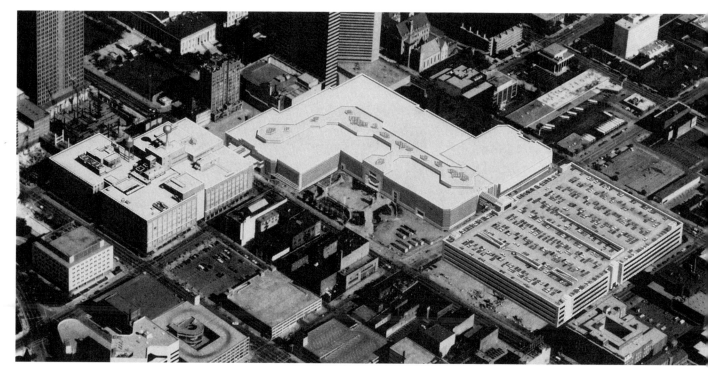

401 Columbus City Center; Columbus, Ohio. Brown/McDaniel, 1989. The in-town mall and its connected garage imprint the city with suburban land-use patterns.

402, 403 ZCMI Center; Salt Lake City, Utah. Victor Gruen Associates, 1967–77. *Photos: Hal Rumel Studios.*

[EXTERIOR] Incorporating several existing buildings at the corners of the block, the shopping center adds a two-level mall containing some sixty-five retail shops as infill, plus a new nineteen-story office building.

[INTERIOR] An indoor street roofed over by an illuminated ceiling.

404 Broadway Plaza; Los Angeles, California. The Luckman Partnership, 1973. *Photo: Balthazar Korab.* With a department store and hotel as anchors, the complex encompasses a two-level shopping plaza and parking garage. Repetitive setbacks on the street facade evoke the frequent doorways that one encounters on the traditional city street, although the project is actually quite self-contained.

405 Deerpath Plaza Shopping Center; Lake Forest, Illinois. Nagle, Hartray & Associates, 1989. *Photo: Hedrich-Blessing.* The clock tower serves as the pivot between the main-street and side-street parts of the project, adding a memorable feature to the townscape. Steep roof slopes, projecting bays, and brick and stucco walls allude to the style of an historic building several blocks away.

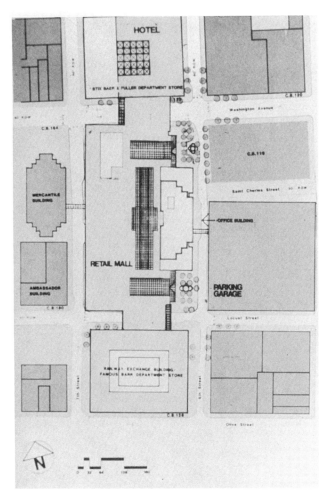

406, 407   St. Louis Center; St. Louis, Missouri. RTKL, 1985.
Photo: Scott McDonald.

[SITE PLAN] The mall, serving as the podium for an office building, is connected by bridges to nearby buildings.

[EXTERIOR] Set back from the sidewalk to create an open plaza, the mall is styled as a luxuriant atrium.

408 Embarcadero Center; San Francisco, California. John Portman & Associates, 1968–81. *Photo: © Timothy Hursley.* As at New York's pioneering Rockefeller Center, the design ties several shopping levels into the city sidewalks.

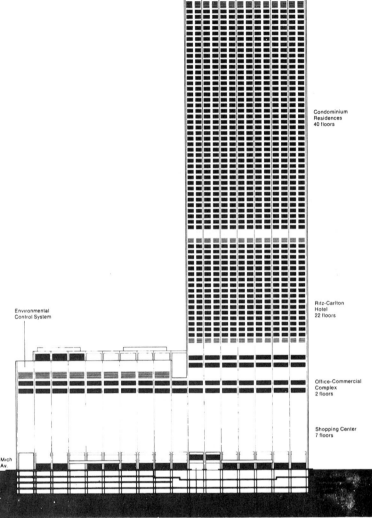

409, 410 Water Tower Place; Chicago, Illinois. Loebl, Schlossman, Dart & Hackl with C. F. Murphy Associates, 1976. *Photo: David Clifton.*

[SECTION] The tower stacks an office-commercial complex, a hotel, and condominium residences.

[EXTERIOR] The mall's street-level windows help to enliven the sidewalk.

411 Trump Plaza; New York, New York. Swanke Hayden Connell, 1983. *Photo: Jaime Ardiles–Arce.* A fantasy world of dancing lights, splashing fountains, glowing marble, and shiny brass, the atrium is a tourist attraction in its own right.

412 Shops at Liberty Place; Philadelphia, Pennsylvania. Murphy/Jahn, 1984–87. *Photo: Lawrence S. Williams.* The bays on the three-story retail podium preserve the continuity of the traditional streetscape. A shopping mall, rather than individual stores, it can be entered at only a limited number of points.

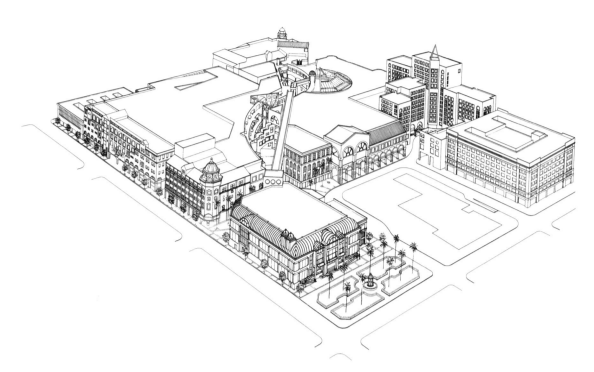

413, 414 Horton Plaza; San Diego, California. Jerde Partnership, 1985. *Photo: Stephen Simpson.*

[AXONOMETRIC] The new shopping center (identified by the large area of the roof) is slipped in behind the traditional facades of older buildings.

[EXTERIOR] Within the center, one experiences the excitement of bold diagonal pathways, fanciful architectural motifs, and a riot of color.

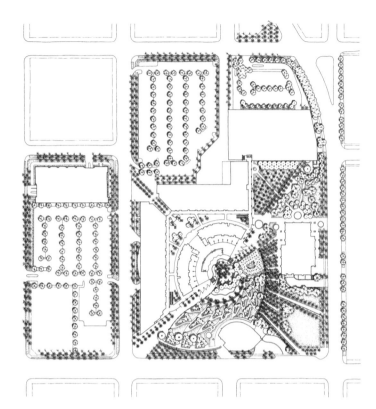

415, 416   The Shops at Arizona Center; Phoenix, Arizona. ELS/Elbasani & Logan, 1990. *Photo: © Timothy Hursley.*

[SITE PLAN] On eight city blocks combined into one superblock, the project includes office buildings, entertainment facilities, parking lots, and crescent-shaped shopping promenades oriented to the lush landscaped setting.

[EXTERIOR] Arizona Center creates an urban oasis.

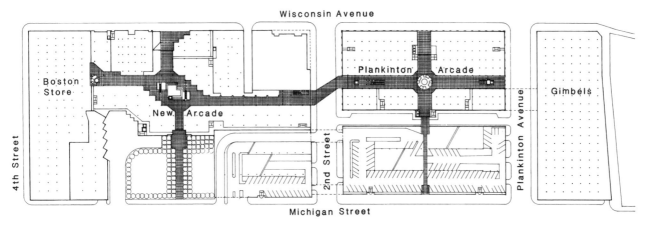

Ground Floor

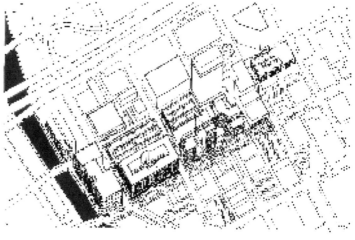

417, 418, 419 The Grand Avenue; Milwaukee, Wisconsin. ELS/Elbasani & Logan, 1983. *Photo: ELS/ Elbasani & Logan.*

[PLAN] A newly configured pedestrian spine links two existing department stores and an historic retail arcade.

[AXONOMETRIC] Various connections link the complex to the public street, parking lots, garages, and convention and performing arts centers.

[INTERIOR] The historic arcade established the design vocabulary for the major expansion.

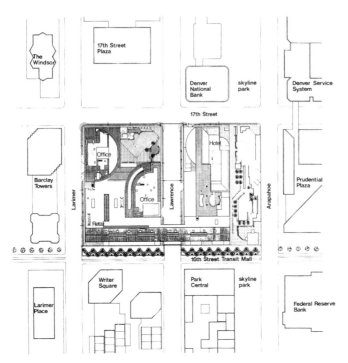

Area Plan
Tabor Center
Denver, Colorado

420, 421   Tabor Center; Denver, Colorado. Urban Design Group, 1985. *Photo: Hooman Aryan.*

[AREA PLAN] In a downtown grid that has been eroded by a series of freestanding buildings in plazas, the tight massing of Tabor Center (facing the 16th Street Transit Mall) reinforces the traditional city sidewalk.

[VIEW] The two-story retail frontage is at a comfortable pedestrian scale, mediating between a tall office structure and the sidewalk. The project includes two office towers and a luxury hotel as well as underground parking.

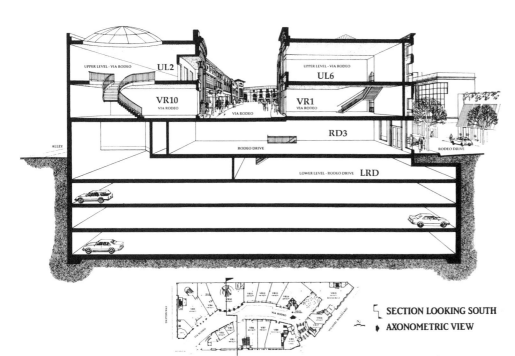

422 Two Rodeo Drive; Beverly Hills, California. Kaplan McLaughlin Diaz, 1990. Served by a common underground garage, the interior of a single block is opened for a multistore development. The central spine evokes a winding medieval hilltop street.

423 CambridgeSide Galleria; Cambridge, Massachusetts. Arrowstreet Architects, 1991. *Photo: Adrian Catalano.* The shopping center's food court and outdoor walkways open to a scenic canal that also serves as an amenity for a developing residential neighborhood.

BETWEEN PLACES

The extraordinary synergy between no-holds-barred real estate speculation and let's-get-it-done road-building programs has launched shopping centers at the amorphous edges of existing cities, farm landscapes, cross-roads settlements, and unattached clumps of office towers, apartment complexes, and ware-houses. Sites such as King of Prussia, Pennsylvania; northwest Dallas; Cherry Creek, Colorado; Research Triangle Park, North Carolina; the interstate in Contra Costa and Orange counties, California; north of Atlanta; west of Chicago; and exurban Washington, D.C., are developing as edge cities, urban villages, technoburbs, and galactic cities. No one knows what to call them, since no one is sure what they are. "Not since more than a century ago, when we took Benjamin Franklin's picturesque mercantile city of Philadelphia and exploded it into a nineteenth-century industrial behemoth, have we made such profound changes in the ways we live, work and play," wrote Joel Garreau, in *Edge City: Life on the New Frontier.* "If the future is Out There," he asked, "will we ever get good at it?"

It surely takes an audacious spirit to plant an urbane galleria on the ragged fringe of a boom-town. The 1970–77 Houston Galleria (figures 424, 425) was built in nondowntown Houston, Texas, thereby sparking a surrounding sub-city that has come to rival downtown itself. Designed by Hellmuth, Obata & Kassabaum, it has a spectacular skating rink that links department store and hotel anchors—paying homage to no less a public landscape than Rockefeller Center. Located at an urbanizing fringe of Dallas, that city's 1982 Dallas Galleria (figure 426), also designed by Hellmuth, Obata & Kas-

sabaum, joins several office buildings and a hotel, all styled with reference to the shopping mall's vaulted form. The scale is bold and big enough to capture the attention of the speeding driver.

Between-place shopping centers are as diverse, varied, and dynamic as the locales they occupy. A shopping center that has endured some three decades of development is South Coast Plaza (1967 on), designed by Victor Gruen Associates, in the edge city of Costa Mesa, south of Los Angeles. Starting as a single stand-alone shopping mall, the development has stretched to three million square feet, now joined with parking for ten thousand cars, several more malls, a cultural center, groups of office buildings, a hotel, and several entertainment complexes. Perhaps the shuttle bus and the viaduct that allows the pedestrian to cross the highway provide some evidence of impending urbanization, but surely the labeling of a little green zone as a "village" and a hotel area as a "town center" has to be counted as wishful thinking.

The manufacture of urbanity, even where there is no city in sight, is a curious trend to note. Corte Madera Town Center (figures 427, 428) in Corte Madera, California, built in 1958 at a highway interchange as a stand-alone, open-air suburban shopping center, was turned into something of a community focus in a 1986 reconstruction by Field Paoli. The addition of a substantial office building at one end and a tall tower in the middle adds a definite public presence. Shop-fronted convenience stores that face the sea of parking spaces at the periphery of the center give the project an unusual degree of extroversion. Outside of Plainsboro, New Jersey,

Main Street features such as real sidewalks, small-town storefronts, second-story offices, and even some curbside parking lend a sense of place to the 1987 Princeton Forrestal Village. Designed by Bower, Lewis, Thrower, this stand-alone shopping center on a highway strip lined by office parks and conference centers seems like some kind of quasi-urban oasis.

The reorganization of the highway strip itself is a phenomenon of the nineties. Look to the stretch of U.S. 1 in Boca Raton, Florida, where the failure of an older enclosed-dumbbell mall provided the opportunity to redevelop another kind of place. An old shopping center on the site having been razed, since 1990 Mizner Park (figure 429) has been developed in several stages toward a stand-alone traditional town. Designed by Cooper, Cary, the project has at its center a landscaped park created by a public-private joint venture.

Fruition of long-range plans has created a downtownlike setting in Reston, Virginia, a planned new town that was completely suburban for the first thirty years of its history. The community now having sufficient density to warrant the development, the 1990 Reston Town Center (figures 430, 431), designed by RTKL, banks on its central location, rather than the formulaic pair of department store anchors, as the draw.

Planned pedestrian communities across the country are intended as future Main Street settings, with mass transit, libraries, museums, post offices, town halls, commercial and government offices, schools, churches, day care, housing, entertainment spots. Are they suburbs by another name, or may we imagine that towns and cities will flourish again in the new millennium?

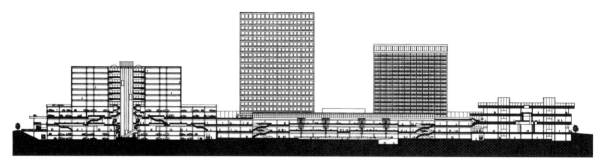

424, 425 Houston Galleria; Houston, Texas. Hellmuth, Obata & Kassabaum, 1970–77. *Photo: George Silk/courtesy of HOK.*

[SECTION] One of the first malls to break with convention by climbing to three levels, the mall is anchored to a department store and hotel.

[INTERIOR] The 620-foot-long mall was trend-setting for its continuous glass-roofed vault, monumental height, abundant natural illumination, and spectacular skating rink in the center. The design distracts from the long distances that the shopper must walk.

426 Dallas Galleria; Dallas, Texas. Hellmuth, Obata & Kassabaum, 1982. *Photo: Courtesy of HOK.* The complex unabashedly celebrates automobility, having highway ramps that enter directly into ample multilevel parking decks that lead to each of the mall's three levels.

427, 428 Corte Madera Town Center; Corte Madera, California. Field Paoli Reconstruction, 1986. *Photo: Marvin Wax.*

[EXTERIOR] Built in a sparsely settled area just off a highway interchange, the stand-alone, open-air shopping center presents an image of urbanity. To encourage leisurely strolling, the design exploits small scale, color, texture, and a wealth of architectural features.

[PLAN] The irregularities of the path configuration are intended to humanize the pedestrian environment.

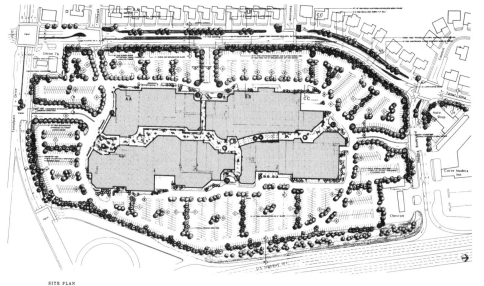

SITE PLAN

429 Mizner Park; Boca Raton, Florida. Cooper, Cary, 1990. *Photo: © Stephen C. Traves, 1988.* Sociably furnished with a fountain, gazebos, and benches, two parallel "avenues" are lined by street-level shops and covered walkways. Apartments are above, and offices are in a separate tower. There is a multilevel parking garage facing the highway.

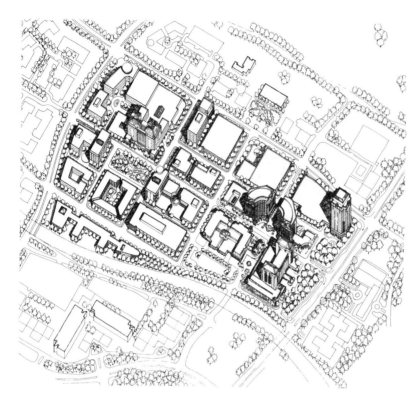

430, 431 Reston Town Center; Reston, Virginia. RTKL, 1990. *Photo: David Whitcomb/RTKL.*

[AXONOMETRIC] The center is mainly out-of-doors, laid out on a traditional grid plan.

[STREET VIEW] The design addresses the diversity characteristic of traditional towns and cities.

POSTSCRIPT: MY TOP TEN

While giving my view of why and how we've built what we've built in America, I've kept my opinions to myself, wanting to set the reader free to form his or her own criteria and judgments. Now, at the end of the book, I am happy for the opportunity to highlight one or more buildings from each category (except—no surprise—public housing and shopping centers), not as "best" architecture, but as buildings that have particular resonance for me.

1. Richard Neutra, Moore House
2. Frank Lloyd Wright, Pope Leighey House

I expect a house to encourage meaningful living, a sense of security, order, comfort, convenience, beauty, and adaptability to change. The design must be appropriate to purpose. Sensational effects of light and space, handsome finishes, and eloquent construction details contribute to livable design, but won't produce it. These two classics of contemporary house design remain outstanding—dignified despite their modesty, inspiring notwithstanding their familiarity. I'm encouraged to think that these criteria might also be satisfied by the works of a growing number of relatively young architects practicing today, such as Fernau and Hartman on the West Coast, William Bruder in the Southwest and Turner Brooks in New England.

3. Paul Rudolph, Orange County Government Center
4. Kallmann, McKinnell & Knowles, Boston City Hall

Aware that the decade of our birth firmly stamps our values and beliefs, I recall that Franklin Delano Roosevelt was the Moses that led my nation to safety when I was in grade school, Harry Truman and Dwight David Eisenhower protected American values during my high school and college days, and John F. Kennedy and Lyndon B. Johnson opened my heart and mind to civic and societal concerns while I was a young mother, stirring an interest in architectural history and historic preservation that has deepened through the decades. I want government to be strong, bold, and progressive, and I expect the government building to dramatize those values.

I was initially drawn to the United Nations headquarters because of its touchingly optimistic Modernist goals, but my selection ended with two confidently expressionistic buildings: Orange County Government Center, whose extraordinarily dynamic and suggestive spaces seem to provide breathing room for all the idealism, energy and creativity of the sixties; and Boston City Hall, whose emphatic physicality asserts the power of government to change society for the better.

359

5. John Russell Pope, National Gallery of Art

6. Louis I. Kahn, Kimbell Museum

As a museum visitor, devoted to a wide range of art, I care deeply about its proper fit with architecture. Because the works of art display to such advantage at John Russell Pope's original building for the National Gallery of Art, I forgive its stuffy classicism in the enjoyment of handsome proportions, gentle illumination, and elegant materials and details. I sometimes have to struggle to come close to the art when I visit Frank Lloyd Wright's magnificent Guggenheim Museum, and although I'm engaged by the bold concept and the exquisite execution of Marcel Breuer's Whitney, it's rare that the art and the building work in concert for me.

Only Louis Kahn's Kimbell Museum provides a perfect aesthetic experience. Its gentle configurations of space, honest sensuality of materials, and extraordinarily eloquent light all work together to make the viewing of art a totally enthralling experience.

7. Eliel Saarinen, Christ Church, Lutheran

8. Eero Saarinen, Kresge Chapel at the Massachusetts Institute of Technology

Neither father (Eliel) nor son (Eero) succeeded in creating a secure place for the unknowable in a nervous society. But both convince me of the seriousness of their purpose and the integrity of their effort, and neither religious edifice passes quickly from memory. The exterior of Eliel's quietly modern Christ Church, Lutheran, struck me for its polite, dignified presence in a residential neighborhood. The inside, for its extraordinarily peaceful atmosphere. By contrast, Eero Saarinen's Kresge Chapel impressed me with its individualism, courage, and confident atavism.

9. Louis I. Kahn, Salk Institute

Sifting through my criteria, I'm intrigued to consider how the very architecture of learning institutions stirs thoughts of why, what, and how we learn. The liberal in me cheers the openness and optimism of The Architects Collaborative's Josiah Quincy School in Boston and Richard Dattner's Intermediate School 218 in New York City, both directed to progressive goals. But my choice settles on Kahn's Salk Institute, a building whose profound discipline and poetic execution seem to me exquisitely attuned to the creative urge in all of us.

10. I. M. Pei & Partners, John Hancock Building

I'm amazed and awed by the supreme technology of the tall building, even while bothered by its disregard for the surrounding street and city. The great classics of the fifties and sixties still enrapture me: undiminished by time are the clarity and elegance of Mies' Seagram Building or the freshness of SOM's Lever House, in Manhattan; as powerful as ever is the frank vigor of SOM's Brunswick and John Hancock buildings, in Chicago. Zeroing in on a choice, I discover that I am most stirred by the ethereal, quixotic beauty of the John Hancock Building in Boston by I. M. Pei & Partners—a building that stirs my admiration for the human capacity to dream the unknown.

I hope that this opens a spirited dialogue among those of us who care deeply about architecture and cities. What's new? What's good? What's not? Please visit me at my website and let me know: www.nyct.net/~rifkind.

RECOMMENDED READING

Contemporary Architecture—General

Alexander, Christopher, et al. *The Oregon Experiment.* New York: Oxford University Press, 1975.

Banham, Reyner. *Age of the Masters: A Personal View of Modern Architecture.* New York: Harper & Row, 1975.

Betsky, Aaron. *Violated Perfection: Architecture and the Fragmentation of the Modern.* New York: Rizzoli, 1990.

Burchard, John, and Albert Bush-Brown. *The Architecture of America: A Social and Cultural History.* Boston: Little, Brown, 1966.

Curtis, William. *Modern Architecture Since 1900,* 2nd ed. New York: Oxford University Press, 1988.

De Long, David G., et al. *American Architecture: Innovation and Tradition.* New York: Rizzoli, 1986.

Diamonstein, Barbaralee. *American Architecture Now.* New York: Rizzoli, 1980.

———. *American Architecture Now II.* New York: Rizzoli, 1985.

Drew, Philip. *Third Generation: The Changing Meaning of American Architecture.* New York: Praeger, 1972.

Drexler, Arthur. *Transformations in Modern Architecture.* New York: Museum of Modern Art, 1979.

Emanuel, Muriel, ed. *Contemporary Architects.* New York: St. Martin's, 1980.

Frampton, Kenneth. *Modern Architecture: A Critical History,* 2nd ed. London: Thames & Hudson, 1985.

Giedion, Sigfried. *A Decade of Contemporary American Architecture.* New York: George Wittenborn, 1954.

———. *Space, Time and Architecture,* 5th ed. Cambridge, Mass.: Harvard University Press, 1967.

Gropius, Walter. *Apollo in the Democracy: The Cultural Obligations of the Architect.* New York: McGraw-Hill, 1968.

Guedes, Pedro. *The MacMillan Encyclopedia of Architecture and Technology.* New York: McGraw-Hill, 1979.

Hall, Peter. *Cities of Tomorrow: An Intellectual History of Urban Planning and Design in the Twentieth Century.* Cambridge: Basil Blackwell, 1988.

Hayes, K. Michael, and Carol Burns, eds. *Thinking the Present: Recent American Architecture.* New York: Princeton Architectural Press, 1990.

Herdeg, Klaus. *The Decorated Diagram: Harvard Architecture and the Failure of the Bauhaus Legacy.* Cambridge, Mass.: MIT Press, 1983.

Heyer, Paul. *American Architecture: Ideas and Ideologies in the Late Twentieth Century.* New York: Van Nostrand Reinhold, 1993.

———. *Architects on Architecture: New Directions in America,* rev. ed. New York: Van Nostrand Reinhold, 1994.

Hitchcock, Henry-Russell, and Arthur Drexler. *Built in U.S.A.: Post War Architecture.* New York: Museum of Modern Art, 1952.

——— and Philip Johnson. *The International Style.* New York: Norton, 1966.

Jackson, Lesley. *Contemporary: Architecture and Interiors of the 1950s.* London: Phaidon, 1994.

Jacobus, John. *Twentieth Century Architecture: The Middle Years 1940–65.* New York: Praeger, 1966.

Jencks, Charles. *Architecture Today,* rev. and enl. ed. New York: Abrams, 1988.

Jordy, William H. *American Buildings and Their Architects: The Impact of European Modernism in the Mid-Twentieth Century.* Garden City, N.Y.: Doubleday, 1976.

Larson, Magali Sarfatti. *Behind the Postmodern Facade: Architectural Change in Late Twentieth Century America.* Berkeley and Los Angeles: University of California Press, 1993.

Macrae-Gibson, Gaven. *The Secret Life of Buildings.* Cambridge, Mass.: MIT Press, 1985.

Marder, Tod A., and Jeffrey Wechsler. *The Critical*

Edge: Controversy in Recent American Architecture. Cambridge, Mass.: MIT Press, 1985.

McCoy, Esther. *The Second Generation.* Salt Lake City: Peregrine Smith, 1984.

—— and Barbara Goldstein. *Guide to U.S. Architecture: 1940–1980.* Santa Monica: Arts + Architecture Press, 1982.

Miller, Naomi, and Keith Morgan. *Boston Architecture: 1975–1990.* Munich: Prestel, 1990.

Mock, Elizabeth. *Built in U.S.A. Since 1932.* New York: Museum of Modern Art, 1944.

Mumford, Lewis. *From the Ground Up: Observations on Contemporary Housing, Highway Building, and Civic Design.* New York: Harcourt, Brace, 1956.

Noever, Peter, ed. *Architecture in Transition: Between Deconstruction and New Modernism.* Munich: Prestel, 1991.

Norberg-Schultz, Christian. *Meaning in Western Architecture.* New York: Praeger, 1975.

Papadakis, Andrea, ed. *Deconstruction in Architecture.* New York: St. Martin's, 1988.

Placzek, Adolf K., ed. *MacMillan Encyclopedia of Architects.* New York: Free Press, 1982.

Robinson, Sidney K., and Elizabeth A. Scheuer. *The Continuous Presence of Organic Architecture.* Cleveland: Contemporary Arts Center, 1991.

Salvadori, Mario. *Why Buildings Stand Up: The Strength of Architecture.* New York: Norton, 1992.

Scully, Vincent, Jr. *American Architecture and Urbanism.* New York: Praeger, 1969.

——. *Modern Architecture,* rev. ed. New York: Braziller, 1974.

——. *The Shingle Style Today or The Historian's Revenge.* New York: Braziller, 1974.

Searing, Helen. *In Search of a Modern Architecture.* New York: Architectural History Foundation, 1982.

—— and Henry Hope Reed. *Speaking a New Classicism: American Architecture Now.* Northampton, Mass.: Smith College Museum of Art, 1981.

Smith, C. Ray. *Supermannerism: New Attitudes in Post-Modern Architecture.* New York: Dutton, 1977.

Smith, G. E. Kidder. *The Architecture of the United States.* 3 vols. Garden City, N.Y.: Anchor, 1981.

——. *Source Book of American Architecture: 500 Notable Buildings from the 10th Century to the Present.* New York: Princeton Architectural Press, 1996.

Smith, Thomas Gordon. *Classical Architecture:*

Rule and Invention. Layton, Utah: Peregrine Smith, 1988.

Spencer, Brian A., ed. *The Prairie School Tradition.* New York: Whitney Library of Design, 1979.

Stern, Robert A. M. *Modern Classicism.* New York: Rizzoli, 1988.

——. *New Directions in American Architecture.* New York: Braziller, 1969, 1977.

—— et al. *New York 1960: Architecture and Urbanism Between the Second World War and the Bicentennial.* New York: Rizzoli, 1995.

Tafuri, Manfredo, et al. *Modern Architecture/2.* New York: Rizzoli, 1986.

Venturi, Robert. *Complexity and Contradiction in Architecture.* New York: Museum of Modern Art, 1966.

Von Eckhardt, Wolf. *Mid-Century Architecture in America: Honor Awards of the American Institute of Architects.* Baltimore: Johns Hopkins Press, 1961.

Whiffen, Marcus, and Frederick Koeper. *American Architecture 1607–1976.* Cambridge, Mass.: MIT Press, 1981.

Wigley, Mark, and Philip Johnson. *Deconstructivist Architecture.* New York: Museum of Modern Art, 1988.

Wilkes, Joseph, ed. *Encyclopedia of Architecture, Design, Engineering and Construction.* New York: Wiley, 1990.

Wiseman, Carter. *Shaping a Nation: Twentieth-Century American Architecture and Its Makers.* New York: W.W. Norton, 1998.

Wright, Sylvia Hart. *Sourcebook of Contemporary American Architecture from Postwar to Postmodern.* New York: Van Nostrand Reinhold, 1989.

Zukowsky, John, ed. *Chicago Architecture and Design 1923–1993.* Chicago: Art Institute of Chicago, 1993.

Architecture—Specific Building Types

Billington, David P. *The Tower and the Bridge: The New Art of Structural Engineering.* New York: Basic Books, 1983.

—— and Myron Goldsmith, eds. *Techniques and Aesthetics in the Design of Tall Buildings: Fall Meeting of the American Society of Civil Engineering, Houston, 1983.* New York: American Society of Civil Engineering, 1984.

Bowly, Devereux. *The Poorhouse: Subsidized Housing in Chicago 1895–1976.* Carbondale: Southern Illinois University Press, 1978.

Brown, Michael. *The New Museum: Architecture and Display.* New York: Praeger, 1965.

Clausen, Meredith L. *Spiritual Space: The Religious Architecture of Pietro Belluschi.* Seattle: University of Washington Press, 1992.

Craig, Lois, et al., eds., *The Federal Presence: Architecture, Politics, and Symbols in U.S. Government and Buildings.* Cambridge, Mass.: MIT Press, 1978.

Davis, Douglas. *The Museum Transformed.* New York: Abbeville, 1990.

Davis, Sam. *The Form of Housing.* New York: Van Nostrand Reinhold, 1977.

Dober, Richard P. *Campus Design.* New York: Wiley, 1992.

Doremus, Thomas L. *Classical Styles in Modern Architecture: From the Colonnade to Disjunctional Space.* New York: Van Nostrand Reinhold, 1994.

Fish, Gertrude. *The Story of Housing.* New York: Macmillan, 1979.

Foley, Mary Mix. *The American House.* New York: Harper & Row, 1980.

Frieden, Bernard J., and Lynne B. Sagalyn. *Downtown, Inc.: How America Rebuilds Cities.* Cambridge, Mass.: MIT Press, 1989.

Glaeser, Ludwig. *Architecture of Museums.* New York: Museum of Modern Art, 1968.

Goldberger, Paul. *The Skyscraper.* New York: Knopf, 1981.

Gruen, Victor. *Shopping Towns U.S.A.: The Planning of Shopping Centers.* New York: Reinhold, 1960.

Guise, David. *Design and Technology in Architecture,* rev. ed. New York: Van Nostrand Reinhold, 1991.

Hildebrand, Grant. *The Wright Space: Pattern and Meaning in Frank Lloyd Wright's Houses.* Seattle: University of Washington Press, 1991.

Hitchcock, Henry-Russell, and William Seale. *Temples of Democracy: The State Capitols of the United States.* New York: Harcourt Brace Jovanovich, 1976.

Hoyt, Charles. *Public, Municipal, and Community Buildings.* New York: McGraw-Hill, 1980.

Huxtable, Ada Louise. *The Tall Building Artistically Reconsidered: The Search for a Skyscraper Style.* New York: Pantheon, 1984.

Kennedy, Robert Woods. *The House and the Art of Its Design.* New York: Reinhold, 1953.

Langdon, Philip. *American Houses.* New York: Stewart, Tabori & Chang, 1987.

Loud, Patricia Cummings. *The Art Museums of Louis Kahn.* Durham, N.C.: Duke University Press, 1989.

Macsai, John, et al. *Housing.* New York: Wiley, 1982.

McCoy, Esther. *Case Study Houses 1945–1962,* 2nd ed. Los Angeles: Hennessy & Ingalls, 1977.

Mock, Elizabeth. *If You Want to Build a House.* New York: Museum of Modern Art, 1948.

Molloy, Mary Alice. *Chicago Since the Sears Tower: A Guide to New Downtown Buildings.* Chicago: Inland Architecture Press, 1990.

Montgomery, Roger. *Bay Area Houses.* New York: Oxford University Press, 1976.

Moore, Charles, et al. *The Place of Houses.* New York: Holt, Rinehart & Winston, 1974.

Plunz, Richard. *A History of Housing in New York City: Dwelling Type and Social Change in the American Metropolis.* New York: Columbia University Press, 1990.

Rathburn, Robert Davis. *Shopping Centers and Malls, Book 2.* New York: Retail Reporting Corp., 1988.

Redstone, Louis G. *New Dimensions in Shopping Centers and Stores.* New York: McGraw Hill, 1973.

Rowe, Peter G. *Making a Middle Landscape.* Cambridge, Mass.: MIT Press, 1991.

Rubenstein, Harvey M. *Central City Malls.* New York: Wiley, 1978.

Saliga, Pauline. *The Sky's the Limit: A Century of Chicago Skyscrapers.* New York: Rizzoli, 1990.

Schmertz, Mildred. *Office Building Design.* New York: Architectural Record Books, 1975.

Scott, N. Keith. *Shopping Centre Design.* London: Van Nostrand Reinhold (International), 1989.

Searing, Helen. *New American Art Museums.* New York: Whitney Museum of American Art, 1982.

Sergeant, John. *Frank Lloyd Wright's Usonian Houses: The Case for Organic Architecture.* New York: Whitney Library of Design, 1976.

Sherwood, Roger. *Modern Housing Prototypes.* Cambridge, Mass.: Harvard University Press, 1978.

Smith, Elizabeth A., ed. *Blueprints for Modern Living: History and Legacy of the Case Study Houses.* Los Angeles: Museum of Contemporary Art, 1989.

Stephens, Suzanne. *Building the New Museum.* New York: Princeton Architectural Press, 1986.

Turner, Paul Venable. *Campus: An American Planning Tradition.* New York: Architectural History Foundation, 1987.

Wagner, Walter F., and Karin Schlegel. *Houses Architects Design for Themselves.* New York: McGraw Hill, 1974.

Walker, Lester. *American Shelter: An Illustrated Encyclopedia of the American Home.* Woodstock, N.Y.: Overlook, 1981.

Woodbridge, Salley B., ed. *Bay Area Houses*. Layton, Utah: Peregrine Smith, 1988.

Wright, Frank Lloyd. *The Natural House*. New York: Horizon, 1954.

Wright, Gwendolyn. *Building the Dream: A Social History of Housing in America*. New York: Pantheon, 1981.

Architects

Books on individual architects and firms continue to proliferate. Some notable examples are:

Brownlee, David B., and David G. De Long. *Louis I. Kahn: In the Realm of Architecture*. New York: Rizzoli, 1991.

Bruegmann, Robert. *Ralph Johnson of Perkins & Will: Buildings and Projects*. New York: Rizzoli, 1995.

Clausen, Meredith. *Pietro Belluschi: Modern American Architect*. Cambridge, Mass.: MIT Press, 1994.

Fitch, James Marston. *Walter Gropius*. New York: Braziller, 1960.

Giedion, Sigfried. *Walter Gropius*. 1954. Reprint, New York: Dover, 1992.

Hanna, Paul. *Frank Lloyd Wright's Hanna House*. Carbondale: University of Illinois Press, 1981.

Hines, Thomas. *Richard Neutra and the Search for Modern Architecture*. Berkeley and Los Angeles: University of California Press, 1994.

Krinsky, Carol Hershelle. *Gordon Bunshaft of Skidmore, Owings & Merrill*. Cambridge, Mass.: MIT Press, 1994.

Littlejohn, David. *Architect: The Life and Work of Charles W. Moore*. New York: Holt, Rinehart & Winston, 1984.

Muschamp, Herbert. *Man About Town: Frank Lloyd Wright in New York City*. Cambridge, Mass.: MIT Press, 1983.

Newhouse, Victoria. *Wallace K. Harrison, Architect*. New York: Rizzoli, 1989.

Saliga, Pauline, et al., eds., *Architecture of Bruce Goff 1904–1982: Design for a Continuous Present*. Chicago: Art Institute of Chicago, 1995.

Scully, Vincent, Jr. *Frank Lloyd Wright*. New York: Braziller, 1960.

Storer, William A. *The Architecture of Frank Lloyd Wright*. Cambridge, Mass.: MIT Press, 1974.

Wiseman, Carter. *The Architecture of I. M. Pei*. London: Thames & Hudson, 1990.

Zukowsky, John, ed. *Mies Reconsidered: His Career, Legacy and Disciples*. New York: Rizzoli, 1986.

Contemporary American Life and Urbanism

Cantor, Norman. *Twentieth Century Culture: Modernism to Deconstruction*. New York: P. Lang, 1988.

Cayton, Mary K., et al., eds. *Encyclopedia of American Social History*. New York: Scribners, 1993.

Garreau, Joel. *Edge City: Life on the New Frontier*. New York: Doubleday, 1991.

Gillette, Howard, Jr., and Zane L. Miller. *American Urbanism: A Historiographic Review*. New York: Greenwood, 1987.

Hayes, R. Allen. *The Federal Government and Urban Housing: Ideology and Change in Public Policy*. Albany: State University of New York Press, 1985.

Huxtable, Ada Louise. *Unreal America: Architecture and Illusion*. New York: New Press, 1997.

Jacobs, Jane. *The Death and Life of Great American Cities*. New York: Random House, 1961.

Kowinski, William S. *The Malling of America*. New York: Morrow, 1985.

Kunstler, James Howard. *The Geography of Nowhere*. New York: Simon & Schuster, 1993.

Mayer, Martin. *The Builders: Houses, People, Neighborhoods, Government, Money*. New York: Norton, 1978.

Meyerson, Martin, et al. *The Face of the Metropolis: The Building Developments That Are Reshaping Our Cities and Suburbs*. New York: Random House, 1964.

Nash, Gary B., et al. *The American People: Creating a Nation and a Society*, 2nd ed. New York: Harper & Row, 1990.

Relph, Ralph. *The Modern Urban Landscape*. Baltimore: Johns Hopkins University Press, 1987.

Rybczynski, Witold. *Looking Around: A Journey Through Architecture*. New York: Viking, 1992.

Teaford, Jon C. *The Rough Road to Renaissance: Urban Revitalization in America 1940–1985*. Baltimore: Johns Hopkins University Press, 1990.

Trachtenberg, Stanley, ed. *The Postmodern Movement: A Handbook of Contemporary Innovations in the Arts*. Westport, Conn.: Greenwood, 1985.

Von Eckhardt, Wolf. *Back to the Drawing Board: Planning Livable Cities*. Washington, D.C.: New Republic Books, 1978.

———. *A Place to Live*. New York: Delacorte, 1967.

Wachs, Martin, and Margaret Crawford, eds. *The Car and the City: The Automobile, the Built Environment, and Daily Urban Life*. Ann Arbor: University of Michigan Press, 1992.

Warner, Sam Bass. *The Urban Wilderness*. New York: Harper & Row, 1972.

Wolf, Peter. *The Future of the City*. New York: Whitney Library of Design, 1974.

Wuthnow, Robert. *The Restructuring of American Society and Faith Since World War II*. Princeton, N.J.: Princeton University Press, 1988.

Zukin, Sharon. *Landscapes of Power: From Detroit to Disney World*. Berkeley and Los Angeles: University of California Press, 1991.

Architectural Periodicals

A wealth of information on specific buildings and developments can be located through *The Avery Index to Architectural Periodicals* (Columbia University). Particularly useful journals include the following: *Architectural Record; Architecture; A + U: Architecture + Urbanism; Assemblage; The Chicago Architectural Journal; Faith and Forum; The Harvard Architecture Review; Inland Architect; Journal of the Society of Architectural Historians; Perspecta: The Yale Architectural Journal; Process: Architecture;* and *Progressive Architecture.*

Architectural Guidebooks

Reflecting the burgeoning interest in contemporary architecture, local and regional guidebooks are tending to report more fully on the recent past. The bookstores of the American Institute of Architects (Washington, D.C.), and The Society of Architectural Historians (Chicago), and the Urban Center Bookstore of the Municipal Art Society (New York City), Hennessy and Ingalls (Los Angeles), and Form Zero (Santa Monica) are good sources for such books.

Index